About Shane Bryant

Shane Bryant was born in Sydney and grew up in Dapto on the New South Wales south coast. After joining the Australian Army at the age of seventeen, he eventually fulfilled his ambition to qualify as an explosive detection dog handler. He later worked as a police dog handler, a private investigator and a not-very-successful real estate salesman. In 2006, he returned to his first love, working with dogs, and took a job in Afghanistan as a civilian dog handler contracted to provide support to the US Army and other coalition military forces. He served 10 years in Afghanistan and Iraq as a military contractor in frontline and management positions.

About Tony Park

Tony Park was born in 1964 and grew up in the western suburbs of Sydney, Australia. He has worked as a journalist, public relations consultant and a press secretary. He also served 34 years in the Australian Army Reserve, including a tour of duty in Afghanistan in 2002. He is the author of 18 other thriller novels, all set in Africa. Tony and his wife, Nicola, divide their time equally between a home in Australia and a house on the edge of the Kruger National Park in South Africa.

WAR DOGS

Shane Bryant with Tony Park

First Published by Pan Macmillan in 2010
This edition published in 2020 by AJP

Copyright © Tony Park, Shane Bryant 2010
www.tonypark.net
The moral right of the author has been asserted.

War Dogs

EPUB: 9781922389022
POD: 9781922389039

Cover design by Paris Giannakis

Publishing services provided by Critical Mass
www.critmassconsulting.com

This book is dedicated to my five beautiful children: Corey, Lauchlan, Demi, Kyron and Jaylen. Every minute I have been away, you have always been in my heart and thoughts.

CONTENTS

Contents

GLOSSARY

.50 cal – .50 calibre Browning heavy machine gun. First used by the American Army in World War I and still in use today.

1 CER – 1 Combat Engineer Regiment.

240 – 7.62-millimetre light machine gun, adopted by the US Army as a replacement for the Vietnam-era M60 machine gun.

A-Team – Officially Operational Detachment Alpha, a twelve-man US Army Special Forces team.

AC-130 'Spectre' – C-130 Hercules cargo aircraft configured as a gunship, armed with 40-millimetre cannons, six-barrelled 20-millimetre 'Gatling' guns and 105-millimetre howitzer.

AK-47 – Russian-made Kalashnikov assault rifle, in widespread use with both Taliban and Afghan government security forces.

Alice pack – The common name for the US Army's aluminium-framed LC-1 backpack.

ANA – Afghan National Army.

Apache – US Army helicopter gunship, also used by the Dutch in Afghanistan.

B-Team – Officially Operational Detachment Bravo, US Army Special Forces administrative and headquarters element overseeing a number of A-Teams.

B1 Bomber – US Air Force supersonic strategic jet bomber, designed to drop nuclear bombs on Russia, but now in use in Afghanistan.

BBDA – Back blast danger area, the out-of-bounds area behind an anti-armour weapon while it is being fired.

Bison – Canadian armoured troop carrier, a smaller version of the light armoured vehicle.

Black Hawk – US Army troop carrying and medevac helicopter.

Brown Ring – Code name for regular supply run circuit flown by Chinook helicopters to firebases in Uruzgan Province.

C-17 – US Air Force medium-lift cargo jet.

C-130 – Four-engine Lockheed Hercules cargo aircraft.

CAI – Canine Associates International.

CANSOF – Canadian Special Operations Forces.

Carl Gustaf – Swedish-made 84-millimetre shoulder-fired anti-armour weapon used by US Special Forces.

CH-47 Chinook – Twin-rotor cargo helicopter, first used operationally in the Vietnam War, with variants still in service today.

Dooshka – Soviet-made DshK 12.7-millimetre heavy machine gun.

ETT – Embedded training team, coalition military personnel assigned to train and mentor Afghan security forces.

FOB – Forward operating base, outlying fortified encampment typically used by a Special Forces ODA.

GMV – Ground mobility vehicle. Also known as a 'gun truck', a humvee with a turret on its top and open rear load space. A heavy weapon launcher, such as a .50 calibre machine gun or Mark 19/Mark 47 grenade, would be mounted in the turret, and two 240 machine guns (or similar) mounted in the rear.

Haji – US Army slang for an Afghan male, derived from the name given to believers who have made a holy pilgrimage to Mecca.

Hesco – Steel mesh container lined with hessian and filled with earth, and used as a barricade.

Hooch – US Army slang for a dwelling.

Humvee – Short for 'high-mobility multipurpose wheeled vehicle'. US military four-wheel-drive.

IED – Improvised explosive device, usually a roadside bomb.

JTAC – Joint terminal attack controller, US Air Force air-to-ground controller, responsible for coordinating air strikes and air support.

M4 – Standard US Army Special Forces 5.56-millimetre assault rifle, a shortened version of the M-16 rifle.

Mark 19/Mark 47 – Automatic belt-fed grenade launcher that fires 378 40-millimetre grenades per second.

MEDCAP – Medical Civic Action Program that provides medical care to Afghan civilians.

PKM – Russian-made 7.62-millimetre belt-fed light machine gun in common use with insurgent and government forces in Afghanistan.

Psyops – Psychological operations.

PUC – Person under consideration, such as a suspected Taliban or al-Qaeda member targeted for questioning or arrest. (To 'PUC' someone means to capture them.)

RPG – Rocket-propelled grenade, fired from a Russian-made RPG-7 launcher.

SAS – Australia's elite Special Air Service Regiment.

SF – Special Forces

Soldier's five – Australian Army term for a short lesson, or briefing, given by one soldier to another.

Space-A – Space Available transport.

Terp – Stands for 'interpreter', an English-speaking Afghan interpreter assigned to coalition troops.

TIC – Troops in contact, under fire or engaged in combat with the enemy.

Turtleback – A humvee with a fully enclosed roof.

VCSI – Vigilant Canine Services International.

AUTHORS' NOTE

War Dogs was first released in Australia in 2010. This worldwide edition has been expanded and updated.

PROLOGUE
Uruzgan Province, Afghanistan

February 2007

The rain had stopped but it was still so cold up in the mountains, it hurt.

I took out a plastic bag of dog food and fed my dog, Ricky, then looked after my needs with some chunked-and-formed crap from an MRE – Meal Ready to Eat, or Meal Rejected by Ethiopians. I was in the team sergeant's humvee. Before he did his evening walk-around the other vehicles, he told us what was what.

'They're all around us,' the grizzled Green Beret said, almost as though he were relishing this revelation. 'I got a feeling we're going to get hit again tonight, so stay sharp.'

I nodded. Two TICs – troops in contact, what the Americans called firefights – in one day had been pretty full on, I thought. God knows what the night has in store.

'We're getting lots of ICOM chatter. They're out there and they might be looking for another fight.' The team sergeant added that headlights moving around the hills had been spotted, which was a bad sign, as villagers knew that, due to a curfew, they needed to be indoors by six in the evening. You could assume that anyone driving around at night was doing so for disturbing reasons. 'Don't worry too much, though. We got Spectre overhead tonight.'

It was good to know the AC-130 Spectre gunship was orbiting up there somewhere, unseen and unheard, ready to unleash its awesome fury if needed. The AC-130 was a converted four-engine Hercules transport aircraft, which was loaded with guns and ammo. It had 40-millimetre cannons, six-barrelled 20-millimetre electric Gatling guns and even a 105-millimetre howitzer on board.

Someone had radioed that they'd seen movement, at about 300 metres from our position, which was why Spectre had been called on line. I could hear it droning above us now and so could whoever else was out there among the rocks and boulders. I felt better – no-one fucks with you when they know Spectre's overhead.

Like everyone else in the team, I had to take my turn on picket – my guard duty shift – during the night. The US Army – particularly its Special Forces (SF) – isn't as slack regarding discipline in the field as some people like to make out. Smoking wasn't allowed at night, so I had taken up chewing tobacco to help keep me awake. I'd chew it while we were driving around on missions as well, to help keep me alert and to give me something to do while I was sitting behind my gun. The tobacco doesn't usually taste too bad, like a strange-tasting chewing gum. Some of the flavours, such as raspberry, are really disgusting, but I usually went with peppermint. The Americans are all into chewing tobacco and call it 'taking a dip'.

As usual, I had a one-hour shift. One of the only things I was scared of in Afghanistan was fucking up and letting the team down. They treated me as one of their own. When I was pulling my night shift, other people's lives were in my hands. I sat in the truck behind the 240 light machine gun, chewing tobacco and spitting the juice into an empty half-litre plastic water bottle. I stared out into the bleak mountain night, and listened to the muted voices coming from the radios of other vehicles in the convoy.

I was colder than I'd ever been while in the army in Australia. Those days seemed a lifetime away.

When my relief came up to the truck, I eased myself down and walked around for a bit to get some feeling back into my feet, then went to check on Ricky. He was tied under the truck, curled up on his own sleeping bag. 'Good boy,' I whispered to him.

I spat out the last of the chewing tobacco and wished I could have had a proper smoke before going to bed. I unzipped my Gore-Tex bivouac or bivvy bag – kind of like a waterproof swag – and slid into the sleeping bag inside it, still with my boots and all my gear on. If the team sergeant was jumpy, it was for good reason, and I had to be ready to stand-to in the middle of the night. I laid my M-4 in the bivvy bag and tried to get comfortable on the unforgiving rocky ground. I was shattered, but sleep didn't come easily as I replayed the day's events.

It had turned out that the second ambush we'd been through, earlier that day, was just one guy with a rifle taking pot shots at us, but it had turned into a full-on TIC from our side. The Taliban always had spotters in the villages, hills and mountains, keeping an eye on us whenever we were on the move. Sometimes they'd open up on us, which, I guess, was their way of screwing with us – delaying and making us expend some ammo that we then wouldn't have if the shit went down for real. It was a high-risk strategy for the spotters, though, as the American SF guys were always looking for a fight, and if someone called game-on, they were ready to play. Sometimes the spotter would get away, but other times they'd nail him.

I dozed off, but woke again, busting for a piss. I checked the display on my watch. 'Shit.' It was three in the morning. When I unzipped the bivvy, I immediately felt the almost stinging cold on my face. Reluctantly, I walked a few metres away. Steam came off the ground. When I got back to my sleeping bag, I stepped on it in the dark and heard a growl. The sleeping bag started to wriggle.

'Ricky?'

He'd crawled right inside my warm sleeping bag.

'Cold, boy?' I whispered. I opened the bag and saw him looking at me. When I reached in to drag him out, he gave another low growl.

'Very funny. Move, boy.'

Ricky growled once more. I ran a hand through my hair and shook my head. I couldn't blame the poor guy. He was probably freezing. I took a peek under the truck and saw that his water bowl was frozen over. 'Fuck. At least move over, man,' I said.

Ricky growled a little again as I shoved him, but he made just enough room for me to slide back inside. We couldn't both fit, but Ricky nestled against me near the bag's opening. I couldn't do it up, but as I had German shepherd hair wrapped around my shoulders and face, the cold wasn't too bad. Ricky seemed happy with this compromise and shifted a bit. He sighed.

'Night, buddy,' I said to him. Bloody dog, I thought, smiling as I tried to unwind and get back to sleep.

ONE

A picture of a man and a dog

1989, Kapooka, Australia

The soldier standing in the barracks block corridor tried to move his weight from one foot to the other surreptitiously. The bombardier's spit-polished boots shrieked on the linoleum floor as he executed a perfect about-turn further down the line of green-uniformed recruits.

'I SAID, DON'T MOVE, YOU FUCKING IMBECILE.'

'Sorry, Bom...'

The bombardier, which is what the artillery calls its corporals, squeaked his way down the corridor to the recruit who'd been human enough to move, and stupid enough to try to apologise for it. He stopped a few centimetres from the guy's nose. 'DON'T FUCKING SORRY ME.'

The spittle must have hit the recruit in the face. I concentrated on standing perfectly still, and hoped the beating pulse in my neck wasn't visible to the bombardier's all-seeing eyes.

Sometimes you'd get a secret laugh or sly smile out of one of the instructors' insults, but not this time. I can't even remember who'd done what wrong, but the bombardier had made us all fall in and stand perfectly still in the corridor. Even for Kapooka, it was a bizarre and, in its own way, sadistic punishment – just standing still and silent, hour after hour. We would march all day, or so it seemed, and we'd do the run, dodge, jump obstacle course, and we'd do more physical training and at the end we'd be sore, and sorry for ourselves, but at least we'd been on the move. I didn't mind the exercise, because I was a pretty active kid, but making us keep rock still in one position seemed all the crueller because of the active lives we'd been leading. If standing to attention in the corridor, not moving or speaking for two-and-a-half hours, was supposed to teach us something, it didn't work, because I can't remember it.

Lining the wall of the corridor were big blown-up drawings illustrating all the different jobs you could do in the Australian Army. There were guys posed next to trucks, an infantryman with a rifle and fixed bayonet, an artillery dude next to a big gun and a bloke in the turret of a tank. The one that most interested me, though, was of a soldier kneeling beside an Alsatian dog. For some reason, as soon as I saw that picture I knew that this was what I wanted to do in the army. Those blokes in the pictures all looked determined – happy, even – and they'd all gone through the shit that we were experiencing today. I sincerely hoped the real army wasn't going to be like Kapooka.

The bombardier continued prowling along the corridor, watching, waiting for another victim to move. Out of the corner of my eye, I saw the guy who had moved his feet stick out his right hand, his arm bent at 90 degrees at the elbow,

which is how you put your hand up if you are standing to attention. 'Bombardier,' he said in a high-pitched voice.

The lino now screamed as the bombardier executed an
about-turn and came marching back down the line. 'Put-your-
fucking-hand-down,' he said slowly and quietly, sounding
even more menacing. 'I SAID, NO FUCKING MOVEMENT.'

'But, Bombardier, I need to . . .'

'SHUT UP!'

The guy apparently had a death wish and for a moment
I felt sure that the non-commissioned officer was going to
punch him. Instead, the bombardier repeated his order and
walked up and down the line, telling us all that we needed to
learn some fucking self-control.

A little while later, with the pain burning through the thick
soles of my boots and my shoulder muscles starting to cramp,
I heard it. I think everyone heard it, no matter how far along
the corridor they were, but no-one wanted to look. Soon, I
could smell it.

I risked moving my gaze to the recruit who had asked for
permission to speak. The front of one leg of his green trousers
was stained black, and a puddle of piss was fanning out on
the lino, around his boots.

It was my mum who encouraged me to join the army.

I was born in Leichhardt, in the inner-western suburbs
of -Sydney, where we lived until I was five. After that, we
moved to Dapto, on the New South Wales south coast, which
was a big change from the city's cramped terrace houses and
narrow streets.

I have two sisters and a brother, and am the oldest by five
years, so I found myself doing quite a bit around the house
after my folks split up when I was in fifth class. Later, my

mum had twins, a boy and a girl, Reece and Naomi, from her second relationship.

Dapto's big claim to fame is its greyhound dog racing track, but I don't think this had anything to do with my future career choices. Dapto's not by the beach and is pretty suburban, so I didn't grow up a surfie, spending all my time on the sand, smoking dope and driving a panel van.

I wouldn't live in Dapto now, but it was a good place to grow up. I started playing rugby for Wollongong, the nearest big city, when I was fourteen and that kept me occupied during my early to mid teen years. I always wanted to be outdoors, either riding my pushbike or playing sport, rather than hanging around the house.

Dogs became a part of my life pretty early on. I really wanted a Doberman, but mum bought me a cattle dog instead, which I called Sheba. I really liked being with her, and I'd walk her every day, along with a mate of mine who also had a dog. Sheba was a good friend and always happy to see me. At that stage, though, I had no thoughts of ever working with animals.

I wasn't good at applying myself at school, and I couldn't wait to get out and start doing something – anything. I just wanted to escape. Looking back, I wish I'd applied for a trade, or kept up with my studies. My mum wasn't going to force me to stay on until Year Twelve, and she decided that if I wanted to leave, I should think about joining the army. My dad had been in the army, in the transport corps, so it wasn't as though Mum was unfamiliar with the military life and all that it involved

The defence force recruiters, from the army, navy and air force, came to our school, and after their talks I spoke to the army guy. I'd already decided that if I were going to join one of the services, it would be the army. I told Mum this, and she called the recruiting office and arranged for someone to come to our house and talk to me about it some more.

The recruiter started the ball rolling and, before I knew it, I was on the train to Sydney for my medical and psych evaluation. I was told I had high blood pressure, so I had to go for more tests once I got back to Dapto. The doctor gave me the all clear and suddenly I was being sworn in as an Australian Army recruit.

I was seventeen years old and on a bus with a bunch of blokes I didn't know, on my way to the 1st Recruit Training Battalion at Kapooka, near Wagga, in southern New South Wales. I was looking forward to starting my career and earning some money. The army recruiters had been friendly and supportive, and there were a few of them travelling with us.

There was a relaxed feel about the trip. We stopped at a roadhouse on the way to Kapooka and got some lunch, and everyone was in good spirits. The countryside was mostly wide open grazing lands covered with short, yellow-brown grass; very different from the rolling emerald-green hills of the south coast where I'd spent most of my life. The coast gets decent rainfall and it's good dairy country, but out here in the inland, it was dry, tough country. I'd never really been away from home, and my senses were a bit overwhelmed.

It was about six in the evening by the time we reached Kapooka. When the bus stopped, the driver opened the door and a group of MPs – military police – in bright red berets got on board. It was as if someone had just flipped a switch on my life.

'GET OFF THE BUS!'

We all looked at each other, and a couple of the guys smirked at the screamed command.

'I SAID, GET OFF THIS FUCKING BUS NOW AND FALL IN OUTSIDE. MOVE IT!'

We suddenly all knew this was for real, and bumped into each other as we got out of our seats and pushed our way to the door.

'NO FUCKING TALKING. GET OFF THE BUS. GET YOUR SHIT AND LINE UP OUTSIDE!'

Talk about a reality check! Once we'd had our names marked off, we didn't stop running. Over the next few days we were issued with uniforms and a pile of other gear including a pack, webbing pouches and belt and harness, water bottles, boots, mess tins, hats, raincoats, sheets, blankets, towels and even a toothbrush. We were given everything we'd need to start our lives all over again. It was May, and although it wasn't yet winter, that place was cold. Anyone who's been to that part of Australia knows how bitter it can be when the chilled wind whips across those empty plains and you wake to find the grass white with frost. It was extreme – freezing in winter and baking, stinking hot in summer. I would discover there was nothing that could remotely be described as mild about the place or the experience.

'HALLWAY TWENTY-SIX, WAKEY, WAKEY. OUTSIDE!'

Had I even slept? The next morning, it seemed like I'd had my eyes closed for ten minutes when our section commander was screaming at us to wake up. 'GET OUT HERE AND BRING YOUR SHEET WITH YOU, OVER YOUR SHOULDER!'

Screaming, screaming, screaming. Bombardier Wilson was an absolute arsehole. It was the section commander's job to get in our faces and tip our civilian world upside down, and Wilson seemed to love his job.

We were sleeping four to a room, and had to parade in the hallway with our top sheets over our shoulders to make sure that each of us had pulled his bed apart. In the past, some smart arses had tried to take a short cut by making their beds perfectly and then sleeping on top of the blankets so they could save a few precious minutes of morning routine, but the instructors knew all the short cuts in the book.

Wilson went on at us from the moment we woke to the moment we passed out in the evenings. He'd follow us into the bathroom to make sure we were shaving. It was rush, rush, rush all the time, and guys would have bits of toilet paper sticking to their faces where they'd cut themselves. I was seventeen and had barely started shaving, but still had to go through the motions. Mates of mine back home were in school, sneaking drinks and cigarettes, surfing or playing footy, but I was a teenager who had to iron his fucking pyjamas, on pain of punishment.

Everything had to be perfect.

Sheets had to be pulled tight and tucked in with hospital corners. The stripes on the scratchy, red-brown blankets had to run right down the centre of the beds, and sheets had to be turned over at the top precisely the length of a rifle bay-onet. Everything we owned had to be kept in its designated place. Uniforms had to be ironed and hung facing the same way, and our civilian clothes were locked away so that there were no reminders of the lives we'd left behind. Socks had to be folded just-so, and there were rules about how far each item of clothing or belt buckle or toothbrush could be from the next.

Nights were filled with the smell of Brasso and spray starch, as we strove to get our uniforms in a state fit for the following morning's inspection. Minor infractions were punished with screams of abuse and the violent ransacking of whatever had been done incorrectly. Blankets and sheets were ripped from beds and tossed out the barracks first-floor window to land in the dirt and grass below. If Bombardier Wilson found a water bottle a few millimetres out of place in a locker, he would reach in and slide everything onto the floor, and the hapless recruit would have to start all over again.

There was no free time. The army owned us, body and soul, and every minute of every day was filled with some sort of activity. We'd run in the morning, our cheeks and noses, bare arms and legs stinging from the cold, our breath freezing in front of our faces. Panting, gasping, sometimes throwing up, we realised how easy our lives at home had been. Having played rugby helped me a bit, but they were pushing my young body to its limits, and beyond. During crisp, cool days under empty blue skies, we drilled and marched, learning to walk all over again, as though we were toddlers. Always there was the yelling, the abuse, and the bombardier's nose almost touching yours as he delivered each day's fresh insult, punctuated with tiny drips of spittle.

'CLOSE YOUR FIST WHEN YOU MARCH OR I'LL STICK MY COCK IN IT, BRYANT!'

'EYES FRONT OR I'LL RIP THEM OUT AND SKULL-FUCK YOU TO DEATH, YOU STUPID BASTARD!'

'SWING THOSE FUCKING ARMS BREAST-POCKET HIGH WHEN YOU MARCH, OR I'LL RIP THEM OFF, STICK THEM IN YOUR EARS AND RIDE YOU AROUND THE PARADE GROUND LIKE YOU'RE A FUCKING HONDA!'

Breakfast, lunch and dinner became our only respite. I looked forward to meals and shovelled the food into me. Our bodies had become machines and our brains weren't far behind.

When we weren't marching or drilling, our foggy minds were being filled with map reading, military law, first aid or radio procedures. A few of the guys were excited at the prospect of the weapons lessons but there were weeks of training before anyone pulled a trigger. During the lessons, the bombardier didn't scream, but he was no more tolerant of mistakes, especially safety breaches. Still, there was at least a feeling the instructor was genuinely trying to teach you something, rather than just hoping you'd remember it through constant ranting, belittlement and abuse.

As we recruits grew more confident and started getting into the groove of life at Kapooka, we could laugh and joke in private about some of the things the instructors did. There was a dark side to that barren, windswept, soulless place as well, though.

I've got mates who are still in the army who have been posted to Kapooka to be instructors and they tell me that, these days, recruits are issued with cards that they can hold up to instructors to let them know when they've had enough of their bullying and abuse. That sounds extreme to someone like me who survived the old system, but we did have some serious problems. Two recruits went absent without leave during my time at Kapooka. One jumped a train and was so exhausted that he fell asleep and rolled off and injured himself. The other guy made it to Melbourne, where he hanged himself in a public toilet.

Things often went too far, as with the recruit who had pissed himself rather than move from his spot in the corridor. I understand that they're trying to break you down and then rebuild you, but things had to change at Kapooka and, apparently, they have. Although I didn't know it at the time, and neither did the army, I'd joined the Australian Defence Force at what was probably a turning point.

13

Our uniforms back then were the same plain green heavy cotton ones that troops had been wearing, pretty much unchanged, since the end of World War II. They had to be starched and ironed with razor-sharp creases and our black leather boots had to be spit polished, which took hours. Our rifles were the big, old 7.62- millimetre self-loading rifle (the SLR) and the F1 sub-machine gun, which dated from the late 1950s and early '60s. Back then, in 1989, Australian soldiers hadn't been to war since Vietnam in the '60s and '70s. Our training methods, including the virtually unchecked abuse our instructors meted out, belonged to another era.

Within a few years, the army would switch to polyester-blend camouflage uniforms that didn't need ironing; to a lighter, smaller calibre rifle, the 5.56-millimetre F88 Steyr; and would be serving in modern peacekeeping operations in places such as Rwanda and Somalia, where knowing who was your friend and who was your enemy was even more confusing than in Vietnam. By the turn of the 21st century, the army would be fighting an enemy different from any we'd ever encountered, in the deserts and mountains of Afghanistan and Iraq.

*

Failure was never an option for me – I hate the thought of letting myself down. I set myself small goals in order to keep my sanity and make it through Kapooka. At seventeen I was the youngest recruit in the platoon, but could see that men who were older than me were finding the hard slog of training just as difficult as I was. This inspired me, because I wanted to prove to everyone, especially myself, that I could pass this tough course at my age.

As we progressed, we'd be given rewards, like we were dogs in training, and the smallest thing could mean so much. The first time I got to leave the base was like a dream. We were allowed to go into Wagga, and, while we were forbidden to drink alcohol, we could wander around the shops, have a soft drink, look at girls who weren't wearing baggy, unflattering green skins and, most importantly, not be in Kapooka. Later, even though I was still seventeen, I was allowed with the other recruits to start having a few beers in the boozer, the canteen on base.

During the days, we spent increasing time on the range, zeroing and trying to qualify with our SLRs. We also got to fire a heavy-barrelled automatic version of the SLR, called the AR. I'd only ever fired a .22 rifle before joining up and, even after my training at Kapooka, I was never a fantastic shot. As it's turned out, I've carried a firearm for work most of my adult life, although, unlike some of the Americans I've served with in Afghanistan, I'm not a gun freak. Weapons are a tool of the job to me; nothing more.

Like a lot of people on the course, the only thing I enjoyed about basic training was the march-out parade at the end of it. I really felt as though I'd achieved something. Halfway though our course, Bombardier Wilson had broken his leg playing rugby and had been replaced by a medic corporal, who was about as different from the abusive artilleryman as he could be. Wilson came back to Kapooka to have a beer with us the day we graduated and, despite all the ill-treatment we'd been through, we were happy to have a drink with him – as soldiers, rather than his scared, white-faced recruits.

About three years after recruit training, I was playing rugby at Holsworthy in south-western Sydney, where I was based, and when the other team ran on to the field, I saw Bombardier

Wilson among them. He grinned at me in recognition and I nodded back at him. That day, I didn't care whether our team won or lost; I spent the whole game chasing him around the field.

It was payback time, and when I caught up with him, I smashed him.

I thought for a while about applying to be an army medic or physical training instructor, but ever since I'd seen the picture of the army dog handler in the corridor at Kapooka, I'd been sure what I wanted to do. As it happened, I was posted to the Royal Australian Engineers, the corps that controls the army's explosive sniffer dogs.

There was something about dogs, and working with them, that really appealed to me. I like a dog's companionship–it gives me a sense of fulfilment and peacefulness, like the feeling some people get sitting on a beach watching waves roll in. Dogs really are loyal to the last beat of their heart. Nothing's simple in the army, though, and it was four years before I could actually do a dog handler's course.

When I finished at Kapooka, I was sent, with the rank of sapper, to the School of Military Engineering at Holsworthy to learn how to be a combat field engineer during my initial employment training. Engineer training was interesting, with the course covering a whole heap of subjects, including building bridges, water purification, clearing land mines and booby traps, small boat handling, demolitions, and rope work. It was good to be learning new things, as opposed to marching and being screamed at. We got weekends off, and I'd go home to Dapto to see my girlfriend, Jane. I'd first met Jane two weeks before leaving for Kapooka. She was fifteen at the time, a friend of a friend and she worked in the McDonald's at Albion Park Rail, near where I lived.

After I finished training, I was sent to 1 Field Engineer Squadron at Holsworthy, where I screwed up, big-time, very early on. I was on guard duty at the front gate and one morning I managed to sleep in because an overnight blackout had cut the power to my alarm clock. There was no sympathy, though, and I was given two weeks' restriction of privileges. I was charged and fined, and spent a lot of time doing drill, cleaning garbage bins, sweeping roads and cutting hedges, working until ten o'clock most nights. It was a good lesson for a young digger to learn – that people depend on you doing your job and there's no excuse for failure.

Even when I was I was on restriction of privileges and being punished, I was still army-mad. I thought I'd like to try out for the SAS selection course, and asked the sergeant of the guard if I could start running with a full pack and webbing during my punishment period. He told me I was too young even to apply for the SAS, that I should wait until I was 21 and had more experience, but I persisted and he gave me the OK. He probably thought I was crazy, and I think some of the other people on base thought the sergeant was beasting me by making me run with my pack on.

After my punishment was finished, I had enough on my plate without training for the SAS in my spare time, and it increasingly looked like Jane and I were going to settle down together. I did an army driver's course, and when I was posted to 1 Field's airborne troop, I was sent to the Parachute Training School at Nowra, near where I'd grown up on the south coast. The first few jumps, in particular, were exhilarating and, unlike Kapooka, we were able to get pissed every night.

Not every aspect of the army, I was learning, had to be as full-on as Kapooka. The parachute course was intense, and everyone was focused on learning the flight and emergency drills, but there was still time for some humour. One day, everyone on the course was sitting in the big timber-panelled lecture room, paying attention to the instructor. As he was talking, the door behind him opened softly and another instructor, totally naked except for a paper bag over his head with eye holes cut out of it, snuck in, padded silently along the stage behind the lecturer, then slipped out another door. As hard as we tried, some of us couldn't help laughing. The instructor wanted to know what was so funny, but no-one said a thing. He looked behind him and saw nothing. As soon as he returned to his lecture notes and continued speaking, the naked phantom -reappeared, and darted behind him and out the first door.

While the parachute course was fun, I wasn't getting any closer to my dream of working with dogs. There was only one military dog handler's course per year and I always seemed to miss it. However, in the airborne troop we also learned how to do hand searches for bombs and would often work with the dog teams, both in training and in real-life searches for bombs and explosives with the police and other civil authorities.

I really enjoyed watching dogs and their handlers working together as a team, especially when the handler would let the dog off its lead to do its job. The dogs always seemed so eager to please their partners, and responded to every command as though they were perfectly attuned to them. I was fascinated by how a handler would position himself to channel a dog into searching different areas, and the way he would anticipate the dog's every move and read its body language. There was understanding, respect and friendship there. I knew that I always felt better with a dog by my side, so how much better could life get if I were paid to work with dogs like these guys did? The longer I had to wait to get on the dog handler's course, the keener I became.

The work of searching, in training and for real, continued. When the former President of the United States, George Bush Snr, came to Australia on a state visit, the airborne troop was part of the team tasked with searching his hotel room and other venues he'd be in. We prided ourselves on our professionalism, although when one of our guys, Wrighty, was searching with a small hand mirror inside a fuse box at the Maritime Museum in Sydney, he did manage to black out a whole section of the building by short-circuiting something.

There was a huge bang, like an explosion which, given the job we were doing, startled everyone. We went to see what had happened and Wrighty was just standing there, stunned. His hair was sticking out – he looked like the boxing promoter Don King – and his eyebrows had disappeared. The glass had blown out of his hand mirror and the metal was all buckled.

One of my mates, Chris Arp, went up to Wrighty to check him out. 'How are you not dead?' Chris asked in amazement.

'I don't know.' Wrighty said. 'I should be dead.' He's still got that mirror, to this day, as a souvenir.

The president's Secret Service detail was also checking places, but they weren't keeping too close an eye on their own vehicles, because one of my mates, Wainy, managed to nick one of their numberplates, which we proudly displayed in the unit boozer.

The dog teams searched the president's hotel room first, and then we went in to do a second, detailed, check, following the dogs so that our scents didn't confuse them. We used mirrors to check in hard to see places, methodically searching from left to right, and from the lowest to the highest parts of the room.

'So, this is George's room?' Wainy said as we searched the hotel suite.

'That's what the intel said.' Wainy looked at me, and I smiled and nodded. We knew this was a once-in-a lifetime opportunity that we couldn't pass up. At the time, Jane and I had a favourite practical joke that we liked playing when friends stayed at our place, or when we went visiting. I told the other guys about it and they thought it would make for a fitting welcome for the US President. One of them ducked outside and kept watch for Secret Service dudes while the rest of us quickly went to work.

I'd like to think that George and Barbara Bush saw the brighter side, after a long day of public engagements, of trying to climb into a king size bed that had been short-sheeted by some Aussie soldiers.

TWO
Ziggy

1994

Finally, in February 1994, after more than four years' wait, I was able to get into an Explosive Detection Dog Handler's course at the School of Military Engineering.

I'd come a fair way since joining the army as a seventeen-year-old. Jane and I had married in 1992, and while I'd been waiting to go on the handler's course, I'd already done my two promotion courses to become a corporal and had been promoted to lance corporal. The other five students on the dog handler's course were all sappers.

If I had wanted to pursue higher rank in the army, I wouldn't have gone on the dog handler's course. At the time there was only one sergeant dog handler's position in the Australian Army, so, until he retired or died, there was no prospect of me even going higher than being a corporal, which was the next rung on the promotion ladder. All up, there were probably less than 20 military dog handlers in Australia at the time. However, rather than lessening, my determination to work with explosive sniffer dogs had grown stronger over the years I'd been around them as a field engineer and in the hand-search role.

The corporal instructor on the dog handler's course was Mark Wilczynski, who had been a lance corporal dog handler when I was in the airborne troop. When I was working on hand searches, I'd always be asking Mark questions about his job, and whether he'd let me work as the number-two on his team, so I knew him well by the time the course started. I'd also got to know another dog handler, Sean Reason, who had let me work with him and his dog. As it turned out, Mark was the one who would recruit me to work in Afghanistan many years later.

Chris Arp, who had been with me when Wrighty nearly killed himself searching the Maritime Museum, was also on the course with me. Because there were only a few students, and it was a tight-knit unit once you qualified, the instructors wanted to make sure they would get the most out of their dogs and the soldiers who would end up working with them. I didn't know it at the time, but even though he already knew me, Mark had called my troop commander to ask what sort of bloke I was. He did this with all the students on the course so that he could make sure he assigned the right dog to the right man. Dogs, like humans, have very different personalities, and Mark had a good feel for what types of dogs would fit best with different types of humans.

I was assigned a German shepherd cross Doberman named Ziggy, who was so laid-back and friendly he was like Scooby-Doo. Some dogs work at a hundred miles an hour and need little encouragement, but Ziggy was the opposite, as I soon learned. He needed a handler who would give him 100 per cent attention to make sure he worked well and to keep him motivated. Ziggy wasn't a dog that, where work was involved, could be turned on and off. His need to be worked intensively all the time pushed me to develop my dog handling skills to the limit, right from the start. We really had to work as a team. I hope that Mark gave me Ziggy to ensure that I'd get the most out of the course, having been busting a gut for so many years to get on it, and because he knew I liked to be active. Either that, or he was screwing with me.

The course lasted three months. Every morning, the students had to walk all the dogs in the kennels, rather than just the ones assigned to us. We also had to clean the kennels, which, like most things in the army, were subject to regular inspections. If the kennels weren't clean enough, we'd be told to do them all over again. We'd take it in turns either to walk the dogs or clean the kennels.

Sometimes cleaning the kennels could be disgusting work, especially if a dog had been sick. Ziggy had gastro one day and when Chris and I walked into Ziggy's enclosure it looked like the dog had spray painted the entire place, even the ceiling was covered in shit.

As we would not always have a vet nearby, especially if we were in the bush, we were taught basic care of our dogs, so Chris and I decided we should at least take Ziggy's temperature before I took him to the vet. I convinced Chris that as Ziggy was my dog it would be better if I held him while Chris inserted the thermometer.

Though not completely convinced, Chris put on a rubber glove and put some Vaseline on his finger, ready to do the dirty work.

Chris lifted Ziggy's tail. 'Mate I am not touching that thing.'

Still holding Ziggy I leaned around to have a look. Ziggy's arse looked nasty, swollen and red. 'You'll be right.'

'Put a muzzle on him, then,' Chris said.

'Nah, he'll be OK,' I said. Everybody knew that despite his fierce appearance, Ziggy was a placid, gentle dog.

To be sure, Chris smeared on more Vaseline, but the moment his finger came into contact with Ziggy's bum the dog leapt out of my arms like a rocket propelled grenade leaving a launcher and hit the ground, barked and growling at Chris like he wanted rip his bloody arm off.

'Good boy, Ziggy, good boy,' I said, trying not to laugh as I got Ziggy under control.

'We're going to the vets – now,' Chris said, 'you can stick a thermometer up your dog's arse next time!'

Ziggy taught me a lot. In the Australian Army at that time, we were trained to work our dogs off-lead. That is, once we were in an area that needed to be searched, we would unclip our dog's leash and let them roam free, so that they could get on with the job. The advantage for the handler, of course, is that if anything goes wrong and the dog trips a booby trap or a mine, there is less risk of injury or death for the handler. In my experience, the dogs also enjoy working this way, as opposed to working at the end of a long lead. They can get into tight places a lot more easily, and show more expression through their actions when they find something than they can if they're working on a lead. For the handler, working a dog off-lead requires a lot of training and practice. You're controlling the dog in many different ways, through your voice, body language (including hand signals), and through where and how you position yourself.

The dogs in the kennels were a mix of breeds. Many of them, like Ziggy, were shepherds, as this had once been the breed of choice. However, the army had started going for mongrels and crossbreeds with a high retrieval drive, rather than for pure breeds. Explosive detection dogs aren't cross-trained as attack or guard dogs, so the aggressive qualities that shepherds are known for really aren't necessary. Some of the older shepherds were being retired – sent to people's homes to be pets – and the army was looking for the right qualities in its dogs, more than at bloodlines.

The army didn't breed dogs or buy them from breeders. The K9 supervisors would instead keep an eye out in the local newspapers for people advertising that they were looking for a home for a dog, or sometimes people would contact us and offer to donate a dog. The supervisors would go around to the person's house, assess the dog there, and if it looked like it would be suitable, the dog would be brought to the School of Military Engineering for further assessment.

The first thing the supervisors looked for was whether the dog was a fanatical retriever – an animal with a high search-and-hunt drive. It didn't matter how big or small the dog was, as long as it showed it was crazy about running after a ball or a stick, or some other toy, and bringing it back. If you've ever had a dog like that, you know what I mean. It's the one with the wet, slobbery tennis ball in its mouth all the time – the one that you hope your house guests won't start playing with, because you know that he will never stop once he starts searching and retrieving.

Generally, the army would look for dogs that were about twelve-months-old, so that they weren't wasting time rearing puppies but the animals were still young enough to be trained properly. We also wanted dogs that weren't too highly strung. Again, the army was finding that cross-bred mongrels tended to have this quality. As the dogs would be working off-lead, they also needed to be reasonably obedient, so that they would respond to a handler's commands, and not go chasing or biting any bystanders who happened to be in the search area. The other good thing about mongrels was that they tended to get on better with each other in the kennels. Having too many cranky old alpha-male shepherds living side by side, testing each other out, led to aggression between the dogs.

Once I was assigned Ziggy, I was given time to get to know him. I took him for long walks around the School of Military Engineering, past the classrooms and training areas, and along the banks of the Georges River, which backs on to the base. I learned how to groom him properly, and to care for him in barracks and in the field. I'd give him a finger-tip massage, running my hands through his coat to check for ticks and fleas, sores and external parasites such as ringworm. Unless he got filthy doing something during training, I'd only wash Ziggy once a month, which was standard procedure in the army. If you wash a dog too often, its coat loses the nutrients and natural oils that keep it in top condition.

All the other dogs assigned to us on the course were already trained and experienced in detecting explosives. It was us humans who were learning the ropes. Our training covered how to search different areas, from open spaces to buildings. We were taught how to search in teams, and how to work to established patterns, so that we didn't miss anything. We'd train in public venues, such as the 12,000-seat Sydney Entertainment Centre, which is a huge building; we'd have to learn how to break it up into zones that we could cover one at a time.

In the Australian Army, the dogs had been trained to respond to praise, rather than to food rewards. The New South Wales Police, where I would work later, fed their dogs when they did the right thing, but a soldier in the field can't carry unlimited amounts of snacks for his dogs. Our police had learned their food-reward training from the Bureau of Alcohol, Tobacco and Firearms in the United States. Training methods can also depend on the dogs themselves, as some breeds respond better than others to food. The police tend to use labradors, and they love food.

Another point of difference in the Australian Army compared with other organisations using dogs was that our dogs were trained to give an active response when they detected the explosives. They were encouraged to show a change in behaviour – to, for example, bark, or wag their tail when they found what they were looking for – and the handler had to learn to recognise his dog's change in behaviour. This was a signal to their handler that they had found something. In the case of the police, and the companies I've served with in Afghanistan, the dogs are trained to give a passive response – that is, when they first find something, they sit and stare at the source of the explosive odour. Ziggy, my dog, would change his behaviour by standing and staring. Sometimes you've just got to accept that your dog has its special way of doing things, and work with it.

As well as indoor venues, such as the Entertainment Centre, we trained in open spaces, such as Warwick Farm Racecourse; on long stretches of road; and on the ferries on Sydney Harbour. Man and dog – but particularly man – were being tested all the time during the course. In open areas, especially along roads, we had to keep our dogs motivated all the time, as there were few obvious places for them to look and fewer objects to get their attention. They needed to keep searching and we needed to stay focused as well.

*

After graduating from the dog handler's course, I was posted back to my old unit at Holsworthy, which was now called 1 Combat Engineer Regiment (1 CER).

There was an odd situation for a while, as the senior dog handler in the unit was a sapper – the engineers' equivalent of a private – and I was a lance corporal, even though I was a junior dog handler. Eventually, the sapper in charge left and I became the commander of the dog element. Although I had a superior rank, it was a lot of responsibility for me to be given, because there were other handlers with more experience than me.

Still, we all got on well together and I really enjoyed getting stuck into being an explosive detection dog handler. I'd waited long enough to do it. At the time, the New South Wales Police didn't have a bomb dog capability, so the army dog handlers, based at Holsworthy, were the only ones qualified to use dogs to search for explosives. We would get called out whenever there was a bomb threat, and the police would sometimes call on us to help them in proactive operations.

On one occasion, we took part in simultaneous searches of three outlaw bikie gangs' premises around Sydney. We went into one of the clubhouses, which had a fully stocked bar inside. I let my dog off its leash and off it went, sniffing around the clubhouse. When it got behind the bar, it started indicating, by changing its behaviour and staying focused on one area, that it had found something.

'We've already searched behind there. There's nothing of interest,' one of the cops said.

'Well,' I replied, 'the dog's interested, so maybe you'd better have another look, mate.'

The police went behind the bar, got down on their knees, and started scratching around and lifting up the floor covering. Underneath, they found a hidden safe, buried in the floor.

There was nothing in it, but I suspected there must have been some ammunition, or maybe even explosives of some kind, stored in there at one point. The dog wouldn't have indicated it for nothing.

We searched venues both when the Pope and former US President Bill Clinton visited Australia. For big jobs, the army sometimes brought in the Brisbane-based army dog team to work with us. For some reason, the Queensland handlers thought their shit didn't stink and would brag about how they were the best in the country. Whatever, I thought.

Pope John Paul II was going to visit the Maritime Museum, so we were searching it prior to his arrival. I was on one of the lower levels of the underground car park, working my dog off-lead. Two levels above me was one of the teams from Queensland.

'Milo!' I heard someone call. 'Milo? MILO!'

I looked around and saw a border collie, Milo, one of the Queensland dogs, bounding down the car park ramp. It ran past me and stopped to greet my dog, disturbing its search pattern in the process. Running down the ramp, out of breath, was one of the army's 'ace' dog handlers from Brisbane, who had completely lost the plot, and his dog.

'Real' searches, however, were the exception rather than the rule. For the most part, my day followed a set routine of letting Ziggy out of his kennel; exercising him; cleaning his kennel; doing some training with him; accounting for, and packing away, the explosive training aids we'd been using; and taking Ziggy back to his home for the night.

As much as I loved my job, and working with Ziggy, the army was starting to get me down. Life in the army in peacetime involves a high degree of bullshit.

In the absence of a real threat, you go on exercise after exercise, and nothing ever seems to change. Things that are exciting to you as a young soldier, such as living out in the bush, shooting, and playing at war, lose their attraction as you get older. You start asking yourself, when you're sitting in a hole in the ground and it's pissing down rain, what the fuck am I doing here, wasting my life away?

To a certain extent, I don't think the Australian Army really knew how to use dogs, except as support to the civil authorities in searches prior to the arrival of some dignitary. Our dogs weren't trained in attacking, or as trackers, so there wasn't very much for the dogs or their handlers to do when the combat engineer regiment packed up and went out into the bush on an exercise. Our dogs were more at home working in the city, searching buildings or roads, than in the rainforests and scrub of northern Australia. Usually what would happen was one of the handlers would stay and look after all the dogs, and the rest of us would go and help the other field engineers build a bridge or do whatever else had to be done. It was a bit of a waste even having the dogs there. It was different once the army started to become operational again, in East Timor and, later, in Afghanistan. There, the dogs and handlers had a real job to do, looking for explosives and improvised explosive devices (IEDs).

Having waited more than four years to do the explosive detection dog handler's course, twelve months after I'd passed, I was ready to pack it all in. This wasn't because of the job itself, it was just being in the army, and probably due to the particular phase of life I was in. I had a young wife at home, and would be away for six weeks at a time, several times a year, on boring field exercises.

I started thinking that I'd get out of the army and learn a trade, so that I'd have something else to fall back on, later in life. I went to see Mark and my troop commander, and told them how I was feeling. They tried to talk me out of leaving, but by this stage I'd made up my mind, and I put in my papers seeking a discharge.

There was one more exercise I had to attend, in Darwin, before I could go. Just before we were due to leave, I went to the kennels on a Monday morning, back at work after a weekend off, with Chris, who had also passed the handler's course and was in my unit. The dogs were always crazy full of energy on a Monday, after being cooped up in their kennels for two days.

Chris went to his dog, at the far end of the kennels and I went to Ziggy. When I got to him, even before I went into his yard I saw something wasn't right; he was just lying on the ground. It was odd, as normally he would have been bounding up to the gate, jumping up to get me to let him out. I supposed it was possible he was sleeping, though he was on the ground, next to his bed.

'Hello, boy.' Ziggy just lay there. 'Ziggy? Get up, boy.' He still didn't move. I started to worry, and grabbed hold of the diamond mesh fence surrounding the kennels and shook it. The other dogs started barking and carrying on. 'Ziggy!'

Hearing the commotion, Chris came to me.

'Come on mate, get up. Stop being stupid,' I yelled at Ziggy.

Chris eased past me, opened the gate and went in. I was frozen there. I didn't want to go in, to hear what Chris said next.

Chris dropped to his knees and checked Ziggy. 'Mate,' Chris looked up at me and I could see the distress in his face, 'he's not moving. I think he's dead.'

I forced myself to go inside and took Ziggy into my arms. As soon as I touched him I knew Chris was right, that Ziggy was gone, but it took a few seconds for the realisation to sink in.

'No!' I yelled. Chris and I both lost it, tears streaming down our faces. Ziggy was a perfectly healthy dog and I couldn't understand how this had happened. My shock turned to anger. When they saw my face later, my other mates in the handlers' building asked me what was wrong and I told them. I smashed my fist into one of the freestanding partition walls in the office.

I walked back outside and let myself into Ziggy's kennel again, and sat beside his lifeless form. I still couldn't really believe he was dead. As I stroked his head, I thought of the months we'd spent together on the training course, and all the time working as a team since then. Ziggy had been like my best friend. I spent more time with him than I did at home; than with anyone else I knew. We shared every working hour. We were mates. And now he was gone.

The officer commanding, a major, and the troop commander, a lieutenant, heard what had happened and came down to the kennels. They found me there, still sitting with Ziggy, patting him and crying. They were very supportive and, after a time, they walked with me out of the kennels. I went to the car park and just sat there, my head in my hands, still trying to come to terms with the fact that my friend was dead.

Everyone else in the squadron was really helpful, as they knew how much Ziggy meant to me, and gave me time to grieve. A good friend of mine, Pottsy, who worked as a dog handler before transferring back into the squadron as a field engineer, organised a funeral for Ziggy. Pottsy had actually trained Ziggy from when he was a young dog, so was close to him too. The pair of us went to the vet to fetch his body, after an autopsy was done.

'Ziggy died from something called gastric torsion,' the vet told us. 'It's not uncommon in medium-to-large dogs. If the dog has a full stomach and then jumps suddenly, its whole stomach can swing around and twist. The entrance and exit to the stomach are then closed off, and gas can't escape. It might have only taken an hour or so for Ziggy to die.'

'But he was fine when I left him,' I said, still having trouble coming to terms with my loss.

'It's not your fault. Gastric torsion can happen to perfectly healthy dogs. Was Ziggy ever agitated in his kennel?'

I thought about this for a few moments. 'Ziggy was living next to a bitch and there was another male dog on the other side of her. Ziggy and the other male would sometimes snarl and bark at each other.'

The vet nodded. 'Maybe Ziggy and the other dog were jumping up on the wire of their enclosures and trying to antagonise each other, and that's when Ziggy twisted his stomach.'

Putting the pieces together was little consolation, but it was a valuable lesson about one of the possible risks of keeping dogs the way that we did. The vet said we could take Ziggy, and Pottsy and I found some shovels and dug a hole for him out the front of the dog section kennels.

It was raining the day we buried Ziggy. The dog handlers belonged to 1 CER's Specialist Troop and everyone from the troop was there, including my mate Chris and the troop commander who'd found me, distraught, in the kennel. Ziggy was as much a part of the troop as any of the soldiers in the unit, and they all wanted to pay their respects.

Pottsy broke ranks and positioned himself in front of the assembled troop. 'Thanks for coming along,' he began. 'Ziggy was a boisterous dog, as I'm sure you all know, and one of a kind. He was the happiest dog a lot of us had seen in quite a while, and a little eccentric, maybe. He loved what he did, and was very committed. He will be sorely missed by all.'

Pottsy was sniffling a little as he then took his place with the others. I wiped the rain from my face and moved in front of the troop. I'd rather face bullets than talk before a crowd, but I needed to now. It was hard, and I can't really remember what I said.

It's difficult to explain how much time, love and other emotions you invest in a working relationship like the one I had with Ziggy. The fact that he'd died so suddenly, and not peacefully in old age, just seemed to make his death worse and so much harder to deal with. How can words convey what you feel for a mate who's been taken from you?

I pulled my discharge papers, because I didn't want to leave the army on such a sad note. I told the troop commander I'd hang in for at least another twelve months.

As I didn't have a dog, there was no point in me going on the exercise, so, instead, I went back to the School of Military Engineering for six weeks and was re-teamed with a new dog, whose name was K-Lee. She was a cross between a Rottweiler and a border collie. She was tough as nails and smart as well. With the other handlers and the rest of the troop being away, I had time to get to know K-Lee, and walking, playing and training with her helped ease the pain of Ziggy's death.

After everyone was back from the exercise, the army dog handlers took part in an open day at Victoria Barracks at Paddington in Sydney. We put on a display of search techniques, and manned a static display for visitors who wanted to look at the dogs and learn more about what we did. There were members of the New South Wales Police on duty as well, and I got talking to one of the coppers. With the Olympics only a few years away, the police were developing their own explosive detection dog capability.

When I was a kid, I'd been interested in joining the police, but had been put off it because I'd thought that I'd have to have my Higher School Certificate, and as I'd left school in Year Eleven, I'd believed I'd automatically be ruled out. The cop I was talking to at the open day suggested I take a closer look at the application criteria, to see if I could get in because of my army experience.

I did as he suggested, and found that if I'd made it to the rank of full corporal in the army, I'd be deemed experienced enough to apply for entry to the police. I was still a lance corporal – with one stripe instead of the corporal's two – although I had passed all the necessary courses to be promoted. As being a dog handler in the army was such a small, specialised trade, there were no full corporal positions available to me at that time. I talked to the officer commanding my squadron and he agreed to write a letter certifying that I was qualified to be a two-striper and that the only thing stopping my promotion was the lack of vacancies in that rank. In fact, he went a step further, saying that as the head of the local dog handling detachment, I had a lot more responsibility than did most of the section commanders employed elsewhere in the engineer regiment.

I left the army in October 1996 and was accepted for training at the New South Wales Police Academy, at Goulburn in the New South Wales Southern Highlands. The course started the following February.

The academy was a lot more relaxed than Kapooka was, though there was a shit-load more study to do than in the army. Being at the academy was a good experience, but I found it hard, mostly because of all the theory work. We studied law and analysed case studies. We'd be given a scenario, and then have to work out how a person would be charged and under which legislation. We had to do exams and write essays. I hate writing essays and, worse still, we'd have to give class presentations.

The walls of my room at the academy were plastered with bits of paper and cardboard with crib notes all over them. If I'd stuck anything on a wall at Kapooka, I probably would have been shot. I was paying for tutors to help me after hours but, even so, I only scraped through many of the theory subjects as I found writing essays difficult.

Jane and I had two little boys, Corey and Lachie, by this time. They were all living at her parents' place and I'd get there at weekends, making the relatively quick drive from Goulburn to the south coast. I also did a couple of weeks' work experience at Dapto Police Station during the course, which was good fun and, fortunately, was close to home.

Six months after I'd walked through the gates, I finally graduated from the academy. I was made a probationary constable and sent to Sutherland Police Station in Sydney's southern suburbs. The study hadn't finished, as probationary constables still had to sit exams for two years, but at least we were also doing the job of policing. With life becoming more stable, Jane and I started building a house at Albion Park, on the south coast. This was about an hour's drive to Sutherland, but I would carpool with some other police officers who lived near me.

There was a lot happening with Lebanese gangs in south-western Sydney at the time, and I was seconded to Bankstown Police Station, in the heart of one of the city's strongest Muslim areas, for three months. Generally, I found the parents and families of the gang members, and the older people in the Lebanese community, to be really hard-working, up-standing people, but some of the teenagers were a handful. Many had no respect for the law, or for much else, and had fallen in with the gangs. As gang members do, they'd hunt in a pack, but I found that when you dealt with them one-on-one, you broke down that pack mentality and their confidence, and then they weren't so brave.

What I liked about life in the police force was that, unlike being in the army, it was always different. You never knew where you'd be going or what you'd be doing next. You could be dealing with a minor traffic accident in a car park one minute, and the next thing you know, you're facing down an enraged man in a violent domestic dispute.

When I got to Sutherland, I was assigned to work with a top bloke, a highly experienced police sergeant named Steve Winder. Everyone in the station was respectful and wary of Steve because he had a real no-nonsense reputation. He was switched on, intelligent and hard as, knew his law inside and out, and had seen and done it all. Steve was English, but he'd been in the New South Wales Police for 25 or 30 years. At nearly 50, he was a lot older than me, but more than held his own in the gym and out on the street. He was always on the go and I had my arse hanging out all the time, just trying to keep up with him. It wasn't unusual for Steve and me to make three arrests a night, whereas other officers might do three in a week. The other young police thought I'd got the rough end of the stick in being lumped with this guy, but Steve and I clicked from the first day. I learned a hell of a lot just watching him–the way he interacted with people, paid attention to everything going on around him, and simply got on with the job of policing. He taught me how to interview people; what questions to ask to get them talking. I nicknamed him Pop.

Sergeant Winder, and a mate of mine, Nunny, and I were sent to serve an apprehended violence order on a guy in Kirrawee, near Sutherland. He'd been involved in a domestic with his estranged partner and the apprehended violence order against him was to ensure that he kept away from her. We'd received intel from the wife that he was a gun nut who had firearms stashed around his house.

We parked the car and, as we approached the house, started putting on our bullet-proof vests and doing up the Velcro fastenings on the side. At the back of the house was a granny flat, where another bloke was living; he came to the front fence to meet us and tell us that the owner was inside.

What we didn't know was that the man we'd come to serve the apprehended violence order on had also been watching our arrival. The granny flat lodger let us into the house and led the three of us as we moved cautiously down the hallway. We called out to let the owner know we were in there, and asked him to show himself.

The lodger paused in the hallway. At the end of it was an open door through which he could see a wardrobe mirror. 'There he is, there he is! He's under the bed.'

We flattened ourselves against the wall. As we edged closer, we could see on top of the dressing table a speed loader for a pistol, and it was empty. That probably meant the guy had just loaded a revolver with six bullets.

'Come on out, now,' Pop said to him.

The man refused to budge and, if he was armed, there was no way we were just going to charge on into his bedroom and drag him out from under his bed. We were about to declare the incident a siege and call for the tactical response group, when he said he was coming out.

He slithered out, and I pinned him on the ground and cuffed him. He admitted that he was armed and that when he'd seen the three of us walking up the road, he'd considered opening up on us and going out in a blaze of glory. When I slid underneath the bed, I found a .357 Magnum, a big-arse Dirty Harry gun, which he'd, indeed, loaded as we were approaching. Later, we found rifles throughout his house and a couple more, along with 2000 rounds of ammunition, in the boot of his car. We took him to the cells at Sutherland and he was back out on the street in less than a week.

On another occasion, Poppy Winder and I had to go to the home of a man with psychiatric problems and schedule him, which was basically an order that said he had to be assessed by a mental health team. When we arrived at his block of flats and found his place on the second floor, a piece of paper covered with gibberish was pinned to the front door.

Sergeant Winder knocked. 'Police; open up, please.'

'I'm not coming out,' a voice yelled back at us. 'I've tipped petrol all over myself and if you come in, I'm going to set fire to myself!'

Steve called for backup and when the other officers arrived, told them to keep the guy occupied, by talking to him through the door, while Pop and I would go around the back, and try to get in through a window. As the crazy man was two floors up, he wouldn't be expecting us. It was a typically ballsy plan from the hard-as-nails old cop.

We left the other police, ambulance crews and the fire brigade, who had also arrived by this time, and went downstairs and around to the rear of the block, and climbed a fire ladder. Steve prided himself on his appearance, and his uniform was always immaculate and his boots spit polished. As we climbed in through the flat's open kitchen window,

Steve first with me following, he cursed, softly. He'd scuffed the toe cap of his polished boot and was bent over in the kitchen, rubbing it with his thumb.

'What are you doing, Pop?'

'Fixing my boot. Why don't you go sort this bloke out, Shane?' With that, he continued wiping the toe of his shoe.

I couldn't believe it.

I smelled petrol fumes and when I walked out of the kitchen into the lounge room, there was the mad dude, wet with fuel, wide-eyed and holding a cigarette lighter. I put my hands up to calm him, but once he saw me, he gave up straightaway.

Maybe Steve, with his years of experience, could read the situation accurately and knew the guy wasn't going to kill himself. Or maybe it came down to his sense of humour, if that's what it was. His stopping casually to clean his boot while a crazy man was standing there soaking in petrol was designed to ensure I was calm when I approached the man. Steve had given me a chance to take charge and prove myself.

Knowing that Steve had a sense of humour, though, I did my best to mess with him at every opportunity. When he wasn't looking, I'd get his hat, and turn his prized cap badge upside down. This was the perfect way to take the piss out of someone who was a stickler for detail and cared so much about his personal presentation. Someone would always notice, eventually.

One day, I was driving around Sutherland on patrol with Nunny and we found an old toilet bowl on the side of the road; probably left out there by someone who'd been renovating their bathroom. We pulled over and, making sure no-one was watching, loaded it in the back of the patrol car. When we got back to the station, I asked Steve if I could borrow the keys to his car, as I needed to get the breathalyser out. He tossed them to me, and my mate and I went and moved the toilet from our vehicle to the back seat of Steve's, wrapping a seatbelt around the commode to keep it in place. When poor old Steve went back out on patrol, he was pulling people over, meeting and talking to them, never noticing the toilet sitting behind him.

THREE

Highs and lowlifes

1999

When I joined the police, I did so hoping that once I'd done my time in general duties, I could transfer to the dog squad. After nearly three years, I got my chance and was placed in an explosive detection dog handling course in February 1999. I'm sure a few people had their noses out of joint, as other police had to do a suitability test before being accepted into a dog handling course but I went straight into it

Unlike in the army, we got to choose our own dogs, and I chose a nice little labrador bitch called Nova. She was about eighteen months old at the time, probably the youngest and most immature of the bunch, but she was keen and eager to please. The sergeant in charge asked us why we chose our dogs, and was surprised I'd selected her. I told him that I was up for a challenge and liked her attitude.

The course went for two months and was different from what I was used to in the army, as we were trained to work the dogs on a lead, rather than the free-moving off-lead style I'd been accustomed to. Instead of rewarding Nova with a tennis ball to play with when she did the right thing, I had to feed her.

I found that I preferred working off-lead. Working with the dog on-lead is much more restrictive, for both the dog and the handler. It takes longer to search an area, and if the handler gets tired or lethargic or stands still, the dog will sense it and start sitting down. It would look for an excuse to stop working – just as a lazy human would. The other downside of working on-lead is that if the dog does find a bomb, the handler will be standing virtually on top of it. Even though it was against regulations, sometimes when I was searching a building, and out of the public eye, I'd let Nova off the lead, as I'd developed a good relationship with her and she easily took to working this way.

The New South Wales Police had ramped up their detection dog capability for the Sydney Olympics in 2000, and when the games were finally happening, we were right in the thick of everything. Nova and I, and another couple of handlers, Dan and Adam, searched the new Olympic Stadium at Homebush Bay prior to the opening and closing ceremonies, as well as the beach volleyball venue at Bondi Beach. Nova worked well and wasn't nearly as distracted as I was by the female teams who were practising there.

We also did searches during the Paralympics and I think I enjoyed that even more than doing them for the Olympics. You could really see the joy on the Paralympians' faces when they were competing. There was no arrogance or carry-on from any of those sportspeople, and you could tell they were really loving just being there. It was inspiring.

After the Sydney Olympics were over, the police started training dogs in drug detection. While I found this interesting,

I also felt like I'd hit a plateau and that I needed a change. Then something else happened to convince me that being a cop wasn't for me. While I'd been working in general duties at Sutherland, there had been an incident involving a man who'd been arrested and brought to the station to be charged. He was drunk and had beaten up his girlfriend because she wouldn't do what he told her–which was to sleep with another man.

He was aggressive, and when I'd put him in the dock to wait to be charged, he tried to get out, so I pushed him down. He was eventually charged and taken to remand. Later, he reported to prison officers that he had a broken jaw. He laid a claim against me, saying that I'd broken it when I was subduing him in the dock. It was bullshit but, as all complaints against police officers are taken seriously, it was investigated. The process was lengthy and I was put through the wringer several times. There was security camera footage from the police station but, as far as the Internal Affairs investigators were concerned, it didn't show conclusively whether I was innocent of striking the man on the chin. I knew I was innocent, which I continued to assert. It seemed clear to me that something had happened to the guy either in prison or on his way there; perhaps in the van. I mean, if someone's just broken your jaw, you don't sit quietly while being taken through the charging process and led off to jail in a truck, which is what he did.

In the end, the Internal Affairs cops delivered a finding that pissed me off. They found that, on the balance of probability, I had struck the man, but that they didn't have enough evidence with which to charge me. I'd served the police proudly, and gained a commendation for my work in stopping the madman threatening to burn himself to death from doing so. I respected the rule of law, and prided myself on upholding it in the most professional and dedicated way possible. I didn't shirk from confrontation, and Poppy's and my arrest record proved that we weren't the sort of policemen who looked for an easy ride. We had even received a high achievement award for our diligence in making arrests.

I hadn't struck the man in custody–though, God knows, I probably wanted to after what he'd done, but my own people had basically said to me, 'You're guilty, but we can't prove it.' They had taken the word of a drug user, who was trying to pimp his girlfriend, over mine. It left a bad taste.

I had issues on the home front, as well. Jane and I had had a third child together in 1999, a beautiful little girl named Demi, but were having problems with our relationship and ended up separating. I worked with a policewoman, Kim, on the dog squad and she was also having relationship diffi-culties. We began talking to and supporting each other, and ended up getting together.

After the low point of going through the investigation and a costly divorce, I finally decided that I needed a change of pace and more money. I left the police force in March 2001.

An ex-police friend got me a job working surveillance for a private investigation company. It paid better than being a po-lice officer, which was why I took the job. I was living in a flat with my brother, shelling out for rent as well as paying main-tenance to Jane. I hadn't yet moved in with Kim because she was in the process of finalising her own break-up.

The work mainly consisted of checking up on people who'd filed workers' compensation claims. I soon learned that while surveillance work paid OK, the hours were long, and it could get very tiring and boring sitting outside someone's house for hours at a time waiting for them do something in-criminating. It had its moments, though.

There was a case involving a guy, who was maybe in his late twenties and who lived in Bondi. I followed him for several days and nights. He was pretty fit, and I spent an after-noon watching, and secretly videoing, him and his lady friend exercising, running up and down the stairs near the Bondi Pavilion, and along the iconic beach.

After his beach workout, I followed the man across the Harbour Bridge to North Sydney, where he parked his car and entered the Berry Street Tavern. He was carrying a round case, like one of those make-up bags women have in old movies. I had a compact video camera with me, hidden in a laptop bag with a hole cut out for the lens, and, intrigued, I followed him into the pub.

A band was in the process of setting up, with roadies in black T-shirts hooking up amps and doing the old 'one-two, one-two, one-two' on the microphone. I'd lost sight of my target. But when the roadies finished and the lights came on, there was my man, on stage.

He was behind a set of bongo drums and laying down a rapid beat to the first track. He was smiling and so was I, be-cause, as I laid the laptop bag on the table and pressed the switch that started the video camera recording, I knew my long days and nights of following him were finally over. Pretty strange, I reckoned, to be moonlighting as a bongo player when, because of a supposedly injured wrist, you'd lodged a worker's compensation claim and been given money by your employer.

After eighteen months of following people, I was sick of the waiting, the watching and the boredom. I've always had an interest in property – buying, selling and developing it – so

I thought I'd give being a real estate agent a try. Kim and I had moved in together, to a house at Regentville in western Sydney, and I landed a job with a real estate agency at nearby Erskine Park. I'd read a few books about making money in the property market and, at the time, my mum was studying for her real estate agent's licence.

Real estate was a change of pace from surveillance – getting up at the same time each morning, shaving, putting on a shirt and tie, and going to an office, instead of pulling on grungy old jeans and T-shirts, and looking forward to a day of sitting in a car. I liked the work, but my timing was shithouse.

The market was peaking; people were asking ridiculous prices for houses and flats, and no-one was buying. It was the worst time to be on the selling side of the property game. At showing after showing, sometimes only one or two people – or, worse, no-one – would show up for an inspection. I stuck with selling real estate for two-and-a-half years, but it just wasn't working out, and neither was my relationship with Kim, even though we had two great little sons, Kyron and Jaylen, born in 2002 and 2005. She and I separated.

Over the years, I'd stayed in contact with Mark Wilczynski, the corporal instructor on my army dog handler's course. Having left the army, he was working as a contract explosive detection dog handler in Iraq. Mark emailed to say that he wanted me to go and work for him over there, but the company he worked for started losing contracts soon after he sounded me out. However, Mark told me he would keep me posted, as it looked as though there might be opportunities in Afghanistan.

After calling it quits with Kim, I moved closer to where I'd grown up, to Wollongong. Unemployed, I did an underground mining course, as I thought that work in the mines might be something I could be interested in—especially now that I had two ex-partners and five children to help support. The mines weren't hiring at the time so, for a little while, it looked like I was well and truly up shit creek without a paddle.

Fortunately, Mark emailed me again to tell me there was a job going in Afghanistan. I contacted his company, Canine Associates International, and emailed my CV to the human resources people. I met their criteria for an overseas job and they emailed me a contract, which I signed and sent back. I hadn't had a job interview in person with anyone, but I knew that Mark had been pushing behind the scenes for me to be recruited.

Ten years after leaving the Australian Army, I was going to war.

FOUR

Hurry up and wait

2006

Six weeks later, I was in a car with my mum, my sister and my girlfriend at the time, driving along the F5 freeway from Wollongong to Sydney airport.

Things had happened fast. One minute, I'd been out of work, with a mounting tide of debts, including two lots of child maintenance payments, and little hope of finding a well-paid job; the next, I was going to war.

Driving past the Royal National Park, I wondered how different things would be for me in Afghanistan. On television, it looked like it was all dirt and desert. It had been five years since the al-Qaeda terrorists had flown their hijacked jets into the Twin Towers and, while I hadn't been paying a lot of attention to the news, it seemed that things were hotting up again in Afghanistan, after some initial successes of the coalition forces.

I knew about as much about Afghanistan as would the average Australian – fuck all. After September 11, Australia had sent to Afghanistan a task force based around an SAS squadron and, by all accounts, they–and the Americans–had done a good job of routing the Taliban and helping the Afghans elect a new government, under Hamid Karzai. A year later, Australia pulled its troops out of their base at Bagram, near Kabul, and the boys were home for Christmas. The SAS, however, wasn't out of the fray for long, as they were back in action in March 2003, spearheading the advance into Baghdad. After the initial invasion of Iraq, the SAS came back to Australia and the government held welcome-home parades in Sydney and Perth. It was John Howard's equivalent of George Bush landing on the aircraft carrier and declaring 'Mission accomplished'.

But now, as we drove to the airport, there was a story on the radio of yet another car bomb going off somewhere in Iraq and killing dozens of people–most of them innocent Muslim civilians.

'At least you're not going there,' my mum said.

It was the same with my dad, who I'd moved in with after splitting up with Kim. He wasn't happy about me taking a job in Afghanistan but, like Mum, he seemed to think it was safer than Baghdad. I couldn't care less. All I knew was that I was going to war, and the reality of this was finally starting to hit home.

The money the new job paid was important to me, as I needed to get on top of my debts, and would have a financial commitment to my five kids for years to come. During the car ride, I didn't think about the morality of going to war for money, or whether some people would class me as a mercenary, or maybe see something wrong in the fact that the coalition was using paid civilian contractors in a war zone.

I'd been over the moon when I'd got the email from CAI confirming my contract. I'd been directionless after leaving the army and police, and had way more than the two years' experience the CAI required of its handlers. I'd been well trained by the army and the police as a dog handler, but there were few opportunities for me to work as one in Australia, outside of those that government agencies offered. But now, everything appeared to be coming together. It seemed like something, or someone, was telling me that my future was in working with dogs, and that it was what I was meant to do. In Afghanistan, I'd have the chance to put into practice, in a truly operational environment, everything I'd learned from my training and experience while in uniform in Australia.

I was booked to fly with Emirates and thought to myself that if you had to go to war, this wasn't a bad way to travel. I was looking forward to getting through the awkward farewells, boarding the plane, and ordering my first bourbon and Coke. Was I nervous? Maybe. I was excited at the prospect of a new challenge, and also, like any soldier, at finally putting into practice everything I'd learned and trained for over the years.

In one sense, an explosive detection dog handler in the police or the army, when they're working in support of the civil authorities, is in an operational situation when searching for bombs or weapons. If some nutjob sets off a bomb in Sydney and you get caught in the blast, you're just as dead as if the same thing happens elsewhere, but the risk of it happening is obviously far greater in somewhere like Afghanistan.

As I didn't want everyone hanging around for too long when saying their goodbyes, I tried to get them over with before I checked in. However, Mum, my sister and my girlfriend all insisted on staying until the flight was called. It was just as well they did.

I'd arranged to meet another dog handler, who was also going to Afghanistan to work for the same mob as I was, at the airport. His name was Guy, and he was an Australian of Filipino descent, who had been working for the Australian Protective Service. Australian Protective Service provides security for Parliament House, various federal government and defence department properties, and our embassies abroad. It's also responsible for the initial response to terrorist incidents at Australia's major airports and for providing 'sky marshals' on civilian flights. Guy had flown from Brisbane to Sydney and was booked on the same flight that I was. Once we found each other, we hit it off immediately. We queued together to check in. After I was called forward, I dragged my kitbag and backpack up to the scales.

I gave the Emirates check-in woman my name and produced my passport, and she started tapping away on her keyboard. Then she frowned. 'Um, I can't seem to find a booking here for you, Mr Bryant.'

I resisted the urge to swear. 'What do you mean? It's been booked by the company I'm going to work for – Canine Associates International. Sydney to Heathrow, and from there on to Manus, in Kyrgyzstan.'

'Just let me try something else.' She tapped away some more, then shook her head. 'I'm very sorry, but I don't have you booked on any flights.'

'What the ... Guy?' I called to my new colleague.

He came up to the counter, gave his full name and produced his passport. The woman shook her head, apologised and told us that Guy didn't have a booking either. We knew it wasn't her fault, but Guy and I were seriously pissed off.

We left the queue and started making calls. As it turned out, the company hadn't ever confirmed our bookings and paid for our tickets. Everyone we talked to was very apologetic, but that didn't stop this whole thing being a fucking joke. Guy called some friends in Sydney and arranged to stay with them until things were sorted out, while I went back to the people who'd come to see me off and told them the news.

My mood fluctuated on the drive back home. At first, I was angry that I'd said my goodbyes and psyched myself up as best as I could to fly off to Afghanistan and the war. Man, CAI was worse than the army, which usually sets the benchmark when it comes to fucking people around.

As we drove in the fast-flowing freeway traffic through the darkened bush back towards Wollongong, I started to mellow. I would have been happier being on the plane, but at the same time I felt a bit like a condemned man who'd been granted a couple of days' stay of execution. I realised I'd have a little longer to enjoy life in Australia, and resolved to make good use of the time. I'd still be getting stuck into the bourbon, but not at 30,000 feet over some desert.

When I returned to the airport a few days later, it was a relief to find the ticket had now been booked and paid for. I said my goodbyes, and waved as I went through into the departure lounge.

This was it; I was really going overseas. When a smiling flight attendant served me my first bourbon, I settled back into my seat and switched on the in-flight entertainment. This, I thought, *this* is the way to go to war.

The flight, however, seemed to go on forever. We stopped somewhere in the middle of the night–I was so disorientated that I can't remember where–before landing again at Heathrow.

I had to wait for a connection and by the time I touched down at Manus airport, in Kyrgyzstan, I was tired, dirty, and probably a little hung-over. Guy had travelled on a different flight from Sydney, so I arrived in this strange former outpost of the Soviet Union alone.

Kyrgyzstan had aligned itself with the United States early in the war against al-Qaeda and the Taliban, and Manus had become an important support base for the war in Afghanistan. Australian Air Force refuelling aircraft had been kept here in the early days of the fighting, and the air base near the civilian airport was still a major hub for a number of different forces flying their people into and out of Afghanistan.

The uniformed bureaucrats at Immigration looked like extras from some old Cold War spy movie and the whole terminal – a drab, '60s Russian-inspired building – was looking pretty tired. When I finally cleared Customs, I was mobbed in the arrivals hall by a swarm of taxi drivers, but no-one from the company was there to meet me and I had to work out how to get to the Manus air force base.

'Mister, mister, mister … you come with me,' they were all yelling in my face. I was tired and jet-lagged, and had no idea how far the base was from the terminal. I picked a guy at random and asked him if he could take me there. 'Yes, yes, mister. Twenty dollars, mister.'

This sounded like a lot, but I didn't have much alternative but to agree. The air outside was chilly, but at least I wasn't inside an aeroplane. I loaded my bags into the back of the driver's crappy old sedan and got in. 'I take you, Mister. No problem.'

My 20 US dollars bought me a 600-metre drive from the terminal to the front gate of the military base. I was pissed off with the driver, but too knackered to argue with the dodgy bastard. I showed the orders I had with me to an American soldier at the gate, who called the US Air Force police. A guy came and checked my paperwork and let me in.

He directed me to a line of tents, which was the transit accommodation for people coming and going. I found a stretcher and passed out. I was too tired to reflect on what lay ahead, or to care much about the journey of false starts and endless plane trips I'd had.

When I later woke up and started looking around, I asked an American airman where I could get a coffee, and he directed me to a café on base with internet access. I went there, bought a coffee and sat down at a computer. I still didn't know who I was supposed to meet or report to, or where, but while sitting there, I saw a familiar face.

'Hey, Mick!' I couldn't believe it. Here, just wandering past me in this formerly communist country, was Mick McAuliffe, a bloke I'd been in the army dogs with.

'Shane! What the fuck are you doing here?'

Mick had been working in the US and, as it turned out, had arrived in Afghanistan only a couple of days earlier. He was now with the same company I was, CAI. Mick and I caught up on what each of us had been up to, and we went back to the tent, collected my gear and took it to where he was staying.

No thanks to them, I started to get my shit together. The resourceful Aussie had scammed a four-bed room in a proper hard-standing building. There was no sign yet, however, of Guy. He showed up a few hours later and catching up with him felt like old times, even though we barely knew each other.

Guy had been screwed around worse than I had. 'I reported at the gate and they wouldn't even let me in,' he said. 'I had to get a cab into town and find somewhere to make some phone calls.'

From then on, it was a classic hurry-up-and-wait situation. We were stuck on the base at Manus for twelve days. Like all US bases I've been on, Manus was massive, and set up like a self-contained chunk of small-town America. As well as the café and the chow hall, there was a Pizza Hut, a tailor, a barber and a PX – the post exchange shop.

As we couldn't go sightseeing off-base, we had to occupy ourselves as best as we could and, to kill time, I'd walk the aisles of the PX. It was set up like a small, cramped variety store, with different departments. There were television sets, DVD players and ghetto blasters in the electrical section, along with iPods, computers, new-release movies, and CDs, and there was a whole aisle devoted to war-related merchandising. It was bizarre. There were coffee cups, T-shirts, Zippo lighters, ashtrays, and souvenir maps of Afghanistan, all emblazoned with the 'Operation Enduring Freedom' logo – an American eagle clutching a bomb in his talons. One of the classier souvenirs was the beer stein, with a giant ceramic eagle built into the handle, with his head on the pop-open lid. There was a separate range of 'Afghanistan Now' goods – mousepads, embroidered patches and more coffee mugs, featuring an Apache gunship flying across the mountains, with the font and colour the same as in the posters for *Apocalypse Now*. It seemed you couldn't go to war without buying the T-shirt, or the mousepad.

The US Air Force allowed its personnel and civilian contractors staying at Manus two beers every 24 hours and while the system was policed electronically – you were issued with an ID card that was swiped when you bought a drink – I got friendly with a couple of the air force bar staff, who'd palm me the odd extra drink without swiping my card.

As well as military people, there were plenty of civilian contractors passing through Kyrgyzstan en route to Afghanistan. They were a mixed bunch of nationalities – Americans, Canadians, Brits, South Africans, a Tanzanian and Aussies – all ex-military or ex-police. By and large, they were a good bunch, but a couple were fucking idiots – try-hards and wannabes.

Contracting attracts very different people. Some are ex-military, who are there for the money and, maybe, because they want to see some action, and so put themselves and their training to the ultimate test. Some have been on operations and some haven't. There's also the lunatic fringe – would-be Rambos and gun nuts, who have seen too many Stallone and Schwarzenegger movies and want to shoot someone. Of course, I'd rather work alongside someone who's there because they can do the job and need the money than alongside a psycho who wants to find out what it's like to shoot someone, but, unfortunately, the job attracts both types.

Buck Dikes was one American I warmed to immediately. He was a former US Marine and had worked as dog handler with the American police. He was larger than life in every way; a big guy with a good sense of humour, who liked a beer and was an excellent communicator. You couldn't help but like him. He was a bit older than the rest of us – in his late forties – and, naturally, Guy and I immediately christened him Uncle Buck, after John Candy's character in the movie of the same name.

In the background was the constant hum and roar of C-130s and C-17s coming and going to Afghanistan. The other dog handlers and I were travelling on what the Americans called Space-A – space available transport. I was starting to learn a whole new language and Space-A, translated, meant low-priority. Uniformed American personnel got top billing, arranged by rank, and coalition soldiers and airmen were next. At the bottom of the heap were the civilian contractors like me. We'd show up at the Pax terminal at a predetermined 'show time', to see if our names would be called for a flight. When they weren't, we'd filter back to the coffee shop or the PX, or watch DVDs in our rooms. I was used to waiting, thanks to my days in the Australian Army, but it never got any easier.

'Bryant, Shane,' the US Air Force sergeant said, looking around the terminal. I looked up and replied.

Next, he called Buck's name, then Guy's and then Mick's.

'You're on,' said the sergeant.

We dropped our big bags on a pallet, and airmen started covering them with a cargo net and lashing them down. I picked up my daypack, and we filed out of the building and onto the runway. It was May and, while the days were getting warmer, there was still a knife's edge of chill in the black night as we walked across the tarmac to the squat grey bulk of the C-17 transport aircraft.

The temperature momentarily increased a couple of degrees as we passed through the kerosene-smelling wash of the hot exhaust of the two jet engines, which were already turning and burning. A loadmaster wearing a desert-tan flight suit, with a nine-millimetre in a shoulder holster, directed us towards the rear ramp and up into the aircraft's cavernous empty belly. There was only another couple of people on the aircraft, which could seat more than 100. After all this waiting, it seemed they'd found a plane just for us lowly civilian dog handlers. An American flag hung from the ceiling, stretching out proudly by the forward bulkhead. The crewman got inside and raised the ramp, and the stars disappeared from the night sky. The engines began to whine as the pilot increased the throttle, and we rumbled down the runway.

With a noisy clunk the C-17 swallowed its wheels. I was in the air at last, on my way to someone else's war.

FIVE

Welcome to Afghanistan

May 2006

Once the overhead lights went to white, we were able to get out of our seats and walk around the vast hold of the cargo aircraft. You could have played a cricket match in there. I could sometimes make out in the moonlight the shapes of mountains below, capped with snow and bigger than anything I'd ever seen.

The countryside seemed harsh. Cold. Hot. Hostile. How hard must a people be, I wondered, to survive in a place like that? No-one was talking much; I guess we all felt pretty much the same. Brewing away in my gut was a mix of excitement, anticipation and nerves. It wasn't a fear of war, or of getting shot at or dying, it was just a fear of the unknown, and I hoped that when I was put to the test as an operational dog handler, I'd come through all right. Most of us were too keyed up to get much sleep, but Buck, who'd already done time in Iraq as a handler, was snoozing, his head lolling to one side.

As if to emphasise that things were about to change dramatically for all of us, the air force loadmaster retrieved his body armour from a forward seat and Velcro-ed it on.

The red lights went on overhead, and the loadmaster motioned for us to go back to our seats and buckle in. I couldn't see much from inside the C-17, as I was facing inwards and wasn't close to a window. The pilot came in steep and fast, no doubt practising some sort of evasive manoeuvre in case of surface-to-air missiles. I'd read that the CIA had sold Osama and co a shit-load of Stingers when they were all on the same side, fighting the Russians. There were still plenty in circulation, and I'd heard that the same American spooks were offering a million US dollars a pop to buy back any of the shoulder-launched missiles left over from the old days.

When the rear ramp of the C-17 opened, I had to screw my eyes shut, because of the sudden flood of light and the wind-blown dust that swirled in the idling engines' exhausts. As we filed out and across the tarmac, I could feel so much grit on my exposed skin that it was like I was being sandblasted. A forklift raced across to the aircraft, its driver wearing goggles, and a scarf over his mouth. The first thing I smelled was shit. Later, I learned that this was from the badly sited sewage farm at the western end of Kandahar's airstrip.

The row of upside-down egg-shaped arches in front of the terminal might have been the height of modern architecture when they were built, but now they looked like part of the set of a low-budget sci-fi movie set on a waterless, hostile planet. I later learned the terminal was built by the Americans, of all people, in the 1950s as a place for long-haul propeller-driven aircraft to refuel on their way to Europe, but the jet age had made it pretty well redundant.

Kandahar is home to about 300,000 people and is Afghanistan's third-largest city. It's the capital of the province of the same name, located in the south of Afghanistan, near the Arghandab River. Kandahar was kind of a spiritual home of the modern Taliban. During the war against the Russians, loose bands of Taliban, which means 'religious students' fought as a faction of the Mujahideen, the general name for the Afghan freedom fighters. After the war ended in 1989, the Kandahar Taliban emerged as the dominant group in the faction, and took over their home city in 1994. Their influence and numbers spread, and by 1996 they had invaded and taken Kabul, defeating a string of rival warlords and factions.

The Americans and the Northern Alliance, however, had kicked the Taliban out of Kabul in the operations following September 11, and the coalition forces had rolled on to Kandahar. The Kandahar airport terminal, where I had landed, was known as the Taliban's Last Stand, as it was here in late 2001 that a number of diehards had fought US forces to the death. Either the Americans hadn't killed them all or the Taliban had been having a recruitment drive because, from everything I saw around me, we were very definitely still at war.

Mark Wilczynski was there to meet us. He and I shook hands and, as with Mick, it was good to see a familiar face.

'G'day. Welcome to Afghanistan.'

In contrast to the disorganisation we'd experienced so far, Mark had a ten-day program of training and assessment ready for us, but first we had to get squared away and be allocated our dogs.

Our accommodation was in semi-permanent canvas tents, divided into individual rooms with plywood partitions and air–conditioned. There was building going on throughout the base, as it had been clear for some time that the Americans weren't going to be leaving Afghanistan any time soon.

The base was enormous, and home to thousands of US and coalition soldiers. There were Americans, British, Canadians, various Eastern European nationals doing their best to be accepted as part of NATO, and even a few Australians. In addition to the men and women in uniform was another army, of civilian contractors from countries as diverse as Thailand, the Philippines, South Africa, India, Nepal, and more Eastern European nations. Contractors dressed like extras from a Rambo movie strutted around carrying M4s and wearing nine mils slung low in leg holsters. Trucks and humvees added to the dust cloud that hung in the air, and choppers, Hercs and C-17s were constantly landing or passing overhead.

In between the scream of jets coming and going were the shrill whine of drills and the pounding of hammers, as the tents progressively gave way to demountables and more permanent buildings. A spider's web of electricity cables was strung everywhere from concrete and steel poles, and water trucks trundled up and down the streets, waging an ongoing, and largely futile, war against the dust. Work had just finished on a long timber boardwalk lined with shops and fast-food joints. There was Subway, Burger King and a Canadian donut shop called Tim Horton's. As well as a new PX, there were mobile phone shops; a screen-printing place that did T-shirts; and a tactical shop, where I was able to buy some field gear, although the selection and quality of its stuff was pretty crappy. The shops were mostly run by foreigners, from Kyrgyzstan, although there were a few Afghans selling carpets and other souvenirs. Once a week there was a bazaar, where locals would sell fake Russian Army belts, old AK-47 bayonets, and green canvas Mujahideen chest webbing, with pouches for AK magazines and grenades. The boardwalk formed a square and in the middle of it was a dirt soccer field, a fenced-in hockey pitch for the Canadians, and a stage on which visiting entertainers performed concerts or stand-up comedy shows. Later, I saw Aussie rock band The Angels there, and the American comedian Robin Williams.

The two mess halls at Kandahar would feed hundreds of soldiers at a time and the food was good, considering the number of people being catered for. There were three hot freshly cooked meals a day, although I usually went for a salad at lunchtime. Breakfast was cooked to order and the servings were always generous. Each mess had two serving lines, one on each side of the building, and the queue at meal-times would stretch for 20 metres or more. Everyone carried a weapon with them at all times.

I was issued company T-shirts, cargo pants, US Army desert camouflage uniforms, a Kevlar helmet, boots and a sleeping bag, along with a 5.56-millimetre M4 assault rifle and a Glock nine-millimetre pistol and a leg holster. I took eight magazines for the M4 and three for the Glock. As contractors, we weren't given any weapons training, or basic military field craft lessons, as CAI had assumed we'd be up to speed with that side of the business, given our past experience. I'd carried an M-16 in the Airborne Troop at 1 CER, and the M4 was basically the same rifle, only shorter, and I'd been issued with a Glock when I was in the New South Wales Police.

We were responsible for organising all our other gear, so Guy and I went shopping at the tactical store and cobbled together some very unsatisfactory load carrying gear. I bought a plate carrier – a bulletproof vest covered with strips of Velcro, but without the armoured plates inside – and some ammunition pouches, which I was able to Velcro to the front of my improvised vest. Later, back home in Australia, I'd end up spending 600 dollars on a purpose-designed combat vest and it was worth every cent.

CAI had a big operation at Kandahar, with nearly 60 dogs in the kennels. Mark gave me two to choose from, called Ricky and Hellboy. Ricky was a German shepherd and Hellboy was a Belgian Malinois. The Malinois, or Belgian shepherd dog, looks a bit like a smaller, squarer German shepherd. They generally have a -brownish-yellow coat; black muzzle and cheeks; and alert, pricked-up ears. The Royal Australian Air Force and other military and civil agencies around the world use Mals as guard dogs, as they have a high prey drive, which means they like chasing things. They're hard working and have high energy levels, so need lots of attention and to be kept active.

We got to work with the dogs for a bit to see how they behaved, get a feel for their personalities, and find out their strengths and weaknesses. The dogs were put in a range of situations, including searching vehicles. I was leaning towards Hellboy, as when it came to searching, he was much more motivated than Ricky. However, one problem was that Hellboy became distracted and agitated around unusual noises. One of the most common sights on any road in Afghanistan is the jingle truck, a standard lorry that the driver has decorated to an outrageous extent, with bells and tassels, paint and flags, and anything else they can find lying around. Because of the bells, the trucks make a hell of a racket as they move – hence the name – and Hellboy didn't like it. In fact, when it came time to work on a vehicle checkpoint, Hellboy would freak out at the sound of the first approaching jingle truck. When it came to searching open, quiet spaces, Hellboy was the better dog, but as vehicle checkpoints were part of the job description, and loud noises a daily occurrence in Afghanistan, it soon became clear that he just wasn't going to cut it out in the field, so I picked Ricky.

The funny thing was that I later learned from Mark that he had been holding Ricky back from other handlers, to give me the option of working with him when I arrived in Afghanistan. It was just like when he was the senior instructor on the dog handler courses at the School of Military Engineering in Australia – he had a knack of pairing the right man with the right dog.

In between briefings and getting our gear sorted out, we started training in earnest. Mark set up searches, using chunks of explosives placed all around the Kandahar military base. We searched long stretches of road through the camp, inside buildings, around bunkers and storage depots, and vehicles at mock vehicle checkpoints. It was a good way to get a feel for the base and, as in any military setting, the soldiers I was meeting all loved seeing the dogs at work.

Summer was well on the way, and during the day it was hot and dusty under empty blue skies. I worked up a sweat trailing Ricky around on the lead and we'd spend hours together in the sun. It was good to be working a job I knew, with a dog by my side. At the end of each day, I was tired but satisfied.

All the handlers needed to be certified to US military standard, and each man-and-dog team needed to score at least 95 per cent on their proficiency test. In practice, this meant you could only miss one hidden explosive out of every 20. Out in the field, the one you missed could kill someone, so I wanted Ricky and me to be the best team possible. At first I was a bit rusty, but Ricky was a seasoned explosive detective dog who'd been doing the job for real, and it wasn't long before I was feeling really comfortable with him.

Ricky had a good nose but, like Ziggy, he could be laid-back, especially when searching open areas and roads, so we put in some extra training on those. In the proficiency training, we used a variety of explosives, including RPG rounds, which I hadn't had much to do with, and detonation cord from a suicide bomber's vest that the US military had found. Just looking at these training aids reminded me where Ricky and I would soon be heading.

'Come on, boy, let's do this,' I said to him as we began our proficiency test. Ricky performed like a star and any apprehension I'd had soon evaporated. It's all about trusting your dog. Many handlers fail because they're trying too hard or trying to second-guess their dog. It's a team effort, and without that trust you're in trouble.

I felt like a huge load had been taken from my shoulders. This wasn't just about passing the test, but about being back on the job with a dog by my side, with the companionship that brings, and finally putting the tools of my trade to the test in a war zone. Of course I was missing my kids back home in Australia, but I knew that with each passing day, I was few hundred dollars closer to being debt-free and better able to provide for them.

I lay on my back on my single bed in the partitioned wooden room, my hand under my head, thinking about what it would be like once we were sent out of Kandahar. Mark had told me that I'd most likely be assigned to a US SF team, working out of a remote forward operating base. I'd never worked with the Australian SAS, or any other special forces, but after the days of training around Kandahar, I was feeling confident that I could do the job as well as anyone. I was looking forward to beginning the mission for real.

A siren started to wail.

I got up and, when I looked around the partition, the other handlers were all struggling out of bed, barefoot and dressed in a mix of jocks, footy shorts and T-shirts.

'What the fuck's that?' one of the other guys said.

I scratched my head. 'I dunno.'

'What are we supposed to do? Is it an attack?'

Three of us walked outside the tent, without any idea of where to go or what to do. An American soldier was striding past. 'What's up?' I asked him.

'Mortars – incoming!' he said, without looking back at us civilians.

The three of us looked at each other. We hadn't even heard any explosions, so either we'd all been dozing or it had happened in some far corner of the enormous base. We couldn't hear any more blasts, or the sound of rounds leaving the tube.

'What do you reckon?' one of the other Aussies asked.

I pulled out my smokes, offered them around and lit one. 'Fucked if I know.'

I finished my cigarette, and we all drifted back inside the tent and back to bed. If somewhere there were bunkers assigned to us to use in case of rocket or mortar attacks, we never found out where they were. The siren went off a couple more times while we were at Kandahar but we just ignored it.

It's funny how quickly you get used to the things that would be expected to freak you out the most. Afghanistan is the most heavily mined country in the world, and there are bombs, rockets and grenades lying around that date back 30 years or more. Something, somewhere, was always being set off, either deliberately by the explosive ordnance disposal guys, or by some poor bastard standing on something. I might have flinched the first couple of times I heard a random explosion, but after a while it just became background noise.

The Russians had sowed the fields and villages of Afghanistan with butterfly mines, small plastic explosive devices that would fit easily into a child's palm. The mine got its name from its shape, as it looked like it was made from two curved plastic butterfly wings. The mines were delivered via cluster bombs, and, theoretically, the purpose of the design was that when the bombs broke open in midair the butterfly mines would, because of their shape, start spinning and disperse over a wide area. It worked, but the other result of the mine's appearance, whether deliberately or not, was that curious little kids found them irresistible. While I was there, children were still losing fingers, hands and eyes from these things. Even the older kids, who knew what the mines were, would play games with them. They'd grab one by the tip of a wing, and fling it at a wall or a big rock to set it off deliberately. Like the saying goes, it's all fun until someone loses a fucking body part.

After I left Kandahar, I also learned the country was awash with guns; another hangover from the Soviet invasion in 1979, when every man and boy had a weapon and fought the Russians. Afghans are a tough people, made up of tribes and clans who've been fighting each other and various invaders for centuries. It wasn't unusual for village disputes over land, animals and women – in that order – to be settled with AK-47s or Dooshka heavy machine guns and mortars. Gunfire was part of the daily soundtrack.

Mark kept our days busy with more training, which was good, as we didn't have time to think too long or hard about where we'd be going and what we'd be doing. We were issued with body armour, and had a choice of either an old-style bulky US Army camouflage flak jacket, with a high and uncomfortable collar, or the slimline blue vest you often seen reporters and politicians wearing for the cameras when they visit a war zone. Neither was particularly practical, but I chose the camo version and wore my plate jacket with my pouches stuck on over the top of the flak jacket. It was a mess. However, I'd passed all the tests, and was ready to go outside the wire and start earning my money.

It was dark as I waited on the edge of the airfield to board the brown ring Chinook. 'Brown ring' was the code name for the regular supply flights that stopped off at each of the Forward Operating Bases (FOBs) in Uruzgan Province. I was with Jason Bergeron, one of the American handlers, and the pair of us was going to FOB Cobra to relieve two other dog handlers from our company, who were both going on vacation for six weeks.

Jason was about 30 and an ex-US Air Force dog handler. After leaving the military, he'd worked in Texas for a few years as a police drug dog handler, but had left to work as a contractor in Iraq. He'd been in Iraq for a couple of years before transferring to Afghanistan, so had plenty of experience in an operational environment. He was a good man, who would help me find my feet.

I hadn't had a lot to do with Americans before going to Afghanistan, but I already had a few impressions of them. For a start, they were incredibly patriotic and they still, several years on, had a strong sense of having a mission to avenge what had happened on September 11, 2001. They were generally friendly and polite, and I'd already picked up that many were overtly religious compared with Australian soldiers. It wasn't unusual to see guys saying grace before they ate. They also loved their guns.

Uruzgan is right in the heart of Afghanistan, north of Kandahar, and FOB Cobra was so remote, and deep inside the strife-plagued province, that the only way into it was by air. The coalition couldn't risk sending road convoys there because of the level of threat the Taliban posed in the area.

Jason and I had our dogs with us, in their portable plastic kennels, and we each had a couple of plastic footlockers – trunks carrying all our personal gear. When the loadmaster was ready for us, we carried our stuff, and our animals, out to the Chinook, and lugged everything up the ramp and inside. It was hot in there, and the flight crew unzipped the tops of their flight suits and got to work strapping everything down to the floor. They worked and joked with each other with the ease of men who'd done this every day and night for months. Perched out on the rear of the ramp was an M240 7.62-millimetre machine gun. The Chinook's design dated from the Vietnam War era, but I guess there are some things you don't need to change if they're not broken. In the thin mountain air of Afghanistan, the big twin-engine helicopter was the packhorse of the coalition effort.

The Chinook smelled of sweat, kerosene, hydraulic fluid, disinfectant and old vomit. The red nylon cargo seats were stained in places, and I didn't want to think about what had made the mess.

'Shush, boy, it's OK,' I said to Ricky through the metal grille at the end of his travel kennel, as the jet engines started to whine and the rotors slowly began to turn.

'Y'all goin' to Cobra, right?' the loadmaster yelled, over the increasing din.

Jason and I nodded, and gave a thumbs-up. 'All stops,' the crewman yelled. 'First TK, then DR. Don't get off until I tell ya.'

Up in the cockpit, the pilots were checking the glowing red instrument panel and lowering their night-vision goggles. The loadmaster walked outside and was looking up at the tail rotor, which was cranking up to full speed, as he talked to the pilots over his intercom. The loudness hurt my ears and I could see Ricky whining in his kennel. I put my fingers through the grate, and he sniffed and licked them. 'It's OK, boy.'

The loadmaster walked back inside, looping his intercom radio communications cable as he walked, hung the coil behind a seat strap and closed the tail ramp. I gripped my M4, which was resting barrel down between my legs, as we lifted off into the blackness.

The Chinook cruised low and fast over the barren countryside of Uruzgan Province. Through the big round windows, I could make out the mountain ranges off to one side and, occasionally, the weak light of a lamp glowing in a hut, or a room in a mud-brick compound. The compounds, which I later learned each housed an extended family, looked like little forts. Somewhere behind us an Apache followed, swooping from side to side, its sensors searching out the heat signatures of people who shouldn't have been out and about on the ground.

We were flying at night to lessen the chance of the Taliban shooting down the helicopter. On board were US soldiers who were either going back into the fight or, like us, arriving for the first time. With my mishmash of gear and the uncertain look on my face, I must have stood out as the new guy.

The stops at Deh Rawood and Tarin Kowt were fast and chaotic. The crew wanted to be on the ground for the minimum time possible, in case of mortar or rocket attack. As soon as the rear wheels touched the ground, the loadmaster was lowering the ramp. The guys who were leaving us grabbed their gear and weapons, and stepped over and around us and our dogs to beat it out of the Chinook.

With the rotors still turning, the inside of the helicopter filled with choking dust. Other soldiers came on board and, directed by the crew's hand signals and shouts, undid the ratchets and lashings holding down cargo that had to be offloaded. Boxes were slid down the ramp or carried off, and halfway through the unloading, a few other guys got on and took the seats along the side walls that had been vacated. They were grinning and laughing, obviously happy to be getting out of the firebase, for however long it might be. I wondered if any of them were going home for good. Home seemed a long way away to me; too far off even to think about.

The loadmaster was still re-securing cargo as we lifted off. It seemed like we'd only been on the ground a minute or two. As what passed for calm returned to the screaming, vibrating interior of the big helo, the sweating crewman slumped down on the ramp and, one arm resting on the 240 on its pintle mount, gazed out over the empty plains of dirt below.

As at the other two stops, there were no lights to greet us when we landed at FOB Cobra.

'OK, this is you!' the loadmaster called to Jason and me. I was glad someone knew where we were. From the window, this firebase looked exactly like the previous two. Jason and I struggled through the dust and dark without the benefit of night-vision goggles, fumbling around looking for our gear and our dogs, and making sure we never let go of our weapons while we helped the soldier from the ground unload our stuff.

I grabbed the handle on top of Ricky's kennel and lugged it and him down the ramp into the dust storm. Behind me, the

CH-47 lifted off, and a few seconds later my ears were ringing from the silence.

Voices among the dark and the settling grit sought us out. 'C'mon, this way. We'll show you to your hooch; get your shit squared away.'

We loaded our gear into the back of a Toyota Hilux ute and a four-wheel Gator all-terrain vehicle, and were driven the short distance from the landing zone to the gates of the US living area inside the FOB. Our new home looked like some of the Afghan compounds we'd been flying over: a medieval mudbrick fortress with a guard tower. Once inside, we parked in a bare earth square and started unloading the truck. Around the walls were rooms—hooches, the Americans called them. Jason and I were assigned the room normally used by the dog handlers we were relieving.

'Oh, shit, man,' Jason said, as we checked the gear that had come off the vehicle. 'Where are my trunks? We didn't leave them on board, did we?'

I shook my head. 'The loadie said that was the last of it.' Next it was my turn to swear, because I suddenly realised I only had one of my two trunks. Jason had no gear at all, other than his rifle and his dog, and I had half my stuff. The stops at the two previous firebases really had been as chaotic as they'd appeared. There was no calm professionalism operating behind the cloud of dust, just a mad panic to get stuff off and on the chopper and get back to Kandahar as quickly as possible.

'Shit,' Jason said. I saw that this time he was talking about the real thing. His dog—a big, black, psycho motherfucker of a Malinois called Nero—had crapped in his kennel and there was mess everywhere, which was already stinking out our small room. 'I'll have to go clean it out. Man, how much more fucked up can this night get?'

It was about ten o'clock, and we were exhausted from the anticipation of getting there and the blow of finding that we were missing our stuff. I opened my remaining locker and found it was the one with all my military kit, so I was able to give Jason one of my US Army uniforms and some bits and pieces. Fortunately, all I was missing was my personal gear–toiletries, civilian clothes, physical training gear and the like. As I've said, I was used to being dicked around in the Australian Army, but in Manus and Afghanistan, it was beginning to seem like a miracle if anything at all went according to plan. Maybe there was no plan?

The room that would be my home, and Jason's, for the next six weeks had two pairs of bunk beds, two locally made wooden desks, and a couple of chairs. The handlers who had gone on vacation had loaded all their shit onto the two top bunks, and there was little space left for Jason and me to store our gear–not that we had much of it. When Jason came back with Nero in his clean kennel, we put the dogs on the floor between the bunk beds and climbed into bed.

The next morning, I had a chance to look around while Jason and I took the dogs for a walk. Outside the living compound was a larger perimeter, which enclosed the landing zone where we'd landed in the night, and, separate from the US compound, another mini fort where the interpreters and local Afghan National Army soldiers lived. The outer wall of the FOB was made of earth-filled hescos, capable of stopping bullets and RPG rounds. No-one in particular was assigned to show us around or brief us, but Jason had been in Afghanistan for a while and had worked with US SF guys in other FOBs, so he pretty well knew the lay of the land

We shared our part of the compound with the Embedded Training Teams, or ETTs. The ETTs were American soldiers who were attached to Afghan National Army units as trainers and advisers, but lived separately from their Afghani. We also shared with a Psyops, or psychological operations, team. Psyops had the job of telling the Afghans we were here to help, not harm, the ordinary people. They'd produce leaflets, and sometimes use interpreters talking into sound systems on the backs of trucks to blast out -reassuring messages via huge speakers when we were working around a village. The SF guys, the detachment of US Army Green Berets who made up the Operational Detachment Alpha – the ODA, or 'A-Team' – lived in a separate part of the mini fort.

Looking out over the line of hescos, I could see that the surrounding countryside was every bit as barren, dry and in-hospitable as it had appeared from the Chinook at night. I wondered how anyone could survive in this country; how anything could grow here. In the distance beyond low, rolling bare dirt hills was an irregular barrier of white-capped moun-tains, knifing their way into the empty sky. From the start, though, I found a kind of attraction – beauty, even – in the starkness of the landscape. I'd grown up on the coast, with the Pacific Ocean on one side and rolling green hills on the other. Afghanistan could not have been more different, but there was something about those mountains and the hard rock, and parched earth between me and the peaks. I breathed in the dry air and stared out at the mountains. After spending seven-and-a-half years in the Australian Army, and going on one bullshit exercise after another, I had finally arrived in a com-bat zone. I was excited.

The SF guys didn't interact with us a great deal at first. The team was from the 7th Special Forces Group, headquartered at Fort Bragg, North Carolina, and they were coming to the end of their six-month tour. They'd nod and say hello, but I got the sense that they were such a tight-knit bunch of blokes, who had obviously been through so much together, that they didn't have the need, or the time, to welcome strangers into the fold with open arms. Talking to the Psyops guys, I learned that the SF men had lost some of their mates during their tour.

Jason and I took the dogs out of the compound, and down the hill to the small rifle range the team had set up. We zeroed our M4s, firing enough rounds at a target to ensure the sights were correctly set. Afterwards, we did some training with the dogs, in the area where the Chinook resupply helicopters came into land. It was open country, and we could mark out simulated roads. Jason would bury some explosives while I wasn't watching, and Ricky and I would go find them, and then we'd reverse the roles. The training aids we used could be detonation cord, ammunition, mortar rounds, RPGs, or C4 explosive.

When you buried something, you had to let it lay there a while before calling the other handler and his dog in. Explosive detection dogs generally air-scent what they're looking for, which means they smell the explosives on the wind, and it takes some time for the odours to escape up through the soil once the training aid has been buried. A good dog might also notice if the surface of the ground has been disturbed.

It can be challenging for a dog to stay focused when searching a wide open area or along an empty road. Indoors, they have more stuff to sniff and check out, which keeps them interested, but in the outdoors, they can easily get bored. You can tell a good handler and dog team by the way they work open areas. The trick is to know your dog – when and how to motivate him to stay focused and keep searching, and when to give him a rest so that he doesn't zone out.

Our dogs weren't landmine-sniffing dogs, so we had to continually keep them focused on having their noses close to the ground when doing route clearances and searching open country. When it was our turn to search for the hidden explosives, Ricky and I approached the landing zone from downwind. You want to give your dog every advantage—just as you do when doing the job for real—and, if the wind is blowing towards them, their sensitive noses can pick up traces of explosive before they get there.

Ricky did a good job, as did Nero, and after each exercise, Jason and I would reward them by letting them play for a while. I bounced and chucked Ricky's ball to him, and he fetched it and brought it back to me, grinning from ear to ear. Ricky hadn't needed any time to settle into the new environment at the FOB. He was away from the kennel at Kandahar, and out in the fresh air working and getting plenty of attention from me and from the other soldiers at the FOB, once they got to know him. It was all good fun for the dogs, and I was really starting to feel like I was in my element.

In the six weeks we were at Cobra the A-Team did a few missions, leaving the FOB in Black Hawks and Chinooks to go out into the mountains in search of the Taliban.

Jason and I sat on a stack of sandbags and watched a pair of Black Hawks lift off, creating a mini tornado in the dust. 'Man, this is bullshit,' Jason said. 'How come they aren't using us?'

I shrugged, and watched the choppers and their Apache escort gradually disappear over the plains, to be swallowed by the hills. I knew there was no point in pushing the issue, and that we would only be accepted slowly. It was harder for Jason, as he'd already worked with a few different SF teams in Afghanistan and proved himself in battle. I figured the war would find me, eventually, and there was no point coming across like some madman who couldn't wait to get into a fight.

SIX

For real

July 2006

Finally, after weeks of training and marking time, I got the word that I was needed on a mission.

I'd found out on the quiet, from some of the other Americans at the FOB, that the two dog handlers we'd replaced had been bad-mouthing Jason before our arrival. From everything I'd seen, Jason was a thoroughly professional operator and good guy; later, I'd work out that if anyone needed to have shit put on them, it was the guys we'd replaced. However, all the ill feeling might have had something to do with the SF team's reluctance to take Jason and me out on patrol.

In any case, it seemed the team now needed a dog handler, so I reported to the briefing hooch to be given the details of the patrol. Instead of going out by helicopter, I'd be part of a road convoy with the guys from the team, the Psyops detachment, and the ETTs and their Afghan soldiers.

The briefing was a PowerPoint presentation on a widescreen television. There were aerial photographs, and slides with maps showing the route the patrol would take, likely enemy positions and friendly forces in the area. Other slides gave a run-down of what air support would be available to us. There was a lot of information to take in and plenty of abbreviations that I didn't understand. I concentrated on absorbing the details that were most relevant to me, such as what vehicle Ricky and I would be in, and likely choke points along the route where we might have to get out and search for IEDs, or mines. The mission was pretty simple – we were to show our presence and check out a village where the A-Team had recently come under heavy fire.

I was assigned to one of the ETT trucks, a turtleback humvee with a gun turret in the centre of its roof. To my surprise, I would be manning an M240 machine gun in the turret.

After the briefing, I sought out Jimmy, the US Army captain in charge of the ETTs, and made myself known to him.

'Grand to have you along,' he said to me. Jimmy was an Irish American and still had a strong accent from the old country. 'Ever fired a 240 before?'

I admitted I hadn't and, rather than being at all fazed by this, Jimmy organised for one of his soldiers to take Jason and me out to the range, and give me a quick soldier's five on loading and cocking the gun, and the immediate action to take in the case of a misfire or jam on the 240, and the .50 cal, which was another weapon I'd never actually fired. The 240 wasn't too different from the M60 that I'd trained on in the Australian Army, so it was no big drama. I practised loading and unloading, and clearing imaginary obstructions while he looked on; then, under his command, I fired 30 or 40 rounds through the two different guns.

'Good to go,' the US soldier said, indicating that, after my fifteen-minute lesson, I was now qualified to take my position behind the gun and drive into battle in the heart of Afghanistan on a Special Forces mission. There was no briefing on the rules of engagement—what to do and when to shoot—so I figured I'd just take my lead from the other soldiers on board the truck. I had no plans to open fire on the first Afghan man I saw, and figured that if I had to fire to help protect the convoy, it would be pretty obvious where the bad guys were.

In the Australian Army, someone who was new in-country would have been given, probably by a legal officer, a detailed briefing on the rules for opening fire on someone. CAI hadn't given me that information, and I guess the SF guys assumed I would know what to do. In any case, it was hard for me to compare what was going on here with what went on in the Australian Army, because the Australian SAS didn't take civilian contractors along on their missions.

I packed my daypack with enough food for Ricky and me for the two-day mission, and loaded the dog and my gear on to the truck. When the time came to leave, we waited until our slot in the convoy opened up, and joined the line of humvees and the Toyotas and Ford Ranger pickups carrying the Afghan National Army (ANA) guys. Just before we left the outer perimeter, we stopped and the driver said, 'Go to action here.'

I nodded and, pointing the 240 out over the open plains of the valley, grabbed the cocking handle and yanked it back. I'd just chambered a 7.62-millimetre round in the breech, and the machine gun was now cocked and loaded—at the action condition. I reached down and ruffled Ricky's neck. It was show time.

I was stoked to get out of the FOB, as there was little to do there except work out in the gym, surf the internet, and train with Ricky and Nero. For the first time, as we rolled through the local village not far from Cobra, I was able to see something of Afghanistan other than the inside of a coalition firebase.

If the countryside was a world away from where I'd grown up, the villages, huts and compounds where the local people lived were from a whole other era. It was like seeing people from the Middle Ages, with the exception of the odd guy carrying an AK-47, which made me nervous initially. How, I wondered, were you supposed to tell the difference between law-abiding Afghans and the Taliban if everyone had a gun?

Kids waved to us and some of the younger men just eyed us coolly. I saw a couple of little girls playing in the street, but all the older women seemed to have moved inside or out of the way at the sound of approaching vehicles. A donkey brayed, and a family of goats trotted through the dust to escape the convoy. I traversed the gun from side to side, watching and not wanting to let my guard down. I was looking forward to doing my job for real.

In a couple of places, we passed between compounds that lined the side of the road, so that we were funnelled down alleys with mudbrick walls on either side. I scanned the tops of the walls, expecting at any second to see a Taliban pop his head over the side and open fire on us. All was quiet, though.

Soon after leaving the vicinity of Cobra and the outlying village, we left the dirt road and started driving cross-country over the wide valley floor. 'How come we're going off road?' I asked the driver.

'Mines and IEDs,' he said. 'If we do have to get onto the road to go through a pass, or through a wadi, you'll be one of the first to know.'

He was right, because not long into the drive, as we started to climb into the foothills of the mountains, the convoy came to a halt. I asked what was going on and found out that the convoy had moved back onto the road, as it was the only way up a pass through the hills. The lead vehicle had come to a narrow section, hemmed in on either side by the thick mud walls of compounds and steep slopes behind the buildings. Some ANA mine clearers had got out to sweep the road.

'Send up K9, over,' a voice squawked over the radio.

I recognised my call sign immediately. Nevertheless, the ETT vehicle driver said, 'OK, you're on.'

'Right-o, Ricky, let's go, mate.'

My mouth was dry and my heart started beating faster as I climbed out of the turtleback. Ricky jumped down after me and I grabbed hold of his leash. I walked along the line of vehicles, aware of eyes on me all the way. Jimmy waved at Ricky and me as we walked by his vehicle.

'Fuck, boy, I hope we don't miss anything', I whispered to Ricky.

I went past the dozen vehicles that made up the convoy, including the heavily armed, up-armoured humvees carrying the US SF soldiers, and the pickups filled with ANA guys just sitting in the back, festooned with AKs and RPGs – the same weapons their enemies carried. At the head of the convoy, a - couple of Afghans carrying minesweepers were talking to each other, occasionally pointing to the ground.

A Special Forces dude in a baseball cap spat a wad of chewing tobacco on the road. 'Found an anti-tank mine,' he said, talking down to me from behind his Mark 19. 'Y'all got to check the sides of the road for any IEDs and such.'

I knew the job and so did Ricky. Up ahead, there was a real-life TM-62 Soviet-made anti-tank mine, which the SF guys were preparing to blow up in place, rather than try to disarm it. I guessed they were worried about booby traps. We weren't playing with chunks of deliberately hidden explosives anymore. This was the real deal.

I would have much rather worked Ricky off-lead, and kept my distance, but I figured it was too early in the period of my contract to start flouting company rules. All the same, a handler standing well back from his dog suddenly made perfect sense to me. 'Sook!' I said to Ricky, using the common word of command to start him searching. By convention, dogs are trained using words of command in German, and the word for 'track' is actually *such*, though it's pronounced 'sook'. Ricky took off, straining at the lead. He had no idea what dangers might lie ahead; he was only looking forward to finding something so that he could play with his ball.

In fact, from what I'd been told back in Kandahar, according to company policy I wasn't sure I should even be searching the roadside. As several civilian handlers and their dogs had either been killed or injured by roadside IEDs, we were supposed only to search buildings, compounds, open spaces and choke points (a place where a road is constrained by natural or man-made features). It was my first mission, though, and the first time the SF team had asked me to do anything, so, while I acquiesced to Ricky searching on-lead, there was no way I was going to say no to searching the roadside on the way to the choke point. I worked out then and there that I was going to have to make some decisions off my own bat.

Working in a pattern, I quartered the road, zigzagging from side to side and going behind where the Afghans had already swept. They'd been concentrating on the road itself, but it was possible that Ricky's sensitive nose would pick up a buried bomb or waiting IED that their detectors had missed.

After moving up and down the verges and pushing out towards the steeply shelving sides of the cutting, I called out that the area was all clear, silently praying I was right. I returned to the vehicle and the Afghans pulled back a bit. The anti-tank mine was blown in place with some C4 explosive. A pillar of dust and rock shot up into the air, and Ricky gave a yelp. I soothed him. It was ironic that only now, after the danger had passed, he was scared.

With the obstacle cleared, the convoy pushed on, further up into the hills to its night harbour position. I checked with Jimmy that it was OK for me to exercise Ricky, then took him for a walk, though we didn't stray too far from the vehicles. He'd had a good day, apart from the fright when the mine was blown, and I had too. Although I was a civilian, and still not fully accepted by the SF team, I felt good about having contributed something to the mission and not having got anyone killed by failing to spot an IED.

After I fed Ricky, I took a brown plastic Meal Ready to Eat packet from the back of the ground mobility vehicle (GMV). I'd had enough army ration pack food in Australia not to have high hopes for what was inside. The most interesting thing about the American field ration pack was the way in which the food was heated. The Australian Army uses tiny fold-out tin stoves that burn a white pill of Hexamine, a compressed fuel that burns hot no matter what the conditions are like. Even so, it takes a long time to boil a mug of water for tea or coffee, or to heat a tin of food. Aussie patrol rations, usually reserved for the SAS or commandos, are sachets of dehydrated food to which you add hot or cold water. While the patrol rations taste better, they use a lot of water, which can be in scarce supply in the Australian bush. Each Meal Ready to Eat came with a plastic bag with what looked like a pot scouring pad. The pad was actually a heating device, activated by pouring a very small amount of water into it. When the water hit the pad, a chemical reaction took place and it got extremely hot. The main meal in a Meal Ready to Eat, usually containing something distantly related to meat, is in a foil packet, which is dropped into the plastic bag, unopened. Within a few minutes, the foil and the meal inside are so hot that you need a Leatherman tool to extract it. The Meal Ready to Eat heaters, I later learned, had turned out to have other uses in Afghanistan. During the fierce fighting in the Tora Bora Mountains in the early days of the war, US Army medics had used them to warm up saline IV drips, which were near-frozen in the extreme cold, before administering them to wounded soldiers.

Inside the packet I found a pork chop: a slab of something the size, colour and consistency of a rubber thong. This chop was 'chunked and formed', which meant that pork, and anything else lying around the butcher's shop floor, had been ground up and squeezed into a mould with some sort of binding agent. The Meal Ready to Eat had other semi-edible goodies, including peanut butter and crackers, and a long-life chocolate brownie, both of which I stuffed in my pocket for later on.

Even though I was a civilian on my first mission, I was expected to pull my weight, and was to stand picket, in the middle of the night. When my time came, I got up, checked on Ricky and stumbled through the darkness to the ETT vehicle, which was being manned continuously all night. My handover was even briefer than my instructions on using the 240 and the .50 cal.

'Keep a watch out, that way,' the soldier I was relieving said. He made a V with his outstretched arms, indicating my arc of responsibility, then handed me a pair of night-vision goggles. I climbed up into the turret behind the .50 cal, slid the goggles' harness over my head and switched the device on. The mountains, foreboding enough during the daytime, had a ghostly aura in the lime-green wash of the image intensifier's lens. The stars burned like tiny comets, adding to the surreal aspect of the view.

Just as when I'd walked up the road with Ricky, the main thing worrying me was that I might fuck up and that some-one – including me – might lose their life as a result. Compared with missions I'd go on later, nothing much had happened, yet I felt more keyed-up than I ever had in my life. On one hand, I'd put into practice what I'd learned as a dog handler in the army and the police, and was happy with how Ricky and I had acquitted ourselves; on the other, it was like I was learn-ing everything from scratch, with no real idea of what I was doing or what was expected.

Things hotted up the next morning.

We got up early, as soldiers always do, but unlike in the Australian Army, no-one bothered shaving. The cleaning of weapons and eating were the main priorities. This was my first indication that the US Army in Afghanistan – at least, the SF teams – was far more focused on the job of hunting and killing Taliban than they were on the bullshit that dominates life in any peacetime force.

Ricky jumped up into the back of the truck and I attached his leash to a tie-down ring on the floor. The convoy mounted up and headed towards our objective, a village where the team had been hit badly not long before. I'd heard one of their men had been killed in an attack on this place, and the word to stay alert had come down. The vehicles stopped on high ground overlooking the village, and the ANA troops, with their ETT advisers, were ordered to dismount and sweep through, checking the village for arms and insurgents.

I could hear the Irish accent of Jimmy, the US Army captain who'd been helpful to me after the briefing, over the intercom radio communications. He was there with his Afghans, moving from compound to compound, looking for the bad guys. It was fair enough, I thought, that the ANA were given the job of clearing a target, and potentially coming face-to-face with the Taliban, but it wasn't as if they had no support or guidance from the Americans. The soldiers and officers, like Jimmy, were really at the sharp end of America's war.

I had a grandstand view of the operation and not long after the government troops entered the village, there was small arms fire from one of the compounds. I could hear the *pop, pop, pop* of AK-47s and it was pretty amazing to think that people were getting involved in a gunfight down there. The intercom radio chatter started increasing in frequency as the Afghans spoke to each other and the ETTs radioed in reports to the other Americans in the SF team.

'Troops in contact, troops in contact,' Jimmy reported over the radio.

The commander of the sweep decided the compound was too well fortified to take with just his men, and the Afghan troops pulled back a bit. It was, I learned, the way the war was being fought. The ANA were expected to step up and do the dirty work of clearing the village, while the Americans, in their heavily armed vehicles, watched over them and provided fire support. When anyone – Afghan or American – encountered stiff resistance from the Taliban, it was time to call on the air support that was always orbiting somewhere above us. Why risk anyone's life in a bloody ground attack when there's an air force strike aircraft that can be dialled up to do the work for you?

It was fascinating watching all this unfold in front of me, like I was some fucking general watching a firepower demonstration on the range back in Singleton in Australia. The JTAC (joint terminal attack controller), responsible for coordinating air strikes and air support, called for support over the radio and soon an A-10 was orbiting our position, waiting for a target and the word to let loose.

The A-10 Thunderbolt is a beautiful little aircraft. It was developed as a tank-buster, and first entered service more than 20 years ago during the Cold War, when NATO and the Soviet Bloc were facing each other down on either side of the Iron Curtain. With the tearing down of the Berlin Wall and the break-up of the Soviet military empire, there didn't seem to be much need for a jet that could fly slowly and low over a battlefield, picking off tanks and other armoured vehicles. The first Gulf War, however, showed that the A-10 was exactly the type of aircraft the Americans needed. The Warthogs, as they were also known, wreaked havoc in the convoys of cars and tanks and trucks that fled Kuwait when the coalition forces kicked out Saddam Hussein.

They were back in action big time in Afghanistan, and were often flown by Air National Guard pilots—reservists. The Warthog has two turbofan engines mounted above the fuselage at the rear and short, stubby squared-off wings that carry loads of bombs and rockets. Under its nose is a 30-millimetre Gatling gun, which is also deadly against troops and vehicles. Some say it's an ugly aeroplane, but the soldiers on the ground in Afghanistan loved it. Because its engines are up the back and out of the way, it's very quiet on approach, so that the bad guys don't usually know it's overhead until it's too late. Also, it's not a fast mover like, say, an F-18 or an F-16, so the pilot of one can often get a better visual on a ground target than can some other jet jockeys. Earlier on in the war, the Canadian Army suffered terrible losses when an F-16 lit up one of their light armoured vehicles by mistake and killed everyone on board.

Ricky looked up into the clear blue sky and I had to search hard to see the jet coming. True to form, we didn't hear it until it was about to drop its 500-pound bomb. A guy on my truck had his video camera out and rolling in preparation for the strike. The first sign the air strike had gone in was a plume of white smoke rising from the compound. Next, came the delayed boom as the noise of the explosion reached us, and then the shock wave.

'Fuck me.' I couldn't imagine what it would be like to be on the receiving end of that, or how anyone in the compound could have survived.

The explosion had been too far away to bother Ricky, and I guess that, anyway, he must have seen this sort of thing a thousand times before. It was all new to me, though. The bomb had been dead on target and the shooting had stopped. The ETTs and Afghan soldiers moved in after the bombing run to assess its effects. The compound was to-talled, with a huge crater left in the centre of its walled square. Inside, the soldiers found the remains of four Taliban and their weapons. Having made a stand, they'd probably decided they were ready to go to their God, and the US Air Force had helped them on their way. If there were any Taliban left alive down there, the Americans didn't give them time to re-group. The convoy saddled up again, and we raced through the village, as we still had objectives in the mountains to check out.

We passed through hills dotted with fir trees and valleys cut by streams fed by melting snow flows, and came to an open flat area that had clearly been cultivated and recently harvested. I didn't get out of the truck, but the ANA dismounted again and began searching some mudbrick farm buildings while we kept watch over the hills. I could see them loading some sacks, but it wasn't until we got back to Cobra that I found out they were bags of compressed opium, which must have been worth thousands – maybe millions – of dollars. We weren't on a drug-busting mission – rather, we were going out to show our faces and, hopefully, stir up a fight – but the Americans confiscated drugs when they came across them. That haul might have represented a farmer's entire crop, but I didn't spare a thought then for what that might have meant to him and his family. There was too much going on around me; too much to try to soak up.

There were no more TICs on the patrol but on the way back, everyone was hyped as we approached the village where the bomb had been dropped. Our truck was in the middle of the convoy and as the lead vehicles entered the village, they passed between compounds, the walls of which came right to the edge of the road. Up ahead, I could hear the deep bass thump of a .50 cal firing, followed by a couple of explosions. I tightened my hand around the 240's pistol grip.

'What was that?' I yelled to the driver.

'Prob'ly nothing. They're just making sure that if there's any of them fuckers in the compounds, they keep their heads down.'

The Americans were employing a tactic, called reconnaissance by fire, used since the Vietnam War. I think the Aussies used to call it 'pray and spray', as they considered it a waste of ammunition by the US forces. The logic was that if you fired first into an area where the enemy might be – and this was an empty village where we'd had a contact on the way in – you would either make them keep their heads down or provoke a response. Either was OK by the SF guys, as they were always looking for a fight and to keep their own numbers of casualties down.

I looked ahead, out over the barrel of the 240, and saw a bearded SF man standing in his hummer lob a fragmentation grenade over the high wall of a compound. A few seconds later, as we drew close, the grenade went off with a muffled thump and smoke billowed into the sky. Other soldiers were firing into windows and raking the tops of the compound walls.

'Hey,' I yelled to the driver below me again, 'should I start shooting?'

'If you want to, man'

If I wanted to? Shit. It was my first mission and I didn't want them to think I was some wannabe war hero, so I held my fire. I also figured that it would be better to conserve my ammo in case someone did pop his head up over the parapet of one of those compounds and started firing back. Ricky was huddled by my feet in his kennel and I didn't want to worry him needlessly with a rain of hot empty brass cartridges from the machine gun. I tried to scrunch low in the turret behind the 240 and scanned the tops of the walls as we raced through, enveloped in a cloud of dust from the vehicles ahead.

We arrived back at Cobra just after lunch. My hair and uniform were stiff with dust, and I was sweaty and stinking and tired, but I was on a high.

The work didn't finish now the mission was ended. I helped clean out our vehicles, blowing the dust out of the interior with a high-pressure air hose. Weapons had to be cleaned and oiled, and we replaced the ammo that had been fired off. As a dog handler, I was part of a team of my own, so I had to make sure Ricky was fed and brushed and looked after as well. I had a hot meal in the chow hall, and went back to my room to chill out and think about the last couple of days.

I checked my watch and worked out that it was too late to call my kids in Australia on Skype. There was, though, an internet cable in the hooch, which I connected to my laptop. I sent an instant message to my girlfriend at the time, Nikki, to let her know I was back from my first mission.

SEVEN

A dog's life on the FOB

2006

There wasn't much to do on a firebase in between missions, other than training with the dogs and working out. The US SF soldiers are generally big dudes, and about the only form of exercise available in the confines of a FOB was weight training. I put on about twelve kilograms of muscle while working out with the Americans during my time with the SF teams. At first I did my routines by myself, while the SF guys would generally be in pairs, helping each other out.

For me, the weight training was more than just something to do to pass the time. The small, but well-equipped, gym in a room about fifteen by five metres, was a place that I could get to know the other guys I was living with and, slowly, be accepted. The alternative would have been sitting in my hooch with my dog, watching DVDs on my laptop and surfing the internet, or hanging out in the communal TV room. I like to keep busy, so this wasn't an option for me for too long; Jason, however, would fly simulated helicopters and aircraft in internet role-player games for hours.

Ricky and Nero were confined to their kennels in our room when they weren't training or exercising, so Jason and I made sure we trained with them every day, to keep them – and ourselves – active. There were plenty of suitable training areas around the FOB, with a good mix of terrain. We'd have the dogs search inside hooches, behind the kitchen, out on the rifle range, and on some broken ground inside the perimeter, planting explosives and letting Ricky and Nero find them so that they could have some play time.

It was still early days for Ricky and me as a team, so I used this time to get to know him better. The Afghan interpreters (called 'terps') lived separately from the Americans, but they had a shady area with some benches near the main SF building, where they could hang out during the day in case they were needed to translate something. I learned early on that Ricky wasn't real keen on the local people. He'd snarl and show his teeth when we walked by the terps, so I'd have to keep him on a short lead around them. I didn't take him for walks through the Afghan compound, but I did keep taking him back to where the terps gathered so that he could gradually get used to them and not be so aggressive. I knew that eventually we'd be working on foot in villages and compounds, so I needed him at least to be controllable and, ideally, a little more relaxed around Afghans.

While I didn't want my dog to bite the locals, I also didn't want him to become too friendly with strangers. I was happy to let some of the soldiers pat him and say hi, but I didn't want him craving the attention of strangers, and seeking out pats on the head or food. No dog handler likes strangers feeding their animal, as it turns dogs into scavengers. They become easily distracted during searches, either by scraps and rubbish lying around, or because they'll go and bail people up looking for affection and food. I didn't want Ricky eating something or nuzzling someone while he was supposed to be working.

'Hey, man, what's your dog's name?' one of the Green Berets walking across the baked dirt square asked one day. 'OK if I pet him?' As was working out in the gym, taking Ricky for a walk was a good way to start breaking the ice between me, a civvy, and the professional SF soldiers. So, at times like this, I was happy to bend the rules and allow someone else to give Ricky attention. It was all about getting the balance right.

You wouldn't think a working sniffer dog would be picky about his food, but Ricky was. We fed the dogs Science Diet, which is a top-quality dog food that came in 20-kilogram bags, shipped in by chopper. I'd feed Ricky once a day, but sometimes it would take him the whole 24 hours to finish a bowl of food. If I needed him to eat quickly, I'd have to go to the chow hall and get a cup of gravy to mix in with it, then he'd wolf the food down. Occasionally I wouldn't feed him for a day, to let his body clean itself out.

There was an artillery battery of 105-millimetre howitzers at Cobra, and the gunners would go about their business dressed in physical training gear – shorts, T-shirts and runners. The guns were used to soften up targets before we went in on a mission, or as fire support that we could call on if we got into trouble. There was a minimum of regimental bullshit at the SF FOBs. The artillerymen weren't ever going to leave the base, as the range of their howitzers covered our area of operations, so there was no real reason for them to wear full uniform in the scorching heat of an Afghanistan summer.

Ricky hated the guns. I made the mistake early on at Cobra of taking him for a walk near the battery when they were firing and it scared him witless; I don't think he ever got over it. Whenever they started firing, even if he was in his kennel in our hooch, he'd start barking and whining, and curl himself into a ball.

Some people might think that it's cruel to use dogs in war, especially in the explosive detection role. Our dogs have a good life, though.

First up, they're extremely well looked after. They have a balanced diet, and all their shots and medicines when they need them, and their living areas are kept spotless. The dogs are kept in top condition – the handler checks his dog every day for ticks and parasites, and if something goes wrong with an animal, there are military vets in-country to look after them.

Secondly, they're active and engaged. Unlike backyard dogs that lie around all day or run in circles, like crazy things, waiting for their owners to come home and pay them some attention, our working dogs are kept busy all day and rewarded for their hard work. Work is play to them, and they love it.

It's in the company's interest to look after its dogs, as each of them costs between 8000 and 10,000 dollars to train and care for. When the dogs reach the age of eight years, or if they are injured in the line of duty, they're retired and sent back to the US, where good homes are found for them, often with former handlers or company personnel.

If I were a dog, I'd want to be a working dog: either an explosive detection dog, a cattle dog or a sheep dog. I'd want to be active, useful and loved.

Still, while they are well looked after, sometimes dogs, like people, can't take the rigours of life in a war zone. I've seen a couple of dogs get to a point where they couldn't handle gunfire or explosions. Ricky didn't like the noise the artillery guns made but he could still do his job. The company I'm with now, however, had a labrador that would stop working, sometimes for an hour, if it heard a big bang. We can't afford to have a dog that only wants to work part-time, so we had to move it to a quieter location, which isn't a euphemism for killing. Some of the American handlers have taken dogs back to the US with them, and given them a home themselves.

Another dog that suffered from shell shock was called Daisy. She had always been a nice, placid dog, but cracked up after hearing the mortars one too many times. She lived at FOB Wilson, a Canadian base, with her Tanzanian handler. The handler had transferred over to us from Ronco, a US contracting firm that specialises in mine clearance. One day, as the mortars on base were firing on a Taliban position, poor Daisy flipped out and managed to escape her outdoor makeshift kennel. She bolted out the front gates of the FOB, and disappeared into the wild heart of south-central Afghanistan before the handler even knew she was gone.

The Psyops people at the base tried to help the handler find his missing dog. They printed up and distributed flyers, put the word out in the villages around the FOB and even offered a reward for Daisy's return. The Afghans weren't known for caring for their own dogs, so there was a good chance that if they saw a stray German shepherd, someone would shoot poor Daisy on sight.

Three months later I was at the FOB at Deh Rawood, and I told the chief of the team the story of Daisy's escape. Coincidentally, two days later I received an email from one of the other handlers, telling me that Daisy had shown up at the front gates of FOB Wilson, barking away, asking to be let in again. She was lean and hungry, but had managed to survive for three months in the harsh Afghanistan winter. What she lived on, and how she stayed alive, is anyone's guess. It would make a hell of a Disney movie.

The company kept an eye on Daisy for a while and got her back into shape, and slowly reintroduced her to some explosive detection dog training. She seemed fine, and taking to her old life without any sign of stress or fear, even around gunfire. Eventually, Daisy was re-teamed with another handler, and today she is back out in the field, doing fine and doing her job. Man, Daisy must have some awesome war stories to tell the other dogs she meets out at the FOBs.

'What's it like when your dog bites you on the arm when you've got one of those sleeves on?' one of the artillerymen at Cobra asked me one day while I was working out in the gym.

'Dunno. Never tried it,' I said.

The dogs I'd worked with in the Australian Army and the police, I explained to the gunner, were not trained as attack dogs, so I'd never done any bite training. The bite sleeve the guy was talking about resembled a sturdy glove made of leather and canvas that you put on your arm for the dog to latch onto. The artilleryman asked if I'd be interested in trying out some bite training with Ricky, -volunteering to be the crash test dummy.

Jason was up for it and, as it turned out, he'd done some bite work with dogs in the US Air Force. Nero, psycho dog that he was, had apparently also done some attack training, which suited his personality perfectly. He had a history of biting people, including his handler, for real. Jason showed me scars all up his arm where Nero had savaged him soon after they'd been teamed.

'I was in a turtleback hummer one time,' Jason told me, 'and the dude in the turret behind the 240 asked if he could feed Nero. I said, "No", of course.'

'What happened?' I asked.

'Dude fucking fed Nero a cracker out of his Meal Ready to Eat, and Nero nearly ripped his goddamn hand off.'

This answer hadn't surprised me. Nero had multiple personalities. When Jason was around, he was well behaved and even friendly. He'd nuzzle my crotch – nerve-racking, when a dog has the teeth and manners of a hyena – and try to get me to pat him. When Nero was on his own, though, he was a different animal; in fact, he was a fucking animal.

One time, Jason left Nero with me in the hooch when he had to go and clean the kennel after Nero had spewed in it. 'You gonna be OK with him?' Jason asked.

'Sure.'

Nero sat on the floor of the hooch between the bunks with his conk – his ball. Ricky was locked in his kennel, as there was no way we could have the two of them loose together in a confined space. Nero would have eaten Ricky for lunch. 'OK, Nero?' I asked.

Nero looked up at me and bit down on his conk. He flattened his ears and started to growl.

'Settle, dude.'

That made him growl louder, and lower. His lip curled and he showed me his teeth. I looked down at him and thought, fuck, this thing wants to take me out. I got up, slowly, and started backing out the door.

'What's up, Shane?' one of the Psyops guys asked as he walked down the hallway that linked the hooch rooms.

'Um, nothing, man, I just...'

I'd turned my back on Nero for a second and out he came, still growling, pushing the door open. I was the dog handler – the expert – so I couldn't very well scream 'Fucking run for your life!' to the Psyops guy. 'Good boy, Nero,' I said in a less-than-confident voice. Nero snarled. I was sure he was going tear my arse off and chow down on it. I grabbed him by the collar and dragged him – no easy task – back into the room, then banged the door shut on him, while I stayed out in the corridor, catching my breath.

When Jason came back, Nero calmed down straightaway, thank God. He was a one-man dog and when Jason was around, and Nero felt comfortable, he could be quite sociable. But he was also a fear-biter – a dog who bites when he's afraid – and he was also very aggressive when he was in his kennel. The most important thing in a working dog is that it has a good relationship with its handler, but you also don't want a dog that's too aggressive. You have to have the confidence of the soldiers you work with, and if they're apprehensive about working close to your dog, then that dog can be a liability.

Now, in among the mountain of shit the other two handlers had left in their room, we actually found a bite sleeve. It looked sturdy enough, but there was no way I was going to put my arm in Nero's mouth.

The artillery guy was keen to have a go as the rag doll for the bite training, and a circle of soldiers gathered to watch the games begin. Boredom's one of the enemies at a FOB, so a gladiatorial competition between artilleryman and dog was a must-see event. First up, I waved the sleeve in front of Ricky, teasing him with it, and encouraging him to bite down on it and try to take it away from me, as though it were a bigger version of his ball. He seemed to take to this, so the artillery guy put the sleeve on and waved it in front of Ricky.

'Good boy, get him,' I said to Ricky, egging him on as he tugged and worried the sleeve.

Nero was in his element and when he got the green light, he leaped at the poor dude with the sleeve and nearly ripped his fucking arm off. If the artilleryman hadn't been wearing the sleeve, he would have bled out from the way Nero was ripping into him. Nero shook his head from side to side, like he was shaking something to death, and I think the American and his buddies might have thought the man was going to end up with a broken bone. The other soldiers were cheering the dog and laughing while the volunteer was dragged around the square.

The way a dog behaves is partly to do with its particular breed, but it's also a reflection on the handler. Unlike in the regular army or police force, where a handler can spend years with a dog, contract dogs can end up having multiple handlers for relatively short periods of time. A dog that's handled roughly might become angry and resentful. By the same token, Mals like Nero tend to be naturally highly strung and aggressive, which is why they're sometimes selected to be attack dogs.

Like most of our dogs, Ricky had been born in the US and flown to Afghanistan on a military transport. He never did become totally comfortable around Afghans, and when we did start mixing with the local population, he'd occasionally try to bite one of them. He also had a thing about motorcycles – he hated them, and would always try to chase and attack them. I don't think Ricky had ever been mistreated by an Afghan kennel attendant, or by anyone on a motorcycle; he was just, by nature, suspicious of people he didn't know and of two-wheeled vehicles.

EIGHT

Kandahar, Canadians and Koh Samui

August 2006

'Did you smoke anyone, man?'

I finished my cigarette, pinched off the end and put the butt in my pocket. 'What do you mean, "Did I smoke anyone"?'

The big redneck, Chuck, grinned, and kind of rolled his eyes, like he was talking to some dumb arse he couldn't waste his time with. 'I mean, did you kill anyone, man?'

'Um, not that I know of. No.' I'd fired off plenty of rounds during my first missions at Cobra, aiming in the general direction of where the rest of the Green Berets had been shooting, but I'd never actually seen a Taliban, or had any idea if I'd hit anything, or anyone, at all.

'Got me one. Yeah, I plugged one of them Taliban motherfuckers.' Chuck was an American ex-military dog handler, and built like a gorilla. He was one of those guys who screams like a woman giving birth when he bench presses weights.

'Congratulations.' Dick.

It was stinking hot. I was only just realising how hot it could get in this fucking dustbowl of a country; some days, it was hitting the mid forties. We were out on the hard-baked dirt strip at Tarin Kowt, waiting for a bird to take us to Kandahar. I'd finished my stint at Cobra, filling in for the guys on vacation, and was on my way back, via Tarin Kowt, after a little under a couple of months. Chuck and his dog had been working – and, apparently, smoking moth-erfuckers – at Tarin Kowt.

I found a sliver of shade for Ricky, who was in his travel kennel, and filled his water bowl and slid it in. Chuck's dog, another shepherd, named Benny, was cooking in his kennel, out in the sun. We heard the deep *whop-whop-whop* of the Chinook's blades clawing at the hot air, and turned our backs as the chopper flared its nose and touched down, enveloping us in dust, sand and grit.

With the rotors still turning, we lugged our dogs and gear out on to the pad and slid everything inside. I was sweating like a pig and plastered with dirt as I slumped into the cargo seat and buckled up. We lifted off. Past the loadmaster and his door gun, I could see the Tarin Kowt firebase below. I hadn't had a chance to look around Tarin Kowt, as I was only in transit. It was bigger than Cobra, and Australians were based there as well as US SF. The Dutch also had a big presence at the base. There was an Australian special operations task group made up of SAS and Commandos from the 4th Battalion of the Royal Australian Regiment, and a reconstruction task force based around an engineer squadron. There were probably a few guys I'd served with there, but I was now well and truly in the American fold as a contractor.

As the Chinook shuddered and whined with the effort of staying airborne, I checked on Ricky to make sure he was OK.

He was fine. However, I could see that Chuck's dog, Benny, was standing in his kennel, his face pressed against the metal grille door. I ducked my head and saw that his water bowl had been up-ended and was preventing him from sitting down.

'Hey,' I yelled in Chuck's ear, over the scream of the engines, 'you want me to move your dog's bowl so he can sit?'

'Nah, fuck him.'

Chuck had just elevated himself from knob to fuckwit. You don't treat your dog like that. The fact he'd say this in front of a stranger made me wonder what sort of life Benny led behind the scenes.

We touched down in Kandahar, but I wasn't happy to be back at the larger coalition base. I felt like I was just settling in at Cobra and starting to establish a rapport with the SF team there. I'd been on a couple of missions and proved, to myself at least, that I could do the job, but then it was time to go. However, just like in the army, when you work for a private contracting firm, you go where you're told and, besides, the dog handlers who usually worked at Cobra were back from vacation.

As well as training, all the dog handlers and dogs had to work on vehicle checkpoints when they were in Kandahar. The base is huge, with more than one gate, and hundreds of vehicles, military and civil, come in and out every day. Vehicle searches are incredibly boring and, despite searching hundreds of trucks and cars, my dog and I never found a single thing. It was necessary work—even if only as a deterrent—but I'd had a taste of life out in the FOBs, and knew that was where Ricky and I were meant to be.

My mate Guy, the other Aussie I'd almost flown to Kyrgyzstan with, had been out at another SF FOB at Deh

Rawood, while I was at Cobra. He and I teamed up again, and we were ordered to pack our gear and travel to the Canadian army firebase at Spin Boldak, south-east of Kandahar on the border of Afghanistan and Pakistan.

We travelled to Spin Boldak by road, in a Canadian light armoured vehicle. I never felt comfortable riding in those vehicles. It was like riding inside a tin can; I couldn't see out and I wouldn't be able to shoot if anything happened. It's funny, but I felt more secure in the relatively open gun position in the back of a GMV humvee than I did in an armoured vehicle. Although the 80-kilometre drive only took about two hours, I was very conscious that, despite their armour, these things were getting totalled by IEDs all the time. Unlike the US SF, the Canadians were happy to use the roads, which made them an easier target for landmines, bombs and ambushes.

The Canadians were from Princess Patricia's Canadian Light Infantry Regiment. Arriving at their base at Spin Boldak was, for me, in many ways like going back in time to when I served in the Australian Army. On one hand, the Canadians were, by and large, pretty good blokes; but, on the other, this was a conventional regular army regiment, complete with all the regimental bullshit that non-SF units like to carry on with.

It was made clear to Guy and me, early on, in the way we were treated that we were civilians and not part of the military structure. Of course this was true, but in the US SF FOBs we were, eventually, treated as part of the team. We were each expected to function as an extra man on the gun truck and to pull our weight doing picket in the night and chores around the base. The onus was on us, as individual operators, to fit in, but with the Canadians, we were there strictly for use as K9 handlers.

The Canadians, for example, would have had a fit if Guy or I had jumped behind a machine gun on one of their light armoured vehicles during a TIC and started shooting back at the Taliban. It just wasn't done for dog handlers to be anything other than dog handlers in their army.

All that aside, as individuals the Canadians were easy to work with and I made some lasting friends at Spin Boldak. Guy and I were assigned to work mainly on vehicle checkpoints. We'd do set shifts in the morning and afternoon, as regular vehicles came and went from the base, and then we'd be on call for the rest of the day, in case anyone else showed up unexpectedly at the gate. It wasn't hard work but, as at Kandahar, I found searching vehicles pretty boring.

Everyone was expected to go about their business in full uniform, whereas the American SF guys would get around in shorts, T-shirts and baseball caps, and bits and pieces of uniform. Green Berets also grew beards and let their hair grow long, but the Canadian infantry had military haircuts and shaved every day.

Alcohol was technically banned on all US bases in Afghanistan, but often someone would sneak a bottle of Jack Daniel's, or something similar, back from vacation and if you didn't start acting like a drunken arsehole, you'd get away with it. At Spin Boldak, however, there was zero alcohol and zero tolerance for rule breaking. What made it worse was that a French Canadian unit had occupied the base before the English-speaking Canadians and had built several bars. It was just cruel to be sitting in one of those pubs drinking Coke, when you knew the French Canadians had been living it up. There was no internet access in our room and, instead, I was issued a card that gave me a pin number and a certain amount of time on the communal internet computers, and a shared satellite phone if I wanted to call home.

I hadn't realised how good I'd had it at Cobra. There were only two laptops with internet connections at Spin Boldak, and Guy and I had to queue with the rest of the Canadians to have a short time online. It's funny when you think about how soldiers in previous wars communicated with their loved ones by snail mail, and that a phone call was probably an unheard-of luxury. In the middle of Afghanistan—one of the most primitive places I'd ever seen—we had internet, satellite phones, instant messaging and Skype, and it was annoying when we didn't have *unlimited* access. After a while, Guy and I got to be friends with an American ETT detachment—an officer and a sergeant, named Dan and Pat—who were also based at Spin Boldak, and they would connect our laptops to their internet connection, which was run as a separate network from the Canadians'.

The camp sergeant at Spin Boldak was a top bloke, named Darryl. He was good to Guy and me, and Darryl and I soon became friends. One day, I wandered over towards the wooden building with the internet computers, and Darryl intercepted me. 'Sorry, no internet today, Shane.'

'How come? Is the system down?'

Darryl shook his head. 'One of our soldiers was killed this morning.' He explained to me that every time a Canadian soldier was killed in Afghanistan, all their bases shut down their internet and satellite communications to Canada until the family, or families, of the dead, could be notified. This stopped relatives from hearing about it accidentally, on the grapevine or via the media. The soldier who had been killed this time wasn't based at Spin Boldak.

Food was all cooked fresh at Spin Boldak, and I could choose how my eggs were cooked for breakfast; this was a nice change from Cobra, where all the food was cooked in Kandahar, frozen in plastic bags and air dropped from a C-130, before being reheated and slopped on to plates.

'Shane, Guy,' Darryl beckoned to us one evening after chow, as we were heading back to our accommodation. 'Come 'round to my place later on.'

'OK.' I thought he probably wanted just to chat or something, but when I got to the camp sergeant's room, he checked the corridor, ushered me in, then closed the door behind me.

'Have a look at this.' Grinning, he produced two bottles of French red wine from under a camouflage shirt.

'Where the fuck did you get that?'

'One of our guys handed them in. Can you believe it? There was a loose wood panel on his wall and when he was trying to push it back, it came off, and these were hidden behind it. God bless the French, eh?'

God bless the dude who'd passed the bottles into the camp sergeant, more like it. The wine tasted like arse, but it was good to have a drink again and I figured it would be rude not to get drunk with the camp sergeant, who was, after all, responsible for maintaining discipline on base.

The first missions that Ricky and I went on with the Canadians were very different from the patrols I'd done with the US SF. Rather than driving out and looking for a fight, the Canadian infantry's approach was more about providing security for the locals, and winning their hearts and minds, in the hope that the people would support the Afghan government. Guy and I would take turns going on missions, one of us staying behind to do the daily grind of vehicle checkpoints.

One time, Ricky and I left the base in the back of a Bison and went out with the soldiers to a village called Kochi Nawe Awmi, where the Canadians planned to run a MEDCAP – a Medical Civic Action Program. MEDCAPs provided basic medical care to Afghan civilians, and the troops would also distribute some humanitarian aid, such as rice, flour, prayer rugs, shoes, and solar and hand-cranked radios permanently tuned to a government station. To make sure we weren't walking into a trap or an ambush, Ricky and I were given the task of searching some compounds and houses around where the Canadian medics would set up their temporary clinic. This was the first time I'd been out on foot in a village.

With Afghan civilians everywhere, and because it was still early days for me in the company, I followed the rules and kept Ricky on his lead while we began searching. I didn't want him running off and eating a child.

The first time I walked into a mudbrick house was an education for me. The Canadian infantry had emptied the houses and compounds, so Ricky and I were free to search. I paused to run my hand over a wall. The mud was a lot thicker than I had imagined, which, I guessed, gave good insulation from the heat and cold. Also, looking at the structure up close, I realised that it would easily stop a bullet from a 240. On the bare, hard-packed earth floor were the rolled-up bedrolls this family slept on. Hanging from hooks in the ceiling and embedded in the walls were simple cooking utensils. Outside the front door the remains of a small charcoal cooking fire were still warm to the touch. Ricky poked around, sniffing in corners and under the thin mattresses, seemingly as curious as I was about this new, alien environment.

A compound could be home to an extended family, with relatives living in adjoining rooms built into the walls. In the open courtyard of the first one I searched, there were a donkey and a goat. There was animal shit everywhere and, to my surprise, human crap as well. Generally, I was discovering, the people had an area set aside where they all went to the toilet, but on this occasion I found a human turd just lying out in the open. How the fuck, I thought, could people live like this? I was trying not to be judgmental, but this place was so different from Australia, it was beyond belief.

The villagers were gathered in knots around their houses, under the supervision of the Canadians, while I did the search. The women were covered from head to foot in burqas, while little girls, who didn't have their heads covered, would intermittently peek at me and Ricky from behind the young boys, who were a bit bolder. On other occasions, the kids would come right up to me, fascinated by my working dog. While on missions, the Americans would sometimes throw lollies to encourage the kids to hang around them, working on the theory that the Taliban were unlikely to open fire on soldiers surrounded by children. This sounds cynical but the other side did the same thing, and I was sure that sometimes there were Taliban spotters present during those humanitarian aid distribution and MEDCAP missions, mingling with the women and children so that they could get a close-up look at us and our gear.

It struck me that for all their lack of comforts, or perhaps because of it, this village would be a pretty good place for a boy to grow up. The male kids I saw were always laughing and getting up to mischief, and appeared to have free rein of the place. There was plenty of space for them to run around and they seemed to keep themselves entertained. I worked out pretty quickly, though, that it was a different story for the little girls, who, as soon as they were approaching puberty, were covered up and kept out of sight.

The boys had the option of going to traditional Islamic school, in the village *madrassa* but, under the Taliban, girls had been banned from any form of study. The new government had tried to bring back education for girls, but it wasn't unusual to hear of Taliban and their sympathisers chucking firebombs at or firing RPGs into schools where girls were trying to study.

On one occasion I went out with some Psyops guys who were refurbishing a school and helped them paint the place. I put the finishing touches to an improvised blackboard, which, with emulsion paint, was painted straight onto one of the walls. We were pleased with ourselves when we finished the job, but one of the soldiers lowered the mood when he said it might all be for nothing. 'Problem is,' he explained, 'that every time they send a new teacher out, the Taliban get hold of him and threaten to kill him. Most of them don't stay long.'

There were no televisions, or other electrical devices, that I could see in the places I was searching for the Canadians, but nearly every house I looked in had a radio of some sort, including the new wind-up radios that the US and Canadian Psyops soldiers handed out free of charge to civilians, so that they could tune into Afghan government propaganda.

Now, Ricky strained on his lead as a chicken clucked past him in fright. I still couldn't get over farm animals being so close to people's living quarters. 'All clear,' I told the ranking Canadian officer. With the area secure, the Canadians set up a clinic in a building that might have doubled as the village school. There was a partitioned area inside where female medics could treat the women and girls, and a separate area for the men. Outside, a long line of villagers was channelled between two rows of star pickets strung with barbed wire, and Ricky and I switched from explosive detection mode

to crowd control. Our job was to keep things orderly and pre-
vent people from jumping the queue, which a few of them
were trying to do.

Afghans are scared shitless of dogs and consider them to be
very dirty. The worst insult you can give someone in Pashto is
to call him a dog. This gave me an advantage, as I only had
to point Ricky in someone's general direction and they would
usually recoil in fear and start to behave. Ricky hadn't trained
as an attack dog, except for his brief bout with the artilleryman at Cobra, but he could be as intimidating as the next
German shepherd.

Spin Boldak had a bad reputation – and still does – as one of
the main conduits for the Taliban to ship people and arms from
Pakistan into Afghanistan. Still, everything went according to
plan during the MEDCAP. It was orderly and well run, like
everything the Canadians did, and in this kind of operation,
which involved dealing with a big crowd of civilians, military discipline ensured that everything went like clockwork. It
was as different as could be from the bands of woolly-haired,
bearded US SF soldiers roaming the country, looking to pick a
fight with any bad guys they could find.

By the time I finished my stint at Spin Boldak with the
Canadians, I was due for my first vacation. It had been a little
more than three months since I'd landed at Manus, with no
idea of where I was going or what was in store for me.

My initial contract with CAI was for twelve months and
the deal was that I would work for four months at a time and
then get 21 days off, including travelling time. It wasn't great
that travel time was included in the vacation, as it could take
a while to get home, but I couldn't complain. My contract
had started around the time I was supposed to leave Australia, but because of the company's screw ups with my initial

travel arrangements, I'd only worked about ten days of my first month but had been paid for the whole month.

Ricky and I rotated back to Kandahar.

I walked through the gates of the pre-school where my sons, Jaylen and Kyron, spend their days. I'd arranged this with their mum to surprise them, soon after I got back to Australia from Afghanistan.

I couldn't wait to see my boys again. I went in and greeted the teacher, and she told me I'd find my youngest, Jaylen, in the playground. I threaded my way between the miniature tables and chairs, past the colourful artwork on the walls, and out into the playground.

I saw my boy and it felt so good. 'Jaylen?'

Jaylen looked up at me, his expression blank. When I walked towards him with my arms spread wide, he turned and ran from me.

I woke in the middle of the night and sat up on my stretcher. My hair was wet with sweat and I wondered if I'd been yelling in my sleep.

I looked around, momentarily confused, before I realised where I was. I was still in Kandahar, in a tent, waiting for a flight out to Manus, from which I'd go home for my holidays for real. You know how when you wake from a bad dream and it takes you a second to remember what it was about, and that when you do, it sends a shiver down your spine? That's what happened to me, and it chilled me to my core. I realised that I'd only been having a nightmare about Jaylen not recognising me, but this didn't make it any easier to get back to sleep

The next day, I found out that I would be flying the first leg home. Before leaving, I went to check on Ricky in the kennels.

While I was away, he would be fed and watered and walked daily, but no-one would conduct any training with him. To introduce him to a different handler while I was away would only confuse him, so he got a vacation when I did. Ricky loved his work – and I was enjoying it too – but I had a feeling I'd be having more fun on my break than he would be on his. 'See you soon, mate,' I said to him as I left.

My new Canadian mate, Darryl, was also due some leave, and as he was going to Thailand, I decided to spend six days there as well. We flew separately, but met up a few days later, on the island of Koh Samui. It was mind blowing. One day I was waiting for a C-17 in Kandahar, praying I wouldn't get dicked around for days by the US military airlift system, and the next I was lying on a white sandy beach.

I looked around the beach as I sipped from an ice-cold can of Singha Lager and drew on a smoke. There were couples, backpackers and families. They were all having fun in the sun, and most of them wouldn't have spared a thought for the men and women fighting and dying on the other side of the world. I was all right with that, though. I wasn't over there fighting for a cause but to get my finances straight and, after four months of tax-free pay, with fuck-all to spend it on in-country, my bank account was looking a lot better than it had in a long time. A holiday to Thailand would have been out of the question for me just before I left Australia for Afghanistan, yet here I was.

The water was a perfect turquoise and when I waded out into it, the sun on my back, I just stood there for a while, then lowered my body into the sea and closed my eyes. I let the water rinse away the dust and shit of another world.

Later, Darryl and I got shitfaced in the hotel bar and I ended up pole dancing on stage. We had a blast: drinking and partying and gorging on good Thai food at night. During the days, I lazed on the beach, drinking some more, and barely cooled off in the balmy waters. We also hired mopeds, and went around the island on some suicidal rides. Darryl was taking the bike riding so seriously that I expected him to show up each day with leathers and a gang patch.

I'm into tattoos and I found a tattoo artist who drew a superb dragon on my arm, in pen. I went back to the motel and showed my girlfriend, Nikki, who'd flown in from Australia to meet me. She liked it, so the next day I went back and the guy got to work. It was so unlike getting a tatt back home, it wasn't funny. I sat there in his studio, drawing deeply on my cigarette and sipping cold Singha while the tattoo artist did his thing. This was the way to do R and R.

Looking back now, that first vacation was one of my best; not necessarily because of where I went or what I did, but because I had some time to chill out before getting back to Australia. By accident rather than design, I'd given myself a chance to transition from Afghanistan back to the reality of normal life in Australia, by having six days to party, sunbake and generally unwind.

I'd really missed my five kids during the time I'd been in Afghanistan. Their mothers were pleased to have me back – so they could get a break from the children. Unlike other blokes who've separated from their partners, I hadn't been around to take care of the kids every second weekend. However, with two exes and only one of me, I had to take care of all five children for the remainder of my vacation. I was due 21 days, but, besides it including travel time, I'd already burned six on the beach at Koh Samui.

The nightmare I'd had in Kandahar about Jaylen had shaken me up but I still wanted to surprise him the first time

I saw him. I needed to prove to myself, I think, that my son couldn't have forgotten me. I spoke to his mother, and to the teachers at Jaylen's and Kyron's preschool, and arranged to arrive unannounced. As I parked outside I was nervous, but I also knew that I needed to confront my fears. Maybe I'm wrong to do this, I suddenly thought. They were only one and three years old at the time.

When I first walked through the gates, I saw Kyron playing with some of his friends. He looked across the playground and saw me, and when he stood there for a couple of seconds, just staring at me, my heart started to thump. Slowly, he walked over to me, then smiled and gave me a hug. It was so good to pick up my son, and wrap my arms around him. I kissed him and held him tight.

'Where's Jaylen, mate?' I asked Kyron. 'Can you take me to him?'

He nodded, and led me by the hand to one of the class-rooms, where I sat on one of those tiny chairs they have. I'd had a momentary scare at Kyron's shyness and prayed that Jaylen would recognise me. The teacher opened the door and, the moment Jaylen saw me, he ran across and jumped into my arms, even though he was barely walking at the time.

Because my finances were still in a mess, even though I was beginning to earn some good money, I didn't have a place of my own in Australia, so the kids and I were shuffled from my mum's place to my dad's, and then to my sister's. It was hectic, and I had all the kids scattered from arsehole to break-fast time, sleeping on mattresses on lounge room floors and in spare rooms.

While I hadn't been especially stressed by the end of my first four months in Afghanistan, I was after two weeks of looking after five kids.

NINE

Tarin Kowt and training

October 2006

The time at home went too quickly, but I'd mentally prepared myself to spend at least twelve months working in Afghanistan, so I figured the quicker I got stuck into my next four-month tour, the better off I'd be – financially as well as mentally.

After transiting through Manus in Kyrgyzstan again, and having to spend a few days waiting for aircraft, I arrived back in Kandahar and was told I'd be going to FOB Ripley at Tarin Kowt, which I'd only ever transited through previously. I was going to be working with a US SF team, so I was happy about that.

I picked up Ricky from the kennels at Kandahar airfield and, after spending a couple of days working and training with him around the base, the realisation that I wouldn't be seeing my family and other loved ones for another four months started to sink in. Military people who serve overseas on operations in wartime might go for four or six months and when they come home, it's all over – they've done their bit. This was going to be my life, though, commuting to and from a war zone for four months on and three weeks off, so I needed to get used to it. The faster Ricky and I got back to work, I thought, the better.

Ricky and I flew into Tarin Kowt in a Chinook. It was October 2006, and there was a chill in the air that I hadn't felt when I'd left to go on vacation. The Third SF Group had replaced the Seventh, and the new teams in--country were preparing themselves for battle, and for the long winter ahead. The dry mid-year summer in Afghanistan had traditionally been the 'fighting season' for the Taliban and al-Qaeda, and their predecessors during the Russian invasion. Action tapers off during the bitter winter, but there were still a couple of months of reasonably mild weather left.

There was an airstrip at Tarin Kowt that had been built by the Russian military and upgraded by civilian contractors working for the coalition to take C-17 jets. The base was in a wide open valley, with a range of mountains to the south. The town of Tarin Kowt, home to about 40,000 people, was scattered over a substantial area north-west of the base, along a river. North of Tarin Kowt was the Baluchi Valley, a serious Taliban stronghold with no coalition presence. Government control in Uruzgan was like a series of ink blots on a map. Outside the area immediately around Tarin Kowt and the FOBs at Deh Rawood and Cobra, the Taliban had a free run.

Tarin Kowt was bigger than Cobra, and the A-Team there was supported by an Operational Detachment Bravo. Working from an Advanced Operational Base – Tarin Kowt, in this case – the Operational Detachment Bravo, or 'B-Team', in the US SF structure was made up of headquarters, administration and support elements that oversaw a number of A-Teams. It just happened that at Tarin Kowt there was also a resident A-Team, conducting missions, and the B-Team was supporting it and other teams in Uruzgan Province. Big brother B-Team looking over our shoulders meant things might not be quite as free and easy as they had been at Cobra, but at least I was back with the SF.

Even though I'd worked with the Americans at FOB Cobra, it had been with a different group and so I had to begin the process of integrating with the team all over again. It was more difficult at Tarin Kowt, too, because I was put in a room outside the SF compound. Work was being done to increase the number of accommodation rooms in the compound, but the pen-pushers in the B-Team had decided that they didn't want any civilians bunked in with the A-Team. Fortunately, the team sergeant from the A-Team, who I got to know early, and got on well with, was on my side and he was fighting his superiors in the B-Team to get me moved. This was one of the problems with there being another level of command close by – too many chiefs with not enough Indians to boss around.

I was living with the mechanics, tradies, cooks and bottle washers from Kellogg Brown & Root which was the main civilian catering and logistics contractor in Afghanistan at the time. The team sergeant pointed out to the B-Team that I was going to be working with the A-Team and going on missions with them, so it made sense for me to integrate with them, but his argument was falling on deaf ears.

There were some personality problems in that B-Team. One of the sergeants was an African American and when he rode his motorcycle past me one day, Ricky went apeshit and started chasing him. I heard later that the sergeant reckoned I was racist and that I was egging my dog on, which was complete bullshit. As I tried to point out to anyone who would listen, it wasn't black people he hated, it was motorcycles. The guy just didn't like civilian contractors and, while he was entitled to his opinion, the soldiers in the A-Team wanted me in with them and, as far as I was concerned, they should have had the right to make that decision for themselves – not have it made by some bureaucrat in uniform. I stuck to my guns. Eventually, one of the A-Team members rotated out to Kandahar and when his room became vacant, the team sergeant just let me have it and I moved my gear in.

The A-Team guys were great blokes and I made good friends with many of them. They were an interesting group of older and younger NCOs – non-commissioned officers – who were mostly sergeants. As at Cobra, I realised that being accepted by the team meant that I'd have to do my share, both on missions and back at base. Their demolitions specialists were building a storage room in the compound, so I got stuck in and helped them with the construction work. Ricky would hang around while we worked and the guys liked having him there.

An Operational Detachment Alpha, or A-Team, consists of twelve men: two officers and ten sergeants, who must all be SF qualified, cross-trained and multilingual, so that the team can work as a self-sufficient element anywhere in the world. A captain usually leads the team, with a warrant officer as second in command. The rest of the team comprises two sergeants specialising in each of the following areas: weapons, engineering, medical, communications, and operations and intelligence.

Adam, one of the sergeants in the Tarin Kowt team, and I would go to the gym most evenings and spot for each other. He loved Ricky and I took a fantastic picture of my dog sitting on top of a gun truck with Adam behind the .50 cal. Adam was in his late twenties and had served with the US Army in Germany prior to joining the Green Berets. He had married a German girl while posted in Europe.

As they'd just arrived in-country, the team was getting stuck into some intensive training, in which I was expected to take part. This made sense, as they needed to know that if the shit hit the fan, I could use their weapons and communications systems; that my first aid skills were up to scratch; and that I was familiar with their tactics, techniques and procedures. The first team I'd served with at Cobra was no less professional, but they had been in Afghanistan for months, so, rather than spending time training me, they had assumed that I would just pick things up as I went along.

Adam and I and the rest of the team went out to the firing range to do some close quarter battle training – house-to-house stuff in a simulated built-up area, which, as a former army engineer, was something very new to me. This was the sort of stuff that only SF and infantry get up to in the Australian Army. There were no buildings on the range, so, to practise the close-quarter combat, simulated walls and doors had been marked out on the ground and with mine tape strung between star pickets.

We practised entering the imaginary buildings, in slow-time at first, before picking up the pace. First, it was two people at a time and everyone, including me, had a go. Then, as skills were refreshed – or, in my case, learned – the numbers of people entering the building were increased to three, four, and five. Everyone had a go in every position, and it was exciting for me, as a civvie, to lead the team in through the pretend doorway, these highly motived, pumped-up dudes rushing in behind me. I never really expected to have to use these newfound skills but, as I was often operating in villages and compounds, it was good at least to know what would be happening around me if the team ever had to bust into a place for real. Then, the team would clear the building first and I'd be expected to come in with Ricky to search afterwards.

We talked through the use of grenades in clearing buildings – who would throw the grenade, and what the other members of the team would be doing when it exploded. I wasn't working with Ricky during these exercises, as the aim was more me bringing my military skills closer to the level of the Americans'. As well as being fun, the training was another great chance for me to be accepted by the team, so I put everything I had into it.

The team didn't only train in how to kill people. On one exercise, I walked into a building in which there were three American soldiers screaming their lungs out and crying for help. They were covered in blood and I could see a puckered wound in a guy's chest that was pumping out more blood all over the front of his torn uniform. The SF medics had done a gruesomely effective job of simulating wounds. First aid training was a top priority for this team.

With the medics watching, we had to check each 'victim', bandage him and prepare him for Medevac. We each had a turn at practising CPR on a dummy that, we were told, was a man who had stopped breathing. After treating the wounded, we went outside and called in a Medevac helicopter. The training was at such a high level that we even had access to a real Black Hawk; some of us carried the patients out to the chopper on improvised stretchers, while others fanned out into covering positions. The Black Hawk took off and circled the base a couple of times, before coming back so that we could start the procedure all over again.

The training was as realistic as possible, right down to us learning how to administer IV drips. We were given real needles and IV lines to practise with, and paired up. I was with a mate of mine, Dave, who was one of the older members of the team. He was also a smoker, so we tended to hang out together at coffee breaks.

We sat at a picnic table in the compound, and I gritted my teeth as Dave slid a needle into my arm. I'd never put a needle into another person before. I tied a tourniquet around Dave's upper arm and checked the line from the saline drip bag, to make sure the fluid was going through. Next, I took an alcohol swab to clean his skin, then rested the needle against his flesh.

'Shit, man. Ouch!'

I was fucking hopeless at this. 'Sorry, man,' I said, trying not to laugh. It took me a couple of attempts to find a vein and each time I was sticking the needle into another part of Dave's arm. Finally, the needle retracted as the catheter entered a vein. I released the tourniquet to get his blood flowing again, then inserted the line.

We had another couple of goes on each other until we all got comfortable with starting IVs. Again, it was good to know I could do this, in case I had to treat someone in the heat of battle. As we became more confident, we even practised giving each other IVs at night, using night-vision goggles. The training was more full-on than anything I'd ever done in the Australian Army.

While the training continued, I also started going on missions with the team. The weather had turned, and it was raining the day we went on a combat reconnaissance mission to the village of Shah Mansur. 'Combat reconnaissance' meant that we would go there, have a look, and if someone wanted to pick a fight, we'd get into it.

Near the village, Ricky and I were tasked with clearing a kilometre of road. A kilometre doesn't sound like much, but when you're working a dog in the open, and in the rain, it's bloody hard work. The dirt road was well defined, flanked by low mudbrick walls and houses here and there. This helped a bit, as it gave Ricky something to focus on. It's even harder to search empty open spaces.

I was quartering Ricky – moving him from one side of the road to the other – and, at that stage, I was still working him on-lead. The road was slippery with mud, and I nearly fell on my arse a few times as he and I crossed back and forth. I had to keep him moving and motivated, and make sure he kept his nose close to the ground, because any potential IEDs would have been buried. I had to balance the need of the team to get through there as soon as possible with the need to keep Ricky on his game, which meant I had to allow him brief rest periods. He did a good job and we made it through without incident. So much of a dog handler's war is like that, hours of effort with no result, but one mistake can be the end of the team.

When we got back from the mission, Ricky and I were cold, wet and filthy. I took him into the shower block at Tarin Kowt and held him under the hot water while I scrubbed him clean, then towel-dried him. Like most dogs, Ricky didn't mind a bath once he was actually under the water but, given half a chance, he'd do a runner.

After his shower, I took him back to my room and we sat together by the heater. It was good to be warm again, even if the space was full of that awful wet-dog smell.

Back on the rifle range at Tarin Kowt, we did heaps of live firing drills. I racked my Glock and, under the watchful eye of an SF soldier, moved up to the start line.

'Go!' he yelled, pushing the button on a stopwatch. As I walked forward, I fired two shots at a paper target – a double tap. It stayed up. Another target was raised, which I somehow managed to hit. I moved through the maze of mine tape we'd set up to represent building walls and snapped off shots, two at a time. My shooting, as usual, was shithouse, but it was all valuable training and more fun than any shooting I'd done back in Australia.

Unlike the fifteen-minute brief on the M240 I'd had when I first arrived at Cobra, with this team I went out and put a lot of rounds down range through the 240 and the .50 cal. I was also given a lesson on the Mark 19 automatic grenade launcher, which was capable of firing up to 375 explosive projectiles per minute. I fired a heap of 40-millimetre grenades, which was awesome. Watching the bursts erupting at the far end of the range made me think how terrifying coming under fire from this weapon must be. Each grenade had a killing radius of five metres, and was capable of causing wounds up to fifteen metres from the point of detonation. This was useful training, as on a later mission with another team, I was given the job of manning a Mark 19. This weapon didn't exist when I was in the Australian Army.

While I was learning new things, I found that the basic training I'd received in the army and police in Australia was standing me in good stead. The Australian Army is big on fire control and being disciplined with your ammunition and, naturally, in the police you've got to be dead sure of what you're doing before you draw your pistol.

For the first time, I was getting a real feeling of what it meant to be part of a US SF team, and really feeling accepted. As well as joining in with their training, I was expected to attend afternoon prayers, the team sergeant's daily briefing. As a civilian I didn't need to be there, and the team could have probably found 100 reasons I shouldn't have attended, but I was pleased to be invited.

There was a US Army special search dog handler named John, based at Tarin Kowt. John was the first American military dog handler I'd worked with. The special search dogs were trained the same way Australian explosive detection dogs were; that is, they worked their dogs off-lead. John and I trained together, and even though company policy dictated that I search Ricky on-lead, I was keen to get him off the leash and used to responding to my words of command and body language. Ricky responded well to the training, and it was good for both the dog and me that he be able to work this way if I needed him to do so.

Up the hill from FOB Ripley was Kamp Holland, the Dutch base in the province, which was also home to the Australian Reconstruction Task Force. The Australian engineers were working closely with the Dutch and it turned out that I knew quite a few of the blokes who were based there. I'd get on a four-wheel motorbike and visit them, but I wasn't allowed to take Ricky with me on my visits.

The Australian presence was split into two parts. Next door to Kamp Holland was Camp Russell, which housed the Australian Special Operations Task Group, which included the SAS, commandos and specialist engineers from the Incident Response Regiment. Access to Camp Russell, named after the first Australian killed in Afghanistan, Sergeant Andrew Russell, was tightly controlled.

I knew Andrew Russell in my early days in the Australian Army. Before he passed the gruelling SAS selection course and was accepted into the elite unit, he was an army engineer. We served together in the 1 CER airborne troop and I'd later end up going on a mission into Helmand Province, where Andrew was killed when the six-wheel drive Land Rover long-range patrol vehicle he was in drove over a mine.

In true Australian Army tradition, there were dog handlers and dogs attached to the Reconstruction Task Force and, on the other side of some barbed wire, dogs and handlers attached to the Incident Response Regiment. I got to meet a few of the handlers and, while they'd all completed their training long after I'd left the army, it was good to catch up with them and swap stories.

The Netherlands has a reputation for breeding and training some of the best sniffer dogs for de-mining operations in the world, so I was surprised to learn that the Dutch military didn't have an explosive detection dog capability. There were military dogs on the Dutch base, but they were attack dogs, whose job was to provide security, especially for the Apache helicopters. At night, these dogs were let off their leashes to roam free around the helicopters, to deter any Taliban who might have considered sneaking into the base.

In the ranks of the Incident Response Regiment and the Reconstruction Task Force were several engineers I'd served with when I'd been in the army. It turned out that Greg, the squadron sergeant major of the engineer squadron, was a guy I knew from 1 CER. He'd been a sapper in the airborne troop when I'd joined, and a corporal while I was working as a dog handler. It was interesting talking to him, and wondering how I would have got on if I'd stayed in the Australian Army. I didn't have many regrets about the career choices I'd made, though, and I knew I had a better life as a civilian contract dog handler than I would have if I'd come to Afghanistan with the army.

The Reconstruction Task Force guys were working closely with the local Afghan community in Tarin Kowt. Part of their job was rebuilding, or building, civil infrastructure in the province, but they were also running a trade training school for young Afghan men, which taught them the basics of carpentry and electrics. The idea was to give the boys the skills and tools they needed to make a living, and to help support their families. After graduating, the Afghans would be given a toolkit. The word was that some of the tools from the kits were showing up in the local markets, but the Aussies were confident that enough of the young men were working as tradies to make the program worthwhile.

The Reconstruction Task Force might have been concentrating on winning hearts and minds, but the Taliban was just as keen to stop them doing their work as it was to stop the SAS or US SF who were out searching for al-Qaeda and Taliban and killing them.

On board the SF vehicles, we carried a few Carl Gustaf -84-millimetre anti armour weapons. It was a Swedish-made weapon and looked like a stubby bazooka, and I'd trained on it in my early years as a soldier. We in the Australian Army called it the 'Charlie guts-ache', as there was a health risk if you fired more than three or four rounds in succession from it: the back-blast was so severe that, apparently, repeated use could shake up your internal organs. It was, however, an effective, easy-to-use weapon, either against vehicles or for busting holes in mudbrick houses or compounds. I learned that the team was short of rounds and I suggested we try to scrounge some from the Australians, as I was sure they were also still using the Carl Gustaf.

I took one of the team guys with me to visit Greg at the Australian base. I'm sure he thought it was a turn-up for the books, the mighty US military machine begging ammunition from the relatively tiny Australian task force, but he was happy to help us out and we were able to ship a few rounds back to the SF compound.

I'd been happy to help out, too, and wondered if being a civilian made it easier for me to be a middle man. Contractors sometimes found themselves in a bit of grey area when it came to the rules. On one hand, we were expected to follow the law of the land at whatever FOB we were based; on the other, on some matters we probably weren't policed as strictly as the soldiers. For example, an American contractor I knew at Tarin Kowt was getting booze shipped to him from the States. His father was decanting spirits and home-brewed wine into peroxide bottles and mailing it to him.

The A-Team at Tarin Kowt was thoroughly professional and, unlike the guys at Cobra, adhered strictly to the no-alcohol rule. I'm not saying the soldiers at Cobra were less professional but, as they were operating at a remote base without a B-Team looking over their shoulder every minute, they could get away with a bit more. My contractor buddy slipped me some bottles of his dad's bootleg alcohol, but I didn't want to jeopardise the acceptance with the team I'd won, so needed to get rid of it.

Over at the Australian base, they were following the US lead, so the task force there was also 'dry'. There are some funny double standards in the Australian Defence Force. For the last fifteen years or so, there has been no alcohol allowed on Australian Army exercises, or for fighting troops serving overseas on operations. The navy and air force, however, have in similar situations had limited access to booze.

I didn't want to get caught with the alcohol in my room, but it seemed a crying shame to tip it down the sink after my buddy's dad had sent it halfway around the world. I smuggled it into the Aussie base and gave it to some diggers I knew there. I thought of this as doing my bit to strengthen further the bonds between the coalition partners in Afghanistan.

*

I stopped and looked at a bloke in civilian clothes, who stared back at me. 'Don't I know you?'

This was happening to me on a regular basis at Tarin Kowt.

As well as the presence of Australian military people in Afghanistan, Aussie civilians were working myriad roles that in past wars would have been done by people in uniform. I said hello to the man, who turned out to be John 'Robbo' Roberts, who had been a troop commander in 1 Field Squadron when I'd been a sapper. Robbo had left the Royal Australian Engineers after becoming a major. He was a good bloke and, having met again, we'd talk for hours. I found out he had married a Mozambican woman he'd met while serving with the Australian detachment to the United Nations de-mining operation there.

Like me, Robbo had come to Afghanistan for the money, as he was supporting kids from his first and second marriages. He was based in a compound beside FOB Ripley, the SF base. He worked for a company called DynCorp, and his job was to maintain the airstrip at Tarin Kowt and run a contract helicopter. The chopper, crewed by Russians who had served in Afghanistan during their war in the 1980s, was used to move cargo around the province, and to and from Kandahar airfield.

When I wasn't out on missions, I'd often drop in on Robbo, who lived and worked out of two shipping containers. As well as running an airfield and a helicopter, he was the local sly-grog wholesaler. He would buy to order for thirsty soldiers on the base and, thanks to the volumes he was trading in, the price of a bottle of contraband Indian whisky dropped from 100 US dollars to 40. Prior to his contact in Kabul being busted and sacked, Robbo had been able to bring in by road half a shipping container of VB, and keep it under wraps while selling it.

Also in the DynCorp compound were civilian counter-narcotics advisers from the Poppy Elimination Force, a US State Department-funded operation. The Poppy Elimination Force had started life as the Afghan Eradication Force, but its name was changed when it was realised that it wasn't politically correct to be talking about eradicating Afghan people.

Robbo and I would watch the sun set over the mountains while we had a beer or two. We talked about our time in the engineers, and he reminded me that he'd been the troop commander in charge of the infamous search of George Bush Senior's hotel room. He also reminded me of another search of a public building, during a visit by Queen Elizabeth, in which our guys found a loaded pistol and a black dildo in a prominent public official's desk drawer.

One evening, we were sitting up on the shipping container and watching multiple rockets being launched from the back of a truck in the FOB, out in support of a TIC in the valley somewhere to the north.

'We're going to have to be here for years to win this thing,' Robbo said.

I shook my head. 'Not me.'

We sat in silence for a while, listening to the whiz and whoosh of the rockets, and watching their high-arcing comet trails scribing white lines across the red-gold sky.

'Did you hear what happened to the backyard blitz boys?' Robbo asked.

'Backyard blitz' was our term for the efforts of the Australian Reconstruction Task Force engineers, many of whom we'd served with in the past. 'What happened?'

'They went out to a village, and worked their guts out to put in a water supply system but didn't get it finished. When they came back the next day to commission it, they found all the plumbing had been nicked.'

'You're joking.'

'We're not going to win hearts and minds by imposing development and infrastructure on these people,' Robbo said. 'The Afghans have to own the whole process of rebuilding and the outcome. As long as we keep acting like westerners and delivering what we think they need, instead of what it is they say they need, we're going to keep missing the mark.'

I could see that Robbo had a point. The Russians had come and built dams and housing and roads, but their troops and their ideology had been hated, and both were long gone. However, Robbo also told me about a conversation he'd had with a tribal elder of the Alokozay, the local people, who claimed the Russians had massacred about 300 people during the invasion and that their bodies were buried somewhere around Tarin Kowt.

'We're not as bad as the Russians, but we're still foreigners and we're adopting a siege mentality,' Robbo said, looking across the river to the village.

It was not surprising that I'd meet ex-army people, like Robbo, in Afghanistan, but it was an eye-opener to see just how many different types of contractors there were in the country, and the range of jobs they were doing. As well as ex-military and law enforcement people, contracting firms recruited people straight from civilian life if they had the necessary skills.

In a couple of shipping containers in a separate compound near the SF base at Tarin Kowt was a bunch of guys who had turned their hobby – flying remote control aeroplanes – into a lucrative job in a war zone. When we went on missions in populated areas, such as in the town of Tarin Kowt itself, we'd sometimes take these guys and their model aircraft, which was fitted with a camera and called *Tiger Shark*, with us.

The team was providing security for a *shura*–a gathering of senior men, like a council meeting–in Tarin Kowt, and the flyboys came along and launched their plane from a road. The local kids were amazed and I'm sure that any bad dudes who were lurking in the area well understood that this thing buzzing around overhead was keeping an eye on them. The aircraft had a wingspan of about two metres and, as it slowly orbited the neighbourhood, was plainly visible from the ground.

Ricky was fascinated by the aeroplane, and by the toy model aircraft that the ground-bound pilots flew back at base in their off-duty hours. We searched some streets and buildings around the place where the meeting was to be held, and every time the aircraft droned overhead, Ricky would look up and follow its path across the clear blue sky. I was searching him off-lead and he was behaving himself, yet I could tell he wanted to get a closer look at the *Tiger Shark*. I told the guys from the team that, as far as Ricky and I could tell, things were clear and the remote control aeroplane pilot said the same.

The mission was completed without any drama and after we got back to the FOB, I took Ricky for a walk. By this time, the guys from the *Tiger Shark* container were outside, playing with their toy aeroplane. One of the guys had the remote control box in his hand and was scanning the skies. Ricky and I looked up at the sound of the approaching engine.

The pilot started bringing his toy aircraft in to land in a patch of open ground. Ricky was by my side but, as we were on-base, he was off-lead. He looked up again as the buzz of the little engine got louder. The plane was coming in towards us, on final approach for its landing.

Ricky took off.

'Ricky! Get back here, boy!'

Normally obedient, my dog was like an animal possessed. Every instinct he had told him it was time to bring that bird down out of the sky. 'Look out,' I yelled to the guy with the remote control.

'Shit! I'm losing control. It's not responding,' the pilot said.

He was trying to pull the power back on, like a pilot of a real plane who sees danger on the runway and has to abort a landing, but the aircraft kept coming down and down as Ricky bounded towards it.

It was all over in a flash. Ricky leaped at the aircraft when its wheels were almost on the ground, and got the fuselage between his jaws and dragged it into the dust. Our working dogs were supposed to be fanatical retrievers and my boy had decided that he wanted to retrieve that thing right out of the sky, like he was a gun dog!

There was a knock on the door of my hooch. 'Mr Shane?'

'Coming.'

Ricky had been sitting peacefully on the end of my bed, but the sound of an Afghan voice was enough to make him ballistic. He shot away, with the same speed and determination he'd exhibited when he'd gone after the model aircraft. The Afghan must have thought I'd said 'Come in,' rather than 'Coming,' because he had started opening the door before I had a chance to put Ricky back in his portable kennel. The dog reared up on his hind legs and started pawing the crack in the door, snarling and barking at the young Afghan interpreter on the other side.

'Eeeeeeeeek!' shrieked the interpreter, sounding like a little girl who'd been frightened by a mouse. In fact, I'd never heard a guy utter such a high-pitched, effeminate squeal in my life, and although I felt for the poor Afghani, it was also one of the funniest reactions to a dog I've ever seen.

Ricky never lost his distrust of the locals. It was hard disciplining him because, while I didn't want him indiscriminately attacking people, I needed him to be capable of a crowd control role, in which part of his job was sometimes to snarl and look vicious if it looked like people were getting out of line.

I was careful to keep Ricky locked up if I knew locals were going to be in the compound. Still, one day two laundry boys were moving through collecting dirty washing and Ricky darted out when I turned my back on him. I must have left the door to the hooch ajar. The laundry boys dropped their sacks and ran, robes flying behind them as Ricky chased them out into the courtyard and around and around in circles, nipping at their heels.

TEN

Death in the Baluchi Valley

November 2006

We were busy at Tarin Kowt, going on missions for two or three days at a time, sometimes with only a couple of days' break in between. Winter was well on the way and the Taliban, like the Green Berets, were trying to make the most of the last of the good weather, before the fighting season came to an end and the cold set in.

At the time, no-one had been up into the Baluchi Valley for two years; the last people who had dared to do so were the Australian SAS. The Taliban had had free rein of the area ever since, but the SF team at Tarin Kowt was tasked to go into the valley to see what action it could stir up. As we loaded the trucks with food, water and ammo, saddled up and rolled out the gates of FOB Ripley, we knew we'd find a fight. My mate Adam was in the turret of our GMV, behind the .50 cal, and I was in the back.

'Good to go?' Adam asked me. I gave him the thumbs up and settled in behind the 240, with Ricky at my feet.

We were part of a massive convoy of about 30 vehicles, including ANA, and Afghan police. It took us two days' driving to get to Baluchi and as we got closer, our reception from the villagers became colder and quieter. The team was also in search of high-value targets, senior Taliban who were hiding up in, what they considered was, a pretty safe haven.

We came to a village that was much bigger than most I'd been to, which was strung out along a river line and surrounded by very well-irrigated fields. In so many ways, Afghanistan's a country of stark contrasts. This place had lots of greenery and thick bush around its outskirts but then it was as though there were a line where civilisation ended and desert began again.

We were sited, to give covering fire, on some high ground overlooking the village about 200 metres from the nearest houses and compounds, while the ANA, led by some American ETTs, went in to clear the place and see who they could flush out. Things were confusing, because there was lots of movement going on all around us and in the village below, and plenty of intercom radio chatter going back and forth.

Below, there was gunfire, and associated chatter as people started giving each other target indications and reports. Adam and I held our fire, as there wasn't anything for us to shoot at yet and, of course, the last thing we wanted was to brass-up one of our own guys. I had an assigned arc of responsibility to watch over. The idea was that the ANA and police would sweep through the tree line in front of us, from left to right, and then swing towards us. Following Adam's lead, I only fired two or three rounds, and mostly we held off.

Every now and then, the silence alongside our gunfire was broken by the loud *shah-chunk* of a .50 calibre round leaving the long barrel of a Barrett sniper rifle, when one of the team guys found a target. Originally designed as an anti-materiel rifle – that is, for shooting holes in vehicles and equipment – the Barrett came into its own in Afghanistan as a sniper's weapon, given the long ranges on many battlefields. A bullet designed to punch a hole in a light armoured vehicle makes a hell of a mess of a human body.

'Ah, the terps are picking up Taliban radio chatter saying they're gonna be coming in from the south, over,' a voice said over the radio.

In the distance, in front of Adam and me and inside the arc we were covering, were some young boys leading a couple of donkeys. 'Adam? You see those kids?' I asked. 'What the fuck are they doing, wandering around?'

'I dunno, man. Those donkeys are loaded – maybe they're carrying ammo for the Hajis.'

The kids kept moving across our front, not seeming to care about the operation unfolding in their village, which made me think Adam was right – that they had a reason for being down there, and not taking cover or bugging out. It was clear by this stage that there was going to be a serious fight down there.

Behind us came a high-pitched whistling sound and, as I turned around, there was an explosion in the rocks as an RPG exploded not far from our truck.

'Holy shit,' Adam said.

This was puzzling, as, according to the plan, the Afghan soldiers and police were supposed to approach our position from the south but the radio report had told us to expect the Taliban coming from the same direction.

'Movement!' someone yelled down the line. 'In the trees, coming this way.'

I looked back to the front, and pulled the butt of the 240 into my shoulder and sighted down the barrel. I could see Afghans armed with AK-47s dressed in man-jammies, which is what we called the *payrann tambaan,* or *salwar kameez*–long, loose-fitting tops over baggy pants. Most of them were either wearing turbans or small round caps. We had no idea where the RPG round had come from, but it seemed to have been the same direction from which these unknown men were creeping through the trees.

'Here they come,' I said, but I wasn't about to fire until I had clearance.

Adam traversed the .50. 'Shit! Hold off, man,' he said. 'Don't fire, Shane; it's the police.' I realised that Adam must have recognised one of the Afghans. It turned out that he was right and that some of the Afghan police didn't have uniforms. As if it weren't fucking hard enough to tell a Taliban or al-Qaeda dude from a local civilian, even the cops dressed the same and carried the same weapons. Adam had averted a major blue-on-blue friendly fire incident, with all the firepower aimed at those men walking through the tree line.

The intercom radio chatter started getting faster and more agitated as more government forces continued their sweep through the mudbrick houses and fields of corn below us. There was plenty of noise coming from the village, with the *pop-pop-pop* of AK-47s firing and the occasional *crump* of a grenade going off.

'We've got troops in contact, troops in contact, over,' a calm voice drawled over the radio. The American on the radio was one of the ETT advisers working with the Afghan forces.

When targets were sighted and positively identified, we'd get word to lay down some covering fire. I looked down at my dog at my feet. He started barking at the long bursts of gunfire. 'Shush, Ricky, it's OK, boy.' I watched Adam's fall of shot, and swung the 240 around a few degrees and squeezed the trigger, sending a burst of fifteen rounds. It was good to be doing something and, hopefully, helping the guys on the ground.

I listened in while I kept watch down the barrel of the 240, swinging from side to side every now and then, looking for a target, ready to respond. It sounded as though things were hotting up. All along the gun line, people were calling to each other, giving target indications or calling for more ammo. On the intercom radio, someone was looking for someone else, as they'd lost contact with one of the ETT call signs. The ETTs' questions to each other were punctuated by bursts of fire that I could hear in stereo, over the radio, in one ear, and in real time from the village, in the other. Talking to Adam, I worked out that it was Scott who was missing.

Scott, who was from Utah, was a US Army second lieutenant, one of the ETTs. Those guys had one of the toughest jobs in Afghanistan: training the ANA and going into the field with them as embedded military advisers. There would be two or three of them in a team, an officer and senior non-commissioned officers, each assigned to a section or a platoon. The ETTs and their Afghans got into some hellish TICs during some of the missions I went on. The American advisers fought and died alongside the Afghans, and we all had a lot of respect for them and for the job they were doing. Scott was a National Guard officer, which meant he was a reservist.

Usually, the SF teams I was with would stand off and give covering fire while the ANA or Afghan police did the actual house-to-house-clearance of a village or a compound. As it's their war, they were expected to step up and do their share of the fighting, but most times the local troops went in to clear somewhere, there would be a couple of ETTs in the thick of it as well. Now, as the fight went on, I could see ANA men emerging from the village, back the way they'd come. It didn't look good and it seemed as though the Afghans were withdrawing.

Scott was a really nice bloke, who loved Ricky. He had a dog back home, as well as a wife and four kids, and I think he liked hanging out with me and Ricky because it reminded him of the life he'd left behind and was looking forward to getting back to. He'd joined the National Guard after September 11, with the goal of serving his country overseas. He wanted to get into SF, but the ETT job had been a way for him to go straight into combat in Afghanistan.

Scott's fondness for Ricky was typical of the way that soldiers related to my dog. Having a dog in the FOB was about much more than having an extra level of security against mines and IEDs. Dogs don't know about rank or religion, or if you're having a good day or a shitty one. They're always there, ready to give kindness to people who show it to them and who deserve it. Guys – and girls – were always coming up to Ricky, and asking about him and whether they could pet him. There was something about scratching a dog behind the ears, or even just talking to him, that could make a soldier feeling like a cog in a big machine that was going nowhere fast feel human again.

'Yep, looks like they're fucking pulling out,' Adam said to me as we watched the Afghans moving back towards our position.

The Afghans had withdrawn without Scott, their ETT. He was still down there, somewhere in the village, where the

Taliban were shooting back at the fleeing government soldiers. I felt sick, as did every other man watching the scene unfold and listening to people on the intercom radio still trying to get a handle on what had happened to the American officer.

'OK. We're going in to look for him,' a voice said authoritatively over the radio.

This time, the Americans who had been giving covering fire from behind their .50 cals and Mark 19s on the hummers were yanking back on the cocking handles on their M4s, adjusting their gear, checking their ammo and getting ready to get into the fight proper. Their faces were set. Whatever had happened to Scott, they were not leaving that village without him.

The SF guys had Scott's last known position, which was where they headed. No doubt, the Taliban knew exactly what was going through their minds because the Americans came under fire as they retraced Scott's movements.

On the radio, and across the open ground between us and the village, we could hear the firefight going down, and it was intense. The SF were shooting at close range – trading shots with the enemy over 50 to 100 metres. If both sides had been looking for a fight that day, they found it, as the US soldiers continued their fire-and-movement drills, rushing from cover to cover and aiming and shooting at any Afghan who showed his head.

Doors were being kicked in as buildings were cleared all over again. Occasionally, someone would fire a burst on full automatic, laying down covering fire for his buddy, who would rush across a narrow alleyway, between compounds or from tree to tree. Searching for a missing man provides strong motivation even for SF guys, who were generally pretty pumped up in the first place.

144

'Ah, we've got one KIA down here, over.'

Scott had died fighting.

His body was found still propped up on one knee, in a firing position. He'd taken a bullet through the eye and died instantly. He'd put his life on the line to train and lead the Afghans he worked with, and they had fucking bailed on him and left his body there. His buddies brought him out – brought him home.

'Those fucking Afghans just left Scott there, man,' one of the guys said, disgusted. I saw Scott's body, laid on a stretcher, being loaded into one of the hummers.

'They ran,' another muttered. 'Fucking cowards didn't even think about trying to carry him out.'

The Afghans view death – like they do so many other things – differently from us. To them, if they die, it's God's will, and they're resigned to there being nothing they can do about it. Also, I've heard of Taliban guys in TICs who have run out of bullets or RPG rounds and just started walking around, waiting to be shot, because they've already made their peace with their God and assume that this is the day they're going to die. The ANA troops probably didn't think there was anything wrong with leaving Scott's body behind, even though their action riled the Americans, who pride themselves on never leaving a man behind.

To a certain extent, you can start to feel the same way the Afghans do; you give up trying to work out why something happens to one man and not to another, and become pretty fatalistic. I had a friend named Josh, an SF guy who had finished his second tour in Afghanistan, and had flown from FOB Cobra, back to Tarin Kowt, and on to Kandahar for his final leg to the States. He was a big, healthy dude but he died in his sleep, a week before he was due to get home. No-one knew why.

Scott was the only American killed on any of the missions I went on during my time working with the US forces in Afghanistan, but during that period there were, that I was aware of, three ETTs killed elsewhere in the country. The losses among the advisers showed the danger they placed themselves in, sometimes on a daily basis. Barack Obama and Kevin Rudd like to talk about getting the Afghans to take on more of the fighting, and the general public sometimes sees sending 'trainers' or 'advisers' as more acceptable than sending combat troops. What people don't realise is that those trainers and advisers are sometimes involved in heavier combat – and in more danger of being killed and wounded – than, say, a battalion of coalition troops would be when out on patrol in their armoured vehicles.

The Taliban believe in fate. We might believe in luck, but we also believe in knowing how to shoot properly, having our weapons zeroed correctly and in knowing how to do our jobs. I think the Taliban way of fighting, planting IEDs on the side of the road and running away, is cowardly, and I hate the way that villagers who might not be particularly anti-the Americans and the coalition, and are happy to take our humanitarian and medical aid, just stand there and watch our guys get blown away, having known there's a bomb waiting for them. Maybe they're scared of what the Taliban would do to them if they informed our men about the IEDs, or maybe they just don't care.

The soldiers who had gone in looking for Scott had come up against a section-strength group of Taliban – maybe ten or twelve guys – and we knew there were plenty more of them in the area. After the initial anger over Scott's death, people withdrew into their shells and there was an uncomfortable silence hanging over the convoy, which was broken by the voice of the JTAC calling up the air controller, orbiting somewhere above us. We pulled back a bit and the air-to-ground controller called in an A-10 to deliver an air strike on the village. The Taliban had made it clear they were going to stand and fight, so the Americans were free to use whatever tools of war were at their disposal.

The air force hammered that place and, according to later estimates, 80 or more Taliban died that day.

After the TIC we didn't go straight back to the FOB. We continued north towards the village of Nayazic.

The weather turned to shit, with icy rain and wind that stabbed through my jacket, fleece and uniform and that made riding in the exposed back of the GMV under bleak grey clouds thoroughly miserable. The conditions mirrored how many of us felt, knowing that Scott was making the first leg of his final trip home, on the medevac chopper that had been called in to collect his body.

The rain turned the dust to mud, and I felt our vehicle starting to lose traction. The back end swayed as the mud-clogged tyres struggled for more grip. We were lucky, though, and managed to get through the soft stuff, but a vehicle behind us became bogged.

I sat in my seat behind the 240, shivering as the team sergeant moved up and down the line telling everyone to stay alert, while the stuck truck's crew got out their shovels and started digging. Another humvee was manoeuvred around to try to tow the stranded vehicle. This was a perfect ambush position and we couldn't abandon the vehicle and crew, so we just had to sit there in the sleet and rain, freezing our nuts off.

It was like the bad weather was eating away at me, breaking down my resolve and laughing at my feeble attempts to stay warm. I had gloves and a balaclava on, but was freezing. I thought about Scott; killed by the enemy and abandoned by his Afghans on the battlefield.

'Stay alert, people,' the team sergeant said. 'I do not like this shit.'

I was with him.

When we finally approached our remain overnight site, it was so cold that it was almost impossible to get to sleep, and I'm sure most of us were kept awake thinking about Scott anyway. Even Ricky was shivering, and in my after-action report I recommended the company buy some cold-weather coats for our dogs. I held Ricky close, hugging him to keep us both warm.

Before settling in for the night, we had rendezvoused with a Dutch SF patrol from Task Force Viper. Officially, the Dutch government didn't want its special forces working with the Americans, who they considered to be rogue elements but, funnily enough, we would often share our night positions with Dutch patrols that we just happened to bump into. It made sense to be around friendlies at night in the mountains, no matter what politicians sitting in their comfortable homes thought.

As the long night wore on, I remembered Scott playing with Ricky, and telling me about his wife and kids back home; how proud he was of his children and how he missed his own dog. For the first time since I'd come to Afghanistan, I felt like I wanted to give it away. I'd give anything, I thought, to be back in the Australian sunshine. I could have been sitting on the beach having a beer, or out having dinner with my girl-friend. Instead, I was shivering to death in the mountains of Afghanistan.

I'd never felt so low in all my life.

ELEVEN

Deh Rawood: Walking the dog

February–March 2007

I was disappointed to leave Tarin Kowt, as I'd really felt part of the team there, and had made goods friends in Adam, Dave and New John – so called because there were a couple of Johns on the base. The A-Team had given me specialist training of the likes usually reserved for SF soldiers, and I'd seen plenty of action. Sadly, too, with Scott's death, I'd seen the cost of war first hand.

After nearly four months, though, it was time for me to move. I had an enjoyable, but hectic, vacation back home, staying with all five of my kids in a two-bedroom flat my mum owned. It was great being a hands-on father again – taking the kids to sport and dancing, organising meals and bath times, and otherwise spending time with them, but it was over too soon.

When I returned to Afghanistan, I once more teamed up with my Aussie mate Guy, and the pair of us were sent to the

FOB at Deh Rawood. It was about 40 or 50 kilometres south-west of Tarin Kowt, still in Uruzgan Province.

Deh Rawood had been the site of a controversial incident early in the war, back in 2002, when the local Afghans claimed a Spectre gunship had opened fire on a wedding party and killed at least 20 civilians. The Spectre crew claimed heavy calibre anti-aircraft rounds were firing on them, while the villagers maintained they were just following the traditional practice of firing rifles in the air as a form of celebrating the happy couple's marriage. The crew of the Spectre was exonerated, but the Taliban propaganda machine had a field day with the coverage of the civilian deaths. The incident highlighted just how confusing it could be to operate in a country that was still awash with weapons dating from the days of the Russian invasion.

Uruzgan had been a Taliban stronghold in the old days, and was where the Taliban leader Mullah Mohammed Omar came from. From the Chinook, we could see the Helmand River, which runs between Tarin Kowt and Deh Rawood. The river passed through a steep narrow valley as it bisected the mountain range, and on either bank was a green zone where the Afghans had established irrigated fields and grew their crops, including drugs. Beyond the life-giving water's reach, there was nothing but rock and dirt.

As we approached Deh Rawood, we flew over a mountain range that looked like a jagged line of broken beer bottles on top of a security fence. I knew that even without enemy threat, those mountains could be dangerous. My mate John Roberts, who ran the helicopters from Tarin Kowt, had told me that an Mi 26 helicopter full of cargo destined for the Dutch base had crashed in the ranges in bad weather, killing all eight crew on board. Even with the risk of accidents and ground fire, I preferred flying to driving in Afghanistan, though, because of the risk of IEDs.

The FOB was a complex of square compounds, demarcated by hesco walls, with guard towers that overlooked the base, the river next to it, and the town of Deh Rawood on the other side of the river. On the town side of the river, the green zone crept as far as it could until it met the mountains, but on the base side there was nothing but dirt between the FOB and the hills. There was no airstrip at Deh Rawood for fixed wing aircraft, just a square cobbled with smooth river stones where helicopters could land.

As well as the A-Team, there was a detachment of four Dutch Marines at Deh Rawood, working as ETTs, training and advising the local ANA. The Dutch turned out to be a good bunch. They were friendly and laid-back, always taking the piss out of each other.

One of the Dutchmen's favourite pastimes, which we introduced them to, was to have wars with Meal Ready to Eat 'bombs'. To make one, you take a plastic half or one-litre sized drinking water bottle, drain off most of the water and squeeze in one of the little chemical Brillo pads from the inside of the meal's heater bag, put the lid on the bottle, then shake it up. As the pad starts to heat up, the plastic bottle expands, rapidly, because the steamy vapours from the pad have nowhere to go. Depending on the amount of water you use, you can make a crude time bomb, so that the bottle doesn't explode straight away.

One night when the SF teams were all out on a mission, the tactical operations centre – the nerve centre of the FOB – was being manned by one of the DynCorp police mentors, an African American dude called Tony. The mentors were former US policemen who were working with the Afghan law enforcement authorities. The Dutchmen, Guy and I rigged up an extra big water bottle as a bomb, and set it by the door to the Tactical Operations Centre. When it went off, poor old Tony thought World War fucking-III had just broken out and was nearly shitting himself as he went running out to the shelter.

Just as with my first deployment to Cobra, the SF team at Deh Rawood was nearing the end of its tour and near to going home, so they were not too inclined to take a new person under their wing. I still went on missions, but spent most of my off-duty hours hanging out with the Dutch guys. We had a massive television screen and Xbox, so when we weren't out on missions, looking for real bad guys, the Dutch would visit Guy and me, and we'd sit in front of the TV for hours, killing pretend baddies in Ghost Recon.

We could never take a break from training with the dogs. Guy and I would sometimes use the accommodation area, and take turns hiding explosives for each other's dog to search for. One day, when it was my turn, I let Ricky off his lead and talked him through the indoor maze of unused bedrooms, hallways and the recreation area. 'Sook, Ricky,' I commanded.

Ricky searched all the bedrooms, and found nothing in them or in the hallway. When we entered the TV room, we started working a pattern. Ricky stopped near a lounge chair in front of the TV, and sniffed under it, then just sat there. This change of behaviour told me he'd found something. He lowered his head, like he was having a second look, then sat there again. I stayed directly behind him as I walked closer, not wanting to distract him. When I crouched down, I saw the mortar round.

'Good boy, Ricky! Ya-hoo! Good boy.' You exaggerate your praise for the dog, as you do to reinforce a child's behaviour, when it's done something right. Next, I tossed Ricky's ball over his head, so it landed just in front of him, and he scrambled for it. We played with the ball for a while and Ricky was happy. It's not so easy to have fun if your dog finds something for real, out on operations. In that case, you praise the dog at the site of the find, then turn and run, getting yourself and your dog away from whatever it is you've found, and have your enjoyment at a safe distance.

Helmand Province, in the south-west of Afghanistan, is the badlands. It's mostly desert and is a thoroughly inhospitable place. Helmand was where Andrew Russell, who I'd served with in the army engineers before he went to the SAS, had been killed by a land mine.

There had been lots of fighting down there and I was on a mission that just touched inside the province. We'd left from the FOB at Deh Rawood and I was in the GMV, manning the 240, with Ricky at my feet. I was with one of two A-Teams on the patrol, and behind us were the Dutch guys in one of their cut-down Land Rover Wolf vehicles.

You don't get a lot of rain when you're in Afghanistan, so when you do, you tend to remember it. It was now early morning and raining and, as there was no cover over the gun position, I was wet, and I was cold. The vehicle's movement produced a wind-chill effect and it was hard to concentrate on anything other than how miserable it was in the back of that fucking truck.

The first mortar explosion was spectacular. The round must have embedded itself deep in the soft ground because when it hit, it obviously kept going a fair way down, through the mud and slush, before it detonated. When it went off, it sent up a fountain of muck into the grey sky, about 50 metres from us.

I was facing rear and could see two of the Dutch dudes laughing. I was laughing and pointing too, but saying to my-self, that was too fucking close, man.

There's never been a time that I've felt absolute terror while on patrol. The mortars didn't faze me too much and, to be honest, driving through the barrage was a bit of a buzz. How-ever, they were zeroing in and getting closer and closer to us as we moved through. Later on, one of the ANA guys who was with us told me he reckoned the Taliban must have had Pakistani army guys working with them.

'Yes,' the Afghan guy said, 'that fire was too accurate to be just Taliban. I am sure it was Pakistanis.'

I didn't really believe him, but the mortars were close, and in intelligence briefings you'd often hear claims that rogue officers from the Pakistani security service, in the Inter Service Intelligence Directorate, were backing al-Qaeda and the Taliban. Their links went way back, to the days when the Mujahideen were fighting the Russians and the Americans were backing them, with the help of the Pakistanis on the ground. Who knows, maybe Pakistanis had trained these guys.

We couldn't really see where the mortar fire was coming from, but guessed it was from the compounds that made up the village we could see in the distance. The guy in the tur-ret of my vehicle was on a .50 cal and once he started firing, that was my cue to open up as well. I watched his fall of shot, where the big fat glowing tracer rounds were landing, flicked the safety and fired a burst in the same direction. Ricky was between my legs.

I heard a short, sharp zapping noise, and looked down and saw that Ricky was looking up at me. His nose was flicking from side to side, like he was watching something going by. It took me a few seconds to realise that Ricky was actually watching or listening to bullets flying past us. There were now machine-gun rounds coming down-range towards us, from the Taliban positions in the compounds. I put my foot on Ricky's lead to keep him down and crouched as much as I could inside the vehicle while still firing back. Even though the M240 position was up-armoured, the bullet-proof plate normally only came up to my chest. It was mad that the first indication I had had that we were being shot at was from Ricky, but at the same time I was grateful to my dog for the warning.

I glanced up ahead, and saw that all the guys in the vehicles in front of us were taking off their baseball caps and hurriedly putting their Kevlar helmets on. That was another reliable sign that the shit was about to start flying.

In the middle of all this shooting, I saw an Afghan guy running through the mud. He'd been with a flock of sheep that had scattered. There were women and children running too, away from the village into the distance.

'There's civilians, there's civilians; watch out!' someone was shouting from the radio. If you moved through a village and didn't see any civilians, you started to worry, because that usually meant the Taliban were ready for a fight. It was the same thing if you saw all the women and children start running away from a village – sometimes they wouldn't get advance warning from the Taliban of an ambush, so that things would look normal when we first approached.

Ricky was whimpering a bit and I again stood on his leash to keep him safe and out of sight on the floor of the truck. 'Quiet, boy,' I said to him. Ricky had a habit of barking at Afghan civilians when we passed through a village, so I didn't want him poking his head up now, in case he added to the confusion. Also, I didn't want him getting in my way as I swung the 240.

I looked back out over the open country and was momentarily mesmerised by the shepherd continuing to run. He was obviously not Taliban – just some poor bastard caught in the middle of a gunfight. I wiped the drizzle from my face and, over the smoking barrel of the 240, tracked his progress. As he ran, it was as though he started to unravel. A long shawl or scarf he wore was coming loose and trailing behind him like a streaming pennant in the cold wind. He stumbled and, for a terrible moment, I thought he'd been hit, but he kept on running as the shawl fluttered for a moment on its own and then dropped to the mud. The attack had taken him, and the women and children of the village, by surprise.

There's so much to think about during a TIC but everything happens so fast, so it's not hard to see how mistakes get made. I was watching the fall of shot from the .50 in my vehicle; keeping an eye on the civilians; reassuring Ricky; and, at the same time, occasionally checking the vehicle where my mate Guy was sitting. He, too, was taking fire. In among all this, I still had to keep putting rounds downrange. There were mountains off to our right, where we'd been heading, and we started taking heavy machine-gun fire from there as well.

The SF guys decided to clear the village before pushing up into the mountains. My truck and the rest of our team gave fire support while the other team moved up to sweep through on foot. One of the Americans injured his ankle when they were dismounting. These things happen, even if they don't in the movies, and a solider with a broken bone is no less important, and no less of a liability, to the team than one who has been shot.

We kept giving covering fire while the rest of the injured American's team swept through the village. We could hear their shouts and the sound of gunfire as they moved from compound to compound, clearing them one after another. They called the sweep off once they realised the injured guy's ankle was broken and he would have to be evacuated. We continued to give covering fire while the other team got back into their vehicles. Ricky wriggled at my feet, to stay out of the way of the shower of hot brass raining from the 240.

It was getting late, so we pushed on from the village, out of range of the mortars, into the mountains. The cloud was low, because of the rain, and the peaks were shrouded in a dirty grey-white fog. The track was narrow and winding, and the humvee, a huge vehicle, barely fitted on it. With no roadside protection to the right of us, we would have been goners if the driver had miscalculated and sent us over the steep drop into the valley below. As the convoy crawled along, we were ambushed again. The Taliban had chosen the perfect site for it.

You can go for hours and days with nothing happening while sitting in the back of a gun truck and it can be hard to concentrate, but you have to. When the mortars start falling and the guns start firing, you get a buzz, at first, but the slump following it is almost as intense as a high. You're drained after a TIC, and then sometimes, as on this trip, everything arcs up again.

I started firing back, watching the fall of shot of the .50 and the other guns and Mark 19s up ahead. The 40-millimetre grenades left the barrels of the Mark 19s with a *ker-thunk*, *ker-thunk*, *ker-thunk* noise as the belt was fed through the launcher. Shortly after, I could see the grenades, exploding, as little clouds of dust, rock and mud in the hills. There were huge boulders above us; I looked up at them, trying not to imagine the damage they could cause if the Taliban dynamited them or even just pushed them down on us. It's an ancient country populated by people who've been fighting for centuries and I wouldn't put anything past them.

We carried about 4000 rounds for the 240, but I still had to be conscious of not blowing all my ammo in the first half hour of the TIC. Like most of the TICs I've been in, all I could see of the enemy was the muzzle flashes of their weapons. The Americans stood and fought, but in the end the Taliban pulled back into the mountains somewhere, so we carried on until we found some good high ground with all-round visibility where we could harbour-up for the night.

We took up all-round protection positions to cover the approach of the Chinook evacuation helicopter. One of the team members popped a green smoke grenade, and pretty soon the bright colour was mixed in with the greys and the browns of sand and loose mud kicked into a dust cloud by the chopper's giant twin rotors. Everyone kept a lookout while the helicopter was on the ground for those few seconds, as we all knew the bird would be a big fat target for any mortar or heavy machine-gun crews that might have been hiding in the hills, watching us harbour-up.

Later, I heard that the Chinook was carrying some British soldiers who were being taken out to the mountains for the first time. Apparently, they got quite a shock when their helicopter made an unexpected detour to pick up a wild-eyed American who'd just come straight from a firefight – or would have, if he hadn't busted his ankle.

The months had begun to drag as I approached my next leave and I could feel my fuse getting shorter by the day. To make matters worse, when the SF team at Deh Rawood rotated out, the new team came in with some ideas that really didn't suit the way Ricky and I were used to working.

The new team included some super-fit guys and they had a team sergeant who liked to walk everywhere, so we started doing lots of foot patrols. Personally, I didn't mind walking, but Ricky was a nightmare on foot. He still hated Afghans, and walking gave him too many opportunities to try to chase motorbikes and local people.

I had a shitload of gear to carry on patrol. At Cobra I'd go on missions wearing a T-shirt, a Texas Longhorns baseball cap and camo trousers, but this team worked in full uniform, so I'd be wearing a helmet, long-sleeve shirt and trousers, and I now had armoured plates fitted into the old plate carrier vest I'd bought in Kandahar when I first arrived. By now, I had my Gucci load-bearing vest that I wore over the top of my body armour. It held eight 30-round magazines for my M4. On one leg I had my Glock and three magazines in a holster, and strapped to my other thigh was a first aid kid containing field dressings, QuikClot – a powder that slows bleeding – painkillers and swabs. In my Alice pack, I had enough food for Ricky and me for the five-day patrol, wet weather gear, ten litres of water, night-vision goggles, sleeping bag, bivvy bag, Leatherman, camera and a torch. I also carried spare collars, a lead, tennis balls and explosives for Ricky's training. Attached to my belt was a short length of rope with a loop on the end, which I'd made up years earlier, in Australia, for working with detection dogs in the bush. If I got into a TIC, I'd pull Ricky close to me and attach his collar to the loop so that he wouldn't tangle me in his long lead and get in the way. All up, I reckon I was carrying about 30 kilograms on my back.

Patrolling on foot with a dog is not easy. Typically of a dog, Ricky would always want to be leading the way and constantly be trying to pull me further ahead to the front of the team. I had to rein him in continually. As well as looking after myself, I had to make sure I kept Ricky's fluids up during breaks and that he was handling the walk OK.

We'd leave the FOB on foot at night, which was a totally different experience from the other missions I'd been on. The nights were becoming cool and crisp and, away from the arc lights of the compound, the stars burned bright and white. I had a sense of vulnerability as, instead of sitting behind a 240 in the back of a heavily armed and armoured gun truck, it was just me, my rifle and my dog, out in the middle of a cold, dark moonscape. We knew that somewhere in the night sky was an AC-130 or some fast-movers orbiting endlessly on standby and, sometimes, artillery in range, but that didn't lessen the reality that a well-sited ambush or IED could do us some serious damage before we had the opportunity to respond in kind.

During the day we'd rest up and leave a splinter detachment to look after our packs, while we, relieved of some of the weight we carried, would move off to check farms and villages. As tiring as it was, I didn't mind the exercise. The walks would take us across a mix of terrain, from wide open tracts of barren, rocky ground; into steep hills where you had to watch your feet on loose stones; through villages and into thickly cultivated irrigated areas. Once, we entered a massive poppy plantation, which was an eerie place. The plants, with their bright flowers, were taller than the average man and the fields were criss-crossed by narrow tracks the farmers used. Everyone was on high alert, as it seemed a perfect place for any insurgents in the area to hide, or an ideal site for an ambush.

Drugs were everywhere in Afghanistan, representing just one of the many challenges the coalition had to deal with in bringing some sense of order to the country and defeating the Taliban. Personally, I don't agree with the concept of people living in a country we're fighting to defend being allowed to grow drugs that will be sold on the streets in America and Australia. The Americans have been trying to encourage Afghan farmers to move into growing different cash crops, such as potatoes and vegetables, but that's going to take a long time. Warlords have a strong hold on the cultivation and processing of opium in Afghanistan, so that even if a farmer wanted to change to growing potatoes he'd be too scared to do so. The teams I was with didn't like seeing the poppy fields, knowing the destination of the product, but they were in the business of killing Taliban, not burning farms. It was different if we came across processed opium and had the Afghan police with us.

After passing through the poppy field, we entered a small village. As usual, the locals were stand-offish, watching the team from a distance. There were children present, though, and some women hanging back, so there was little chance we were about to be lit up, which didn't mean there weren't Taliban there. Just as the Americans would throw lollies from their vehicles to keep the kids close by, the Taliban would sometimes mingle with women and children as a cover. The ordinary people in the village would be too scared to reveal the presence of a Taliban spy or spotter.

The team captain asked to see the village elders, and a couple of old men with long white beards and turbans came forward. The terp started talking to them and an impromptu *shura* was called. Some other guys from the team, Ricky and I started checking around the village buildings, just to make sure we weren't walking into a trap. When we were satisfied it was all quiet, we were all offered chai, which had been brewed for the meeting. It was the first time I'd had *shin chai*, which is milky, and it tasted beautiful. The day was stinking hot, and the drink was refreshing and washed the dust from my throat.

Ricky was sitting by me, but instead of soaking up the hospitality, growled at one of our hosts. He really wasn't cut out for foot patrols, and I was constantly worried he was going to bite some kid and undo any good the Psyops guys were doing with their humanitarian assistance.

In a *shura* the Americans would ask if the village needed a well or radios, or food or medicines, and slowly the Green Beret officer and the intel sergeant would get around to the real business at hand, of asking if the Taliban had been in the area lately. Generally, the answer was no, as people were more scared of the insurgents than they were of the coalition. We knew that it was quite likely that as soon as we were gone, the non-existent Taliban would appear and ask the elders what they'd been saying to the infidels. Winning hearts and minds was a hard job when the people you were talking to faced the possibility of being hanged or shot just for talking to us.

The Afghans who worked for us, or those loyal to the government, lived in constant fear for their lives. When I was in Cobra, I heard a story about an ANA outpost that the Taliban had overrun. The Afghan soldiers had been tortured with knives and burned, or had had their eyes cut out before they were beheaded or hanged. People in the outside world know all about Americans accidentally dropping bombs on civilians, but they rarely hear how many Afghans are killed by their own kind.

Ricky and I were crossing the Helmand River during a foot patrol. The water was up around my waist, which is deep for a dog, and fast flowing.

Ricky started to panic, as he was losing his footing on the slippery stones, and began to dog paddle. The current caught him and suddenly he went under. I hauled up on his leash, but he started thrashing around and rolled over. It was a struggle for me to stay upright. I was carrying my M4, which I couldn't let go of, and was loaded down with my combat vest full of ammunition, and food for Ricky and me. Ricky was spinning like a crocodile drowning its prey and for a second I thought he might drown. I staggered through the current and managed with my free hand to get hold of his collar. Some Afghan security troops waded out to help me, and I lifted the dog and dragged him, coughing and spluttering, to the surface. By the time I got to the rocky shore, both of us were exhausted. Ricky was quiet after his ordeal, as was I, as I'd had a scare, thinking he might drown.

'Maybe you should have thought about taking your dog off its lead before crossing that river,' one of the team members said during a debrief back at Deh Rawood.

I didn't like this guy, who was always very opinionated. I felt like telling him, 'Yeah, man, and if I did that, my fucking dog would have ended up floating down the Helmand River to Kandahar'. There was no way Ricky could have swum against that current, but I held my tongue as speaking back would have provoked an argument. I don't normally shy away from fights but I'd learned that it was better to stay quiet and try to fit in, rather than go head to head with someone who fancied himself the alpha dog in an SF team.

A few weeks later, we were searching a village when the same guy pointed to some writing on a wall. 'Hey, look, that's written in American.'

I felt like telling him the language was actually English but again kept my mouth shut. I've made many good American friends in Afghanistan but, I swear, some of them think the US of A is the only fucking country in the world.

*

When we were out on missions, I would continue Ricky's training by letting him find hidden chunks of explosive to keep him interested and to give him the chance to earn a reward. It was important to keep the dog engaged and interested, even on patrols. I'd always take two tennis balls (in case I lost one) and some chunks of different types of explosive whenever we went out on a mission. I took the balls in case Ricky did find some real explosives, or weapons or an IED. As stressful as that situation would be, the dog would still have to be given its reward – the chance to chew on its tennis ball – while us humans worked out what to do about the bomb.

When we were searching a compound, as long as it didn't seem too dangerous, I'd sometimes get one of the SF guys to hide a piece of explosive somewhere in a house, or under some boxes, in order to give my dog something to find. The training is no use if, as usually happened, we'd search and search and search and search and find nothing for real. The dog can start to lose interest if it's searching every day and never finding anything or, most importantly for him, getting his reward of a chance to play with his ball.

One day, Guy and I were both on a patrol with the team and decided to give the dogs something to find. When the team stopped for a break, I moved ahead of Guy and buried some explosives on the side of the road. When Guy came through, his dog, Apis, found them and got his reward. This wasn't supposed to be too taxing, just an exercise to keep the dogs focused and active.

When it was Guy's turn to hide the explosive, he headed off up a side track and was gone for a while. 'It's up there, not far off the road,' he said to me when we got back. It was a test of the dogs, after all, not of the handlers.

With the SF guys watching, Ricky and I set off up the road. I let him off his lead and told him to 'sook', and he did his thing, diligently sniffing along the side of the road, but came up with nothing.

I was getting further and further from the team, and had been searching for about 25 minutes. It was getting embarrassing that Ricky couldn't find anything. Up ahead, I saw in a field off to one side some sticks with green flags of old cloth fluttering from them. I'd been in Afghanistan long enough to recognise a cemetery and didn't want to get too close but, as Ricky still hadn't found the hidden explosives, we carried on up the road.

'Come on, Ricky, sook!'

As we neared the cemetery, Ricky's ears pricked up and he trotted forward. 'Hey, boy,' I said to him, but he was edging closer and closer to the mounds of rocks, and the flagpoles that marked each grave. 'Ricky.'

There was no way, I thought to myself, that Guy would have planted the explosives in a cemetery. To my horror, though, Ricky wandered off the road and in among the graves. 'Come, boy!'

But Ricky wasn't going to be deterred from doing his job. For a moment, I thought he might be paying attention to a fresh grave. I figured that if any of the locals saw a dog rooting around in the local cemetery, and if Ricky started to dig up bones, one of us could end up being shot, and we'd have a major firefight on our hands as a dozen pumped-up Green Berets decided to get in on the action as well.

'Ricky!'

My worst fears were unfolding as Ricky sat down next to a pile of rocks that marked a burial site, giving a passive response to tell me he'd found something. 'Oh, fuck, no.' I ran over to Ricky, grabbed him by the collar, gave him his ball and led him out of the cemetery. I strode back down the road to Guy and asked him what was going on. He told me had hidden the C4 at the gravesite where Ricky had given his response.

'What the fuck were you thinking, Guy?' I hissed at him when I got back from retrieving the explosive, trying to stay out of earshot of the rest of the team. 'That's a fucking cemetery, man. I was keeping Ricky away from the graves deliberately.' I couldn't believe that Guy had planted the aid next to a grave. He laughed but I was pissed off – less because Ricky had been digging around in a cemetery than because I'd wasted 25 minutes of break time on what should have been a routine training task.

Karma's a useful thing, though. Guy got his comeuppance for making me look like a dick in front of the SF guys, when later on he completely screwed up the FOB's computer system by accidentally downloading a virus.

On the same foot patrol when Ricky nearly drowned in the river, the ANA searched a compound and found a man of fighting age who'd been shot. He was hooked up to a saline drip and hidden in the room with him was an AK-47. Our terp found the building's owner and hauled him into an adjoining room. From the sounds of thumps and the occasional yelp, you knew the government soldiers were working this bloke over for information. The ANA took both the men away for more questioning.

Even when they weren't clearing a village or compound as part of a cordon and search operation, it was often the ANA or Afghan Security Group who came into contact with the Taliban first. This was because they were usually at the front of a convoy, or out in front of us if we were on foot patrol. Drawn mostly from Afghans of Kazak, Uzbek or Tajik descent who served with the Northern Alliance in its fight against the Taliban, the Afghan Security Group provided security for US bases throughout Afghanistan.

We arrived at a village during a patrol out of Deh Rawood, to pull security while a *shura* took place, and found a knot of ANA soldiers standing around two bodies lying in the dust. It turned out the dead guys were armed Taliban who had been caught trying to enter the village, perhaps with the intent of disrupting the meeting. Everyone took turns at having a look at the bodies.

The black turban one of the dead men was wearing had started to unravel and I could see the stubble of his shaved head underneath. He had a dark beard; the Taliban were against men shaving their facial hair. Fundamentally, this guy had died because he wanted to impose his beliefs and religion on other people.

I'd seen dead bodies prior to my going to Afghanistan. When I was in the army, I arranged with the local police for some of my soldiers and me to watch an autopsy, so that they could have a look at death. Afterwards, we went to McDonald's for breakfast, but none of us could face a burger. As a policeman, I'd seen the bodies of suicides, a young guy killed in a car accident, people who'd died of natural causes and been found by their neighbours and of a murder victim, who had been strangled. At first, you're curious about how the person looks and the condition of the body. The worst part of death when you're working in law enforcement, though, is not seeing lifeless bodies but, rather, dealing with the living – breaking the news to a parent, or a spouse or a child, that someone close to them has died.

I had seen Scott's body carried out, in a poncho, which had gutted me. I felt nothing for the two dead Taliban lying in the dust.

So much of Afghanistan seemed to me to belong in another millennium; even the people wage war like they're involved in a conflict that's straight out of the Middle Ages.

I was near a Psyops truck during a TIC, looking over a village, and heard one of the terps hollering into a microphone, blaring out a message to the Taliban fighters down in the compounds who'd been firing at us.

'What's he saying?' I asked one of the Psyops soldiers.

'He's saying, roughly translated, "Come out and fight, you pussies", and "Your mothers fuck donkeys".'

I laughed. Then I heard an angry-sounding message in Pashto squawking through the intercom radio speaker. 'What was that all about?'

The terp looked at me and grinned. 'That is the Taliban. They are replying to my message. They say, "If you promise not to use your aeroplanes, we will gladly come out and fight you, like men".'

Things were not going well at Deh Rawood, so I went to see the team sergeant.

'I'm sorry,' I said to him, 'but my dog just isn't suited to doing foot patrols. Ricky hates Guy's dog, Apis, and you've seen him when we go out into the villages – he wants to kill every Afghan and every motorcycle he sees.'

I suggested to the team sergeant that I email my company and see if they could get me posted to another FOB.

'You do what you gotta do, man,' he said to me.

It was a hard decision to leave, but I didn't want to risk something going seriously wrong because Ricky just wasn't cut out for the sort of work the Deh Rawood team was doing. He had, of course, almost drowned on the river crossing and, far from helping me bring down the barriers with the team, was almost proving to be a liability.

By contrast, Apis, a German shepherd, was so relaxed around Afghans while on foot patrols that Guy could work him off-lead. There was no way I could do that with Ricky if there were civilians in the area. He wasn't a bad dog, but there was no point pretending the situation was going to get any better. Guy stayed at Deh Rawood and I left.

TWELVE

The time of my life

April–May 2007

Disappointed with how things had gone at Deh Rawood, I flew back to Kandahar, where for a month it was back to seemingly endless, boring vehicle searches at the gates, until I could organise another posting. By this time, the company I'd first joined, Canine Associates International, had gone out of business, and its contracts and staff–including me–had been taken over by a new company, American K9. For the handlers and dogs, it was business as usual.

There were no spots available at any of the US Special Forces FOBs, but Jason, with whom I'd first deployed to Cobra, was due for vacation so I had the opportunity to re-place him at Graceland, a Canadian SF base. Graceland was located near the city of Kandahar, but was separate from the main military compound. I gathered my gear and Ricky, and reported to the airstrip, where a US Army Black Hawk flew us to Graceland.

There was a Mexican dog handler I knew, named Henry, who was working at Graceland, and when we landed he met us and introduced me to the Canadians. The Canadian Special Forces, or CANSOF, were fighting a different type of war in a different way from their US counterparts. The Canadians' area of operations was the city of Kandahar itself, a totally different environment to the sparsely populated mountains I'd been operating in so far.

There were still senior Taliban living in hiding in the Kandahar Province, and directing the insurgents' operations around the country. The Canadians were in the business of finding Taliban suspects, known as PUCs, or 'persons under consideration', by the authorities. Working on intelligence from various sources, they'd identify and locate their PUC, then launch a short, sharp raid to grab the suspect.

They were operating in densely populated areas, amid ancient buildings, narrow lanes, busy roads and ugly Soviet-era blocks of flats. The commander of the explosive ordnance disposal (EOD), detachment asked me a lot of questions about Ricky's personality, to see if he were going to be suitable for the kind of work they were doing and the built-up environment they were operating in. My heart sank but I had to be honest.

'I don't think he's going to be the right dog for this kind of work,' I said to the Canadian. I had visions of Ricky running amok in the streets of Kandahar, attacking every Afghan and motorcycle that caught his eye. He'd be a liability for a bunch of guys trying to sneak up to a house and snatch someone.

It wasn't a total loss, though, as there were vehicle checkpoints to do at Graceland as well. Henry's dog was good around people and we decided that if an explosive detection dog were needed on a mission, Henry would go and I'd stay at Graceland to look after the vehicle checkpoints. It wasn't ideal, but I didn't have long to wait until Jason came back from vacation and I could maybe get a gig at a US FOB before I headed back to Australia for my next leave.

As it happened, there weren't a lot of missions being launched from Graceland. The Canadians were looking for specific targets at specific times and places and, as a result, they wouldn't launch a mission unless every 'i' were dotted, every 't' crossed, and every possible element of support available. Several missions were cancelled while I was there. The US SF I'd worked with were able to be more proactive and flexible in their approach to operations, which basically involved driving out into the mountains, and looking for information or a fight.

Graceland deserved its name, as it was far better set up than was the Canadian base at Spin Boldak. The accommodation was spacious and modern, and I had unlimited use of the internet and a connection in my room. The CANSOF were eating first-rate tucker and had some of the best training facilities I'd seen, including a mock village and extensive firing ranges. However, I found the soldiers a bit stand-offish and the vehicle checkpoints, incredibly boring, which just confirmed to me what I knew already.

I wanted to get back to FOB Cobra, in Uruzgan, where the fast pace of operations out in the mountains and valleys suited me, and suited my dog. If I had to be in this fucked-up country, I wanted to be out with the Green Berets, stirring up shit and looking for a fight in the wilds of Afghanistan.

I finally got my wish, and got back into the game at Cobra.

There were two new teams from the 7th Special Forces Group at the FOB when I arrived, as well as another American

K9 dog handler, Brad, and a US Army special search dog, a Native American guy called Lee, who ended up becoming a good mate of mine. Funnily, this dusty, remote, barren corner of Afghanistan felt like home.

Lee, who I usually addressed by the Indian name I'd given him, Chief Chin Nuts, had a Labrador named Spaulding. Lee took good care of me when I arrived and made sure I got myself squared away in no time. I had brought with me on the chopper out to the firebase a couple of boxes of Tim Horton's donuts, which also helped break the ice.

Lee, Brad and I started training together, which kept us and our dogs active and interested in between missions. We changed our training locations often, which was just as well because when a mortar round did land inside the FOB, it hit where we'd been conducting our exercises the day before.

Cobra was way out in the badlands of Uruzgan, and the only way to keep the FOB supplied was by air. Afghanistan's dust eats helicopters and rotary wing assets were always stretched, so we would be resupplied regularly by air drops from US Air Force C-130 Hercules transport aircraft. We'd all go out to the drop zone when the bird was inbound. The rear ramp of the Hercules would open and out would tumble up to eighteen one-tonne containers, each with a 64-foot diameter green parachute above it. We'd get food, water and fuel this way, and the hard physical work of breaking down the cargo, loading it onto trucks and all-terrain vehicles and rolling up the huge parachutes helped keep us fit. After a drop, I'd also help stack all the used parachutes and air drop equipment into cargo nets, which would later be slung under a Chinook helicopter and flown back to Kandahar for repacking. Ricky would come along and hang out with us while we were waiting for the drops and the pick-ups.

Working out on the drop zone, I became good mates with a US Air Force combat controller named Mike, who oversaw all the aerial resupply drops and air movements to and from Cobra. He was a lieutenant, but had spent years in the ranks and recently been promoted from sergeant, so he'd been around the traps. Mike was my gym partner and was fit as a mallee bull. He was laid-back and friendly, but also incredibly professional and very well respected by the SF teams at Cobra. He and I would sit in his room and watch TV and talk about our families. He was a smoker on the sly and would occasionally bum one from me when we were having our coffee. When we worked out, he'd leave me totally fucking exhausted and, as a result, I started to bulk up.

It was great being back in the fold at the FOB and I found the two SF teams there very welcoming. Because Cobra was so remote from the rest of the army, there was less procedural bullshit than at places such as Kandahar or Tarin Kowt. Technically, the no-drinking rule still applied, but if someone managed to bring back from leave a bottle of booze, we'd all share it while watching a DVD. Even though I had to get to know a whole new group of people, I found that by getting stuck into the mundane chores around the base, such as rolling parachutes and refurbishing vehicles, and not mouthing off about where I'd been and what I'd done, acceptance came, with time.

With the CANSOF at Graceland, even if I'd been allowed on a mission, I would have been transported in a soft-skinned vehicle and not given a machine gun to man. I was a civilian dog handler, and that was what I was treated as, but back at Cobra I was part of the team again, manning a 240 on the back of a gun truck with my dog at my feet.

I was happier being out in the wilds of the mountains and valleys of Uruzgan, even if it was tough country. Like the jagged mountains and stony deserts, the people here were shaped by the environment they lived in. It's a harsh, unforgiving country with stinking hot, dry summers and freezing cold winters. In the summer, the temperature would be pushing 50 degrees, and I'd fry, driving around in the back of a gun truck with just a baseball cap to protect my head. At the hottest times of the year, I'd get the medics to help me give Ricky a saline drip before a mission, to keep his fluids up.

Wind whipped the dust into spinning devils and storms that blotted out the sun. We'd wear goggles and bandannas, but it would still get into your mouth, your nose, your eyes, your hair, your food and inside your clothes. The grit chewed weapons, machines, vehicles and aircraft; a pervasive, destructive enemy in its own right. After days in the sun in the back of the GMV, the back of my neck was chaffed red raw, and sunburned, and my lips were cracked and bleeding.

In winter I'd wear uniforms, T-shirts, jackets, jumpers and a beanie, and wrap myself in a blanket, but still the wind would slice through the layers while I was in the back of the gun truck. I've never been as hot or as cold as I've been in Afghanistan. When it rained, as it had when we'd ventured into Helmand Province, I got soaked in the back of the open-top vehicle.

Ricky had seen it all and done it all in all kinds of weather, but that didn't mean that I–or the teams I worked with–didn't care about his welfare when we were out on patrol. When I mentioned to the team sergeant that Ricky was a bit too exposed sitting on a mound of gear in the back of a gun truck, he gave me his blessing to redesign the vehicle's layout. With the help of some of the other SF guys, we moved the rear M240s from their original fittings at the two back corners of the truck to midway up the load area on each side, and moved some boxes so that Ricky had a tailor-made spot at the rear of the truck. It was easier to load and unload him from here and, unlike me, he now had some protection from the wind as we drove.

The team at Cobra had an air of quiet professionalism, and a lot of that attitude filtered down from the team captain, Mike. He was a super-fit, super-calm, quiet, friendly natural leader.

The team's operations were characterised by aggressive patrolling in the surrounding countryside. We'd sometimes go out at night to nearby high ground called Table Top Mountain, and just watch, looking for enemy activity and people breaking the evening six o'clock curfew. At other times, the team would drive out in convoy looking to provoke a fight with the Taliban. The Americans didn't seem to be motivated by a need for payback against al-Qaeda, or by a desire to increase their body count or 'smoke' people, as Chuck would have put it. Instead, these were professional soldiers looking to do their job in the most effective manner they could and to pursue their country's enemy aggressively. Other teams I'd served with would roll into an Afghan village with 'The Boys are Back in Town', or AC/DC's 'Highway to Hell' blaring from the bank of speakers on top of the Psyops truck, to show the locals they were there to kick arse and take names, but this team did things quietly, and with a minimum of fuss or show.

While they were professional in their attitude, the team members still had a sense of humour and, in between missions, would unwind by taking the piss out of each other. One of the military intelligence guys assigned to the FOB had picked up a stray kitten somewhere and was keeping it in his room; he even made it a kitty litter tray. One day he returned to his hooch and did a double take when he saw a foot-long turd covered in litter. After he recovered from his initial heart attack, he worked out that the calling card had been left by a two-legged cat. The identity of the phantom stayed a secret for a while, though.

The television room became the venue for pre-mission briefings, and Captain Mike would have the floor. At one of them, a laptop and data projector were flashing up a map on the drop-down screen, showing what had happened the last time the team had visited the village of Pasaw, a short drive east of Cobra, two months earlier.

I hadn't been at Cobra then, but could imagine the scene by looking at the first slide. There were a dozen red starbursts showing where close air support had been called in, and aircraft of some description had dropped bombs. Artillery support had also been called in from Cobra and there were more starbursts that indicated where 105-millimetre shells from the guns had landed. It looked to me like the Taliban had been spotted by the team from observation posts in the hills overlooking Pasaw, and then funnelled up the Helmand River valley by the air strikes and artillery barrage, into a killing zone. There might have been only twelve men in an A-Team, but they had a shit-load of lethal ordnance to call on when they needed it.

'Slide,' said Mike, and one of the sergeants clicked the down arrow on the computer. The team was going back to Pasaw and Mike's next slide showed the make-up of the force that would be undertaking the mission. There would be 39 of us: the A-Team, some ANA with their ETT advisers, Afghan police, a Psyops element, and one Australian – me.

I would be travelling in one of four GMVs, in my usual position, in the back with Ricky behind a 240 on a swing mount.

Our vehicle's driver was Ryan, a big, bearded bear of a guy who was one of the Psyops people, and a staff sergeant named George would be in the turret behind the Mark 19.

Mike's slide showed the armament we'd be carrying in the GMVs, the ETT guys' up-armoured humvee, and the two Afghan pick-ups. In addition to George's Mark 19 and my 240, we would be carrying M249 and M60 light machine guns, and a Carl Gustaf 84-millimetre anti-armour weapon in our truck. One of the other GMVs would be lugging the team's 60-millimetre mortar, so our little convoy was packing quite a bit of its own grunt. I also noted that another civilian contractor, a police mentor and mate of mine named Dyn-Corp Joe, and Bari, the team's Afghan interpreter, would be riding in the mortar truck. Bari was a good guy. Unlike the other interpreters I'd met, Bari lived with the team in their compound, which was an indication of his loyalty and the esteem in which the Green Berets held him. Unlike some terps, Bari wasn't afraid of a fight, and had fired his AK-47 in support of the team in several TICs.

Mike told the sergeant at the computer to move to the next slide, and he read out the team's mission, which was to support the local ANA unit and the Afghan police in taking up observation posts over Pasaw and the valley, 'in order to observe and disrupt enemy activities'. It was the military way of saying we were going out to a place where we knew we'd find the Taliban, in order to pick a fight with them.

While most of us would travel in the vehicles, Mike was going to lead a six-man element of Green Berets on foot, through the mountains, to the target. The foot patrol would set up an observation post looking east along the Helmand River, while the four GMVs would deploy in pairs to set up two support by fire positions, a few hundred metres to Mike's west. The support by fire positions faced south and south east, overlooking bends in the river and the cultivated fields in the valleys beyond. The Afghan police, ANA and ETTs would have an observation post of their own, down in the valley, near the village, where the fighting would be.

'The area is populated and moderately built-up around the village, with mostly single-storey dwellings. The overall assessment of the chance of contact – likely.'

Mike's final word gave rise to a few nods. There was a very good chance it would be game-on during this mission.

Mike and the other Green Berets on foot patrol slipped out of the base in the pre-dawn gloom, and the rest of us saddled up and rolled out of the gate as the sky was painting the mountains a pale purple. As we were driving off road most of the way, our progress was slow. The landscape around us lightened to shades of red, then gold. It was going to be a clear, crisp autumn day – perfect for the work at hand.

The guys on foot would actually reach their objective before we did, and would let us know if the way ahead of the convoy was clear. Our progress was slowed by the need to stop regularly so that the ANA minesweepers could get out and check choke points, and like sites, for IEDs. Ricky and I would also be called out to search if the Afghans turned up anything.

We didn't have far to drive – it took no more than 20 minutes – and we assumed our positions in the hills. Ryan and I were in the centre of the three American observation posts, overlooking some fields and the large village of Pasaw with its mudbrick houses, and the bend in the Helmand River. We dismounted, and I took the 240 out of the back of the truck and moved up the hill a short distance behind and to one side of the GMV so that we had a better view over the target. I set the 240 up on its spring-loaded bipod, and laid out a belt of 200 rounds and my Kevlar helmet beside the gun. Staff Sergeant George kept watch from the turret. The next vehicle in our element was about 200 metres away. I left Ricky in the truck, still tied to the floor, as I didn't want him running around once the gunfire started. 'Stay, boy. I won't be long.'

'Incoming,' someone said over the intercom radio. We'd only just moved into our position, and Ryan and I stopped what we were doing and cocked our heads. Now I could hear it, the *crump, crump* of mortar rounds leaving the tubes. Ricky whimpered, as though he knew what was about to happen.

'Here it comes,' Ryan said.

The first bombs detonated off to the left, between us and the river, and we watched as rock and dirt volcanoes erupted into the cool morning air. The Taliban hadn't wasted a minute in welcoming us to Pasaw. George and the rest of the team guys started opening up with their heavy machine guns and automatic grenade launchers. I could see the smaller puffs of exploding 40-millimetre grenades walking a path into the village below.

Bullets started landing just behind us, zinging and pinging off rocks and boulders. An RPG whistled up out of the village in our general direction, but sailed wide of our vehicle and blew up behind us. 'Fuck, man, did you hear that?' I said to Ryan.

'Holy shit,' Ryan replied.

'Troops in contact, I say again, troops in contact.' Cool as a cucumber, Captain Mike was letting the men back at Cobra know over the intercom radio that not only were we all in position, the fight was on already.

'Should we move back a bit into cover?' I asked Ryan. All of sudden, our spot up in the rocky hills seemed very exposed. We had a quick debate, but then ducked down as more bullets cracked into the rocks behind us. It didn't seem wise to move back into the path of the incoming fire, so we stayed put, even though we were in an open area.

'Shit, it's coming from behind us.' Looking around us, I had worked out the Taliban fire was coming from a far-off ridgeline to our rear. George was chugging fat 40-millimetre grenades down into the village, where the RPG had come from. We were taking fire from several different directions. Holy fuck, I thought, I'm going to get hit today.

From the intercom radio chatter, we could tell that everyone was in the same situation, as guys were reporting near misses up and down the line. Another mortar went off near the next truck. I heard the deep, rhythmic *ka-chunk, ka-chunk, ka-chunk* of a Dooshka firing from the village, and saw tracer arcing through the sky. I picked up my helmet, fastened the chin strap and grabbed the 240 by its carrying handle. I moved down the hill a bit to be closer to the gun truck, so that when I needed more ammo, I wouldn't have as far to run over the exposed ground.

Rocks dug into my belly and thighs as I lay down behind the 240, yanked back on the cocking handle and pulled the butt into my shoulder. I looked down over the iron sights into the fields and the village. When I saw the bright light of a muzzle, I squeezed the trigger. Rounds cracked and thumped through the air above and behind me, but I ignored them and concentrated on my elusive target. It was good to be putting some rounds down range, back at the Taliban.

Big Ryan lumbered down to the truck and unstrapped the Carl Gustaf from its mount. Ryan got on the radio, gave his call sign and said, 'We're taking fire up here. Permission to fire the Gustaf into the village, over?' George was hammering away with the Mark 19 at the village and empty brass casings were falling around his feet in the turret.

'Permission granted, over.' Ryan grabbed the launcher and a couple of rounds, and huffed and puffed his way back up to where I was. 'OK, load me up, man.'

Ryan hefted the squat anti-armour weapon up onto his shoulder, set it to fire and cocked it, so that I could open the breech. I took a high explosive round from its plastic tube, pushed it in the open rear of the launcher, then swung the tail section closed and locked it. I tapped Ryan on the shoulder. 'BBDA is clear!' I yelled, letting Ryan know that I'd just checked the Back Blast Danger Area to make sure no-one was behind us, where they could be burned by the coming blast or injured by flying rocks.

Ryan sighted the Carl Gustaf on a spot in the tree line where we'd seen the winking muzzle flashes of a weapon, possibly a PKM 7.62-millimetre Russian light machine gun. I grabbed the big man around the waist and tucked myself in close to help brace him for the firing. Ryan pulled the trigger and a cloud of smoke shot from the rear of the launcher. The BBDA was swept with a shitstorm of gravel, dirt, rocks and dust as the round left the tube. I felt the kick of the shock wave from the launch thump and shake my whole body, but I knew from the three or four times I'd fired the Carl Gustaf on the range at Tarin Kowt that it was much worse for the operator. My ears were ringing. In practice shoots, we'd wear hearing protection, but didn't worry about that in a TIC.

I tried to follow the fast-moving projectile in flight, but it wasn't until I saw the bright flash of orange light and the roiling ball of black smoke that I knew where the 84-millimetre round had landed. 'You're a little short!' I yelled in Ryan's ear, barely able to hear my own words. 'Unload.'

Ryan cleared the launcher and went back to the radio to ask permission to fire some more rounds. I lay down behind my 240 and, watching George's fall of shot, opened fire in the same direction. Empty brass casings and the black metal links that held them together in the ammunition belt piled up beside me as I squeezed the trigger. By watching the puffs of dirt and shredded vegetation my bullets kicked up I was able to 'walk' the rounds towards the target by raising the tip of the gun's barrel.

'OK, we're good to go,' Ryan called to me. I got up and freed another round from its tube as he cocked the weapon. I opened the back of the weapon, and slid the round in and locked the launcher shut again. 'BBDA clear!'

Ryan fired, and the boom and shock wave assaulted me once more. 'Yeah!' he yelled as we watched the projectile explode.

I ran down to the GMV to get some more rounds for the 84 and stopped to check on Ricky, who was cowering in the back of the truck where I'd left him. I gave him a quick pat to still his whining and he yelped to let me know he wasn't enjoying all the gunfire. 'Good boy, Ricky. Don't worry, it'll be over soon.' I was concerned for him, but right now I was a dog handler second and a member of the team first. At times like this, all I could do was rely on the training I'd had with the American SF, and the basic training I'd had with the Australian Army all those years ago.

'Come on, load me up again, Shane.' Ryan was grinning and so was I. Despite the danger of the rounds that continued to zing around us, and the occasional mortar round that still searched us out on the hillside, I was having the fucking time of my life.

You know you could get hit any second but you don't stop to worry about it. We could see a target – well, muzzle flashes at least – and we knew those guys down there were trying to shoot us. No doubt they would have seen the back blast from the Gustaf. But we were firing back with everything we could get our hands on and, most likely, we were riding high on adrenaline. With the noise, the dust and the rush of the incoming and outgoing fire, it was mayhem up on that exposed slope, but I really was enjoying myself.

We got another round away and I lay down behind the 240 again, keen to contribute to the firepower the Americans were sending into the village and the trees below. 'Yeah!' I yelled, echoing Ryan.

'You wanna shoot the 84?' Ryan called over the din of my machine gun. I looked up at him.

'Fuck, yeah!'

I got to my feet and Ryan passed me the launcher, which was hot from the rounds he'd fired through it. I grabbed the cocking handle and pulled it back. Ryan swung open the rear and I lifted the weapon on to my shoulder. He loaded me, tapped me, declared the BBDA clear and wrapped a meaty arm around me to steady me.

Watching through the sights, I waited until I could see the winking light of the PKM gunner again. I pulled the trigger.

'Fuck!' I could hardly hear myself swear as Ryan and I watched the missile's flight. The noise was even worse than when I'd been bracing Ryan and my whole body felt as though it had been slapped by a giant's palm. The round exploded in a black and orange ball of flame and smoke, and a second later I heard the boom as the noise reached us from 600 metres away.

I got back down behind the 240 and opened fire again. When the last of the bullets in the belt was gone, I got up and sprinted down to the gun truck. AK-47 and PKM rounds were ricocheting off rocks and kicking up spurts of dirt on either side of the GMV, but I didn't stop to take cover or cower in the truck like poor old Ricky. Ryan and I were laughing and joking with each other as I stumbled and slipped back up the rocky slope to the 240 and dropped the boxes of 7.62 beside the gun.

It was as though the gunners down in the village and the trees were zeroing in on us, because their bullets were getting closer and closer all the time. Ryan was popping off shots from his M4 while waiting for permission to fire the 84 again. When he got the word, I ran back down to the truck and got some more plastic containers out and reloaded him.

I only fired the one round from the Carl Gustaf, but Ryan must have shot eight, which was insane, as we'd been told in training that if you fired more than three rounds in close succession, the shock wave could start screwing with your internal organs. Big Ryan was like a one-man artillery barrage. I don't know if we killed anyone, but fire had dropped off from the village and trees as a result of the constant rain of heavy weapons fire from the gun trucks.

I'm going to get shot, I thought; but it was a matter-of-fact realisation and I knew that my only option was to keep firing my 240, keep running for more ammo and keep Ryan loaded. There was a roar like a speeding train flying overhead, followed a couple of seconds later by a huge explosion out in the middle of the cultivated fields. Someone had called in the 105-millimetre howitzers from Cobra.

The sound was unbelievable. All the gun trucks were firing at once, and the 105s were screaming and crashing into mudbrick buildings, blowing them apart. From far off, the 40-millimetre grenade bursts were like cotton balls blossoming on the landscape, dwarfed both in size and volume by the artillery shells. Tracer arced out like a mini meteorite storm and through it all, Ryan and I were grinning and cursing and yelling to each other, and laughing like mad men.

Captain Mike and his foot patrol had pinpointed the other Taliban who'd been firing from the ridgeline behind us, and the JTAC called in Dude One-One, an F-15 Eagle that had been circling above us, waiting to join in the action. We listened over the intercom radio and watched the hills in between shooting our weapons. The Dude dropped three bombs and made a low-level strafing run, lighting up the enemy position with his onboard cannon. Later, Mike called in a Dutch Harrier to rake the hillside with rockets.

The enemy fire was dropping off but, without a doubt, this was the closest I'd come in two years to being shot. I was loving it.

We were getting low on ammo, so Captain Mike called it a day after a good morning's work. We were back at Cobra in time for lunch.

I was still pumped up during the short drive back to the firebase. When we got back, there were the mundane, but essential, post-mission chores to do. I helped clean the spent brass casings out of the back of the gun truck, and blasted the 240 with the air hose and sprayed it with oil. I took the empty ammo cans out and replaced them with full ones, and Ryan and I filled up the GMV's fuel tank.

Ricky was happy to be out of the truck and moving around again, I'd throw a tennis ball for him to fetch while we were working on refurbishing the trucks. Ricky would run back to me and I – or one of the SF guys – would throw his ball as far as possible in the compound. He never got sick of playing and the guys liked the simple game too, maybe because it was a means of unwinding after the mission.

Ryan was telling some of the other guys about the number of 84 rounds he'd fired and they were relating their part in the TIC, too; mostly we were talking about how many rounds we'd fired off. There was no whooping or hollering, or high-fiving. The talk was calm and matter-of-fact. It was the SF way to downplay things and act like professionals, rather than like a bunch of gun-toting rednecks.

Mike had deliberately positioned us so that we would be at the maximum range for enemy small arms fire but, as Ryan and I had seen, we were still close enough to have been killed or wounded. 'Check this out,' said George.

Ryan and I moved to the back of the truck, where George was bent over, inspecting something in one of the side panels. 'I felt it. I knew we took some fire,' George said as he pointed out two bullet holes in the GMV's panels.

It was no wonder that Ricky had been whining and barking, and I thanked God he hadn't taken a bullet. Ryan and I had been moving across exposed ground, and ducking in and out of the GMV retrieving ammo, throughout the TIC. I started to come down from my high.

According to the after-action report, the team had fired 8000 .50 cal rounds, 1000 40-millimetre grenades, 9000 rounds of light machine-gun ammo, and the Carl Gustaf rounds that Ryan and I had sent down-range. In addition, the US Air Force F-15 had dropped three bombs and made a strafing run with its 20-millimetre cannon, and a Dutch Harrier jump jet had delivered a salvo of rockets. For all of that, the team captain reckoned in his report that we had accounted for fifteen Taliban killed in action and ten wounded. The most important thing for us, though, was that no Americans or Afghans (or Australians) had been killed or injured.

Back in my hooch, I lit a cigarette and stretched out on my bed. Ricky jumped up and I ruffled him under the neck. I thought about the mission and how close the bullets had come to us. While there had been times during the TIC when I'd thought I might end up getting hit, now that I thought about it, I realised I'd never actually seriously considered the possibility of being shot. The threat of being fired on had never altered the way I thought about the job in Afghanistan or how I acquitted myself.

The truth is that I did not have to go on that mission. Captain Mike had originally judged that he didn't need a dog handler to go out to Pasaw, because of the nature of the terrain and the threat level. I'd heard it was coming up and asked if Ricky and I could go anyway. Mike had agreed.

It wasn't the first time I'd volunteered to go on a mission. Sometimes I'd ride along with the Psyops and intel guys when they visited villages to deliver humanitarian aid and talk to the locals to try to gain information about what the Hajis were up to. I'm not a war hero, or gung-ho, but I volunteered because it seemed like the right thing to do. Going on missions helped break the monotony of life on the FOB, and if my mates were going out to do a job, I wanted to go along with them, even if a dog and handler weren't specifically required. I never took the place of a team guy, but if there was space on a truck, the SF guys at Cobra were always happy to have me along. The CANSOF would never have allowed this, so the very fact that that Mike and his men welcomed me made me want to get out there and do more missions, even when I wasn't needed.

It was weird when I thought about it. When I was seventeen, and being punished for sleeping in on guard duty, I'd busted my arse running around with a pack because I thought I wanted to join the SAS. In the end, I'd become sick of life in the Australian Army and there was no way I'd ever want to re-enlist. Yet, here I was, volunteering to go on missions with the Green Berets to break the boredom and to be part of a team. Doing those missions wasn't a dream come true, or the culmination of a lifetime's effort to be in an SF unit, or anything like that, but it did seem like the right thing to do, and I was happy to be doing it.

A US Army padre came out to Cobra on a Chinook, and set up his little portable field altar in the chow hall to conduct a church parade. I'd only been to a service once before during my time in the field, when I found out an old girlfriend had fallen ill. After the service, I sought out the padre, and he and I stood by the back of a GMV and bowed our heads while he said a prayer for her. This time I went to the service because I felt I was overdue for a talk with God.

I'd been lucky and, by and large, the men around me had been lucky and it seemed right to say thanks for that. I believe in God, but I'm not overly religious. Before leaving on a mission from Cobra, the team would stand in a circle and one of the guys would say a short prayer. Unlike a lot of Australians, the US soldiers never seemed embarrassed about publicly displaying their religious beliefs.

When I bent my head in prayer during the service, I thought about Scott, the ETT, and hoped his family were doing OK, and said a prayer for my kids, their mums, and for the rest of my family. And I said thanks for keeping me and my dog alive.

THIRTEEN

Welcome home

July 2007

When Australian soldiers finish a tour of duty in Afghanistan or Iraq, they come home to a hero's welcome. When I landed at Perth airport, I was treated like a criminal.

I'd been busting to get back to Australia and see my new girlfriend, Nat. I'd paid for an Ariana, the Afghan national airline, flight from Kabul to Dubai out of my own pocket, to save wasting time getting to Manus in Kyrgyzstan. As contractors were eligible for US military flights out of Afghanistan to Manus, we were supposed to fly there first before getting a civilian flight home. Problem was, you could wait for days for a flight from Kandahar to Manus. I didn't care about the money, and while Ariana might not have been everyone's first choice to fly with, doing so was no more dangerous than dodging mortars and machine-gun fire on the back of a gun truck. Besides, I didn't want to waste a minute of this vacation.

Nikki and I had broken up, and I'd first had contact with Nat via a mutual friend, when I was on my second tour at Cobra. I was keeping in touch with a few ex-army mates via a social networking site, and Nat contacted me out of the blue one day to say hi, as she'd been interested to learn I was working with dogs in Afghanistan.

Social networking. The internet didn't even exist when I first got married, and now I'd met via a computer the woman I would end up living with. Not for the first time, I wondered how things would have been during World War II, or the Vietnam War, if soldiers had been able to talk to their loved ones back home every day via Skype or see their faces on the jumpy, grainy screens of webcams. They say that one of the good things about striking up a relationship over the net is that you become friends before you become lovers; Nat and I had a lot in common and we'd met in person for the first time during my last vacation. I couldn't wait to see her again.

Nat worked in an administrative job with the West Australian health department, in Perth, so when I knew what date my next vacation would begin, I arranged to fly straight there instead of to Sydney, planning to spend five days with her. She is a beautiful woman with a lovely personality and kind heart. As I stood in the Emirates aircraft and waited for the passengers ahead of me to file off into the terminal, I was impatient to see her in the flesh, and kiss and hold her.

I was in civilian clothes, not a soldier's uniform, but it was clear to the customs officer who inspected my arrival form that I'd been somewhere there was a war going on. I wasn't expecting a handshake or a pat on the back, but neither was I expecting what happened next.

After clearing immigration and collecting my bags, I pushed my trolley into the queue to clear customs and quarantine. I'd filled out my arrival card and had nothing to declare. When I handed it to the customs officer, he asked me to wait to one side. I checked my watch. We'd landed at five in the afternoon and I knew that Nat was waiting for me, just beyond the sliding doors. 'OK,' I said.

As an ex-policeman, I knew something was up when my card was checked, and rechecked by two other officers. I also assumed I was being watched on closed-circuit TV, so that my reactions could be assessed. I tried to stay calm and patient. I had nothing to hide, and, more to the point, had no clue why I might be under suspicion.

Another officer came over to me. 'I'd like you to come with me to a private search area.'

Shit, I thought. I had expected this but that didn't make it any easier to deal with. 'All right.'

My bags were laid out on a long stainless-steel table, and a couple of officers wearing disposable rubber gloves started opening and unzipping them, and unpacking all my stuff.

'Afghanistan's a hostile country. What were you doing there?' the officer asked.

I took a deep breath to calm my rising anger. 'I've been working as a civilian contractor, as a dog handler, for two years.' I pulled out my wallet. 'Here's my US Department of Defense contractor ID.' I held the card up to the officer, but he made a point of ignoring it, and continued going through my gear.

'Are you in possession of any illegal drugs, weapons or pornographic material?' he asked me.

'No.'

'Do you have any needles or drug paraphernalia in your baggage?'

'No.'

While the arrogant guy continued his search, another officer, who had an American accent, started speaking to me. He told me that he'd served with the US military in Iraq, and his tone was friendlier and more conversational. What was this, I wondered, the good-cop-bad-cop routine? It would have been funny if I hadn't had my girl waiting outside, and if I hadn't been getting so pissed off. I was exhausted from the long flight and in no mood for any more of this.

In my bags I had bits and pieces of military equipment, such as clothes and pouches, and papers with military crests on them and even souvenir SF coins, which the Yanks are mad keen on collecting. Even if the officers hadn't been paying attention to what I was saying, it was quite obvious from the stuff in my bags who I was and what I'd been doing in Afghanistan.

One of the officers held up a piece of paper and started reading it. 'What's this then?' he said triumphantly.

It was a one-page gym routine, from my time working out in the FOB.

'Have you ever taken steroids?'

I wondered how a one-page gym routine could warrant such a question. Having worked in law enforcement, I understood that these guys had a job to do, but their presumption that I had to be guilty of something sucked. Not satisfied with my answers about drugs, they opened my daypack and took out my laptop.

'Is there any pornography, child pornography or that sort of stuff on here?' one of the officers asked, opening the laptop.

'No!' What the fuck, I wanted to yell at him. 'I've got five kids and I'm a former policeman and soldier in the Australian Army. That's insulting.'

The officer ignored me and went through my computer accessories. He held up my portable hard drive. 'What about on here?'

I took a breath. 'There are photos of my girlfriend on there. They're personal, and a bit sexy, but not pornographic.'

The prick's eyes widened. He told me they were going to view the pictures on the laptop and the hard drive. By this time, four officers had gravitated into the private search room, although not all of them were going through my bags. I told the officer that I wanted to be in the other room with them while they were going through my pictures.

'That's not allowed. It's against Customs policy,' he said.

Fuck. I didn't want four jerk-offs staring at and joking about pictures of Nat or, even worse, maybe saving the pictures to other computers or memory sticks.

To make things worse, the officer then tactlessly told me that they had viewed 'lots of private pictures' of male passengers' partners. If this idiot thought that was going to reassure me, he was out of his mind.

Angry and frustrated, there was nothing I could do but stand there and wait for them to finish their smirking trawl through my computer and hard drive. They found nothing incriminating because there was nothing to find. By the time I was finally allowed to go, it was seven o'clock, nearly two hours after I'd landed. Poor Nat was waiting for me, wondering what had happened.

'Hi, babe,' she said as I wrapped my arms around her. It was so good to be home, even if the welcoming committee had been a pack of power-drunk uniformed arseholes.

I wasn't fighting with the Australian Army, but I'd been serving with US forces in Afghanistan, trying to help stabilise a shaky fledgling democracy. My reward, when I got home, was to be accused of being a drug smuggler and pornographer, and treated like a criminal. I was so incensed that I lodged a formal written complaint with Customs about the—in my opinion, totally unprofessional—way the officers had acted. I was told, eventually, that the matter had been investigated and that they had been following procedure. It still pisses me off today.

Nat made the decision to relocate her life and her dog, Tyra, a lazy but cute little Staffy, from Perth to the steel town of Port Kembla on the New South Wales south coast.

With the money I'd earned as a contractor in Afghanistan, I'd been able to get on top of my debts and buy a place of my own, a run-down 1930s house near Port Kembla beach. The place needed a lot of work, but Nat was keen to renovate, saying that the work would help keep her occupied while I was away overseas.

For the first couple of years I'd been in Afghanistan, I'd been working four months on, with 21 days' vacation. As my leave included travel, a day or more was knocked off each end and, after 24 hours of flying and sitting around in airports, I'd arrive home jet-lagged and dead tired.

There was no wind-down time anymore, as there had been on my first leave, when I'd stopped off in Thailand; no time to chill out and just get used to not being in Afghanistan, and to being in a first-world country again. It took me about two weeks to settle down: to get used to not living in a war zone, and to being around my kids and Nat again. By then, it would be time to start psyching myself up to go back to Afghanistan. Vacations were quickly turning from being a source of relief to a source of depression for me, as the high of coming home was replaced all too soon by the sinking feeling in my gut that I'd have to go back. Prior to leaving Afghanistan, I'd be counting down the days until I got home, thanks to a digital clock on the screen saver of my laptop that showed the number of weeks, days, hours, minutes and seconds to go, but once I was home, the clock started ticking the other way.

These days, soldiers in the Australian Army who have served in Afghanistan or Iraq undergo a psychological debrief before they come home, and have access to counselling, if they need it, back in Australia. There's nothing like that for contractors.

It seemed that every time I came home, everyone wanted a piece of me. 'When are you coming home for good?' was the most common question they asked me, and they do to this day. My ex-wives wanted to know, so that they could get back into some sort of routine for my access to the kids, and my mum and dad were always worried about my safety. I heard that in the army psych debriefs, they suggested that when a soldier comes home on leave, or for good, his partner should organise a barbeque or party where all the friends and family get to ask their questions, and that after the big event the person who has come home should just be allowed to chill, and catch up slowly and quietly with those closest to them. It sounded like good advice, which I was never given.

'Why are you going back? When are you going back? When are you coming home for good?' I felt as though I answered the same old questions a hundred or more times whenever I was home on leave.

After I'd met Nat and she had decided to move to Port Kembla, I told American K9 I needed more than a 21-day vacation, minus travel time. My initial contract had expired, and I told them that I was going home for three months and would let them know when I was ready to come back.

As well as wanting to spend time with my kids, I needed to build a foundation for my relationship with Nat. She's an independent person, as am I, and is happy to get on with her life and do what she wants while I'm away but, as we hadn't been together all that long, I knew that we needed more time together. American K9 told me I could have my three months off, but added that there were no guarantees I'd be re-teamed with Ricky. I knew that, unlike in the army or the police force, I couldn't be guaranteed to get the same dog for the whole time I was in-country if I were gone for too long. I had expected and understood the reasons for this, but I felt sad about it.

Ricky was an experienced working dog and it made no sense, either economically or for his sake, for him basically to be locked up in a kennel for three months. Sure, he'd be fed and walked, but there would be no training or work for him without a handler. It would have been too confusing for Ricky to be teamed with someone just for three months.

I needed the time with Nat and the kids, but something still hurt inside when I thought about Ricky. You learn to be professional as a dog handler, and that your dog is not your pet, but there is no denying that you build a relationship. You live, eat and sleep together 24-7, and you do become friends. That relationship is one of the keys to your success as a team. To make things tougher, I knew that even if I didn't get Ricky back as my dog I would probably see him from time to time but we would never work together again.

FOURTEEN

Benny the Bouncer

November 2007

It was different when I got back to Afghanistan this time. Instead of the excitement I'd felt in the early days, and the thrill and satisfaction I'd had from doing the job for real, now I couldn't wait for the next four months to be over.

I used to chat to Nat on MSN and, while I tried to put on a brave face for her, she could tell I was down. 'I'm not getting Ricky back, babe,' I said to her in an instant message.

When I got back to Kandahar, I found out that Ricky had been teamed with another handler, a guy from the Dominican Republic. Ricky was working out of Kandahar and when I went to the kennels, I saw him. He recognised me immediately. It was a tough moment.

I met his new handler, and watched him and Ricky working as a team. I could tell straightaway that the handler was still unfamiliar with him. He was using too much lead control, jerking too hard and too often on Ricky's collar to try to make him obey. Having been able to work Ricky off-lead some-times, I could see that this forced control was aggravating him. I spoke to the guy, to try to give him some guidance on how best to work with Ricky, but I knew I could only go so far. They had to get to know each other and learn how to work as a team. My interfering might only make it harder for both of them. Ricky was the new handler's dog and I had to let him bond with him.

However, that didn't change the fact that all I wanted to do was take Ricky off that bloody lead, and give him a big hug and tell him I was back.

It's sort of a catch-22 situation working with dogs. If you're not a dog lover you're not going to make a good handler, but you've got to treat being a handler like any other job. You need to bond with your dog and establish a relationship with him, yet, as I've said, at the same time you know, as a professional, that the dog isn't your pet and you have to be capable of re-teaming with a new dog at a moment's notice if required. But Ricky had slept on my bed and in my sleeping bag with me in the deathly cold mountain nights, and he'd been at my feet in the gun truck when we were being shot at. He was almost like another child to me, or at least a really good mate.

On MSN I told Nat that I'd been walking another dog, Jan, and that, while he'd showed some promise, it was unlikely I'd be teamed with him. Jan had already been working with an-other handler, who was on leave, and the kennel supervisor couldn't give me Jan to train or work with, as the other han-dler would have the right to stay with him when he got back to Afghanistan, if that's what he wanted.

That left Benny. Benny the Bouncer, they called him, be-cause of his hard-arsed, no-nonsense attitude.

'What do you think about being teamed with Benny?' Nat asked me.

'I've always liked him, but he can be a little aggressive,' I replied.

'You could get him under control, but once they are aggressive, isn't that in their nature?'

I told Nat that I'd known Benny for a while and that I partly put his aggressive behaviour down to the way he'd been handled. In the past eighteen months, he'd had three handlers, including Chuck, the dude who was so fond of smoking people, and who I'd seen not give a fuck about his dog's welfare on board the Chinook from Tarin Kowt to Kandahar.

'Well, babe, give him a go, you can sort him out,' Nat said.

I hoped she was right. Benny the Bouncer was actually a lot more aggressive than I'd let on to her. Once when I'd passed through Kandahar airfield not long after I'd arrived in Afghanistan, I'd seen Benny in the kennels with five metal food bowls in his enclosure. When I asked the trainer what was going on, he said the kennel attendants were all shit scared of Benny, and none of them was game enough to go in and retrieve his empty bowl. They would slide a fresh bowl in each day and then run. When I spoke to Benny that first time, he had a bowl in his mouth and was growling, as though he were demanding food.

I found a lead, opened his enclosure, walked in and snapped the lead on his collar. He didn't growl or bite, or otherwise try to pick on me. I'm not, despite what Nat sometimes says, a 'dog whisperer'. When I go into an enclosure with an aggressive dog, like Benny was, I just don't make a fuss of the dog, or try to be overly domineering. I just get the lead on him quickly and get him out into the open. A lot of dogs are kennel-aggressive; that is, they become very territorial and protective of the space they're in. However, they don't necessarily want to be in there and once they're out walking on a lead, their attitude changes immediately. Nero was like that. I think Benny picked up on the fact that I was there to help him and that I wasn't going to be intimidated by him. I took him for a few walks, just so the poor thing didn't spend all his days locked up.

Maybe Benny remembered me because, when I eventually picked him for a re-team after I'd lost Ricky, we got along like best mates who haven't seen each other for ages but can still pick up with each other straightaway. You make a lot of those kinds of friendships in the army.

The next time I spoke to Nat on MSN, I had Benny with me.

'What's he look like?' she asked.

'He's a shepherd – very alert with pointy ears. He looks like a small black and tan wolf.'

Our kennels at Kandahar backed on to the Australian compound, where the headquarters and rear echelon people for the task force were based. I'd see the Aussies most days and got friendly with a few over meals in the mess hall. I invited a few Australian soldiers over one night, to hang out and visit the kennels.

I'd made great progress with Benny and received some good news. In a couple of days, I would be heading back out to FOB Cobra. The last team I'd served with, including Captain Mike, Mickey and grumpy old George, had all rotated home and a new team had taken over, but Lee the dog handler was still there. I was really looking forward to seeing my mate again and to introducing him to my new dog.

When they came to visit me, the Australian soldiers were just like Americans; a dog was a link to home, and to a life they'd left behind. Maybe for some of the Aussies, seeing the dog also brought back memories of their childhood, and of a time before the planes flew into the World Trade Center, when it seemed it was other people's countries that went to war.

After visiting the kennels, the Aussies came back to my room, along with a couple of other civilian handlers, so it was getting crowded. I got up to go for a piss and, just as I closed the door of the bathroom, I heard one of my handler mates yell, 'Benny, no!'

I burst back into the room and saw a female Australian soldier on her knees with her hand over her face and blood streaming out between her fingers. Benny had bitten a nice big chunk out of her lip.

'Fuck!'

We tried to clean her up as best as we could, but it was obvious to all of us that the party was over and the girl needed medical attention. One of the Aussie soldiers raced back to their lines and woke up their doctor.

'Shit, I'm sorry,' I said to her.

'No,' she insisted through her swollen, bleeding lip, 'It was my fault, I'm to blame. I put my face down near his and I knew I shouldn't have.'

We were all on edge for a couple of days, as at first the word was that she'd have to be flown home to Australia for a skin graft. If that had happened, everyone there that night would have been in the shit, but luckily the task force's medical officer was able to get her patched up in-country.

Benny and I, however, were temporarily grounded. The doctor wanted Benny to be tested for rabies and other diseases, and that meant we had to stay in Kandahar for another ten days before leaving for Cobra. Nat was pleased when I told her the news, as she thought I'd be safer at Kandahar than I would be at a FOB, but I was pissed off. I told her that I was sick of Kandahar already and hated the place. If I were going to be in Afghanistan, I wanted to be out at a FOB where I'd at least be doing my job and where the time would go quicker.

'Did you get a warning from Benny that he was going to bite that girl?' Nat asked on MSN.

'No, he was really good with everyone and he's been coming along in leaps and bounds.'

'Well, being with you, he's with a good person for a change. He'll be fine,' Nat said. And she was right. We were soon back in business and on our way to Cobra.

'I don't like the sound of this one, man,' Lee, the US Army special search dog handler said to me while we were waiting to saddle up for a mission at Cobra. 'It just doesn't feel right.'

I nodded. The convoy's route would pass along a stretch of road and through a long wadi at Yakhdan we called IED alley. The Afghan minesweepers would be searching the track at choke points along the way, and Chief Chin Nuts and I were pretty sure we'd be called out with our dogs to search.

Benny had tested negative for rabies and any other nasties, and I'd finally made it back out to where I belonged, at Cobra. While it was good to be getting back out on missions, Lee's sudden attack of wariness was infectious.

Lee was my best buddy at Cobra. Nothing was ever a hassle for him and he'd do anything to help a friend. He was a happy-go-lucky guy in his late thirties and, like me, had heaps of kids and had been married more than once. We'd talk for hours about our kids and our homes, and our dogs.

'What do you reckon about the US Army using civilian dog handlers?' I asked Lee. As he was an army dog handler, I wondered if he saw us civvies as a threat to his trade.

'I've got no complaints,' he said. 'Hell, yes, there are some that don't belong out here where we are, like at Cobra, but overall I think it comes down to how people are trained, and how the handler thinks. You and me both know the job's important and we save lives. We train every day–even when we're out on patrols–so, I guess, if a man takes the job seriously, knows his stuff and keeps on training, I've got no problem whether he's army or civilian.'

After I returned from vacation and had been re-teamed with Benny, Lee told me he was pleased to see me back at the FOB. Guy went to Cobra to replace me when I went on my extended vacation, and I'd told Lee the other Aussie was a good bloke. Lee had said he would look after Guy.

Not long after arriving at Cobra, Guy went out on a mission and was sitting in my regular spot behind the 240 on the back of a GMV. The convoy was ambushed and while Guy was getting some rounds down range, a Taliban bullet came in from the rear of the vehicle, went straight between Guy's legs and hit poor Apis in the foot.

To their credit, the SF team called in a medevac for Apis, and Guy was flown out with his injured dog–there was no point in the team carrying a handler without a dog on the mission. Apis was treated by the US Army vet at Kandahar and later made a full recovery. Even though he could have gone back to work, he was retired as he'd been wounded. He ended up being shipped home to the US, where he found a home with the family of one of the American K9 project managers.

Guy never returned to Cobra after that incident.

Spaulding, Lee's dog, took after his master, and was a warm and sociable individual. Spaulding got on fine with Ricky and Benny. While we were training, we could let both dogs off their leads, which was something I could never do with Guy and Apis, as Apis and Ricky would have torn strips off each other if they'd been running free. Spaulding was friendly, though. Too friendly, in fact, as, although they were both males, Spaulding loved sniffing Benny's arse and, when we weren't looking, would often try to mount him.

Benny was funny around people. He hated some individuals at first sight and could be unpredictable, like when he'd bitten the Australian Army woman. With others, he was more relaxed, though still a little guarded. He loved Lee, though. When Lee came in the room, Benny would be all over him, rubbing up against him and looking for a pat. It was just the way things were with Lee – he was friends with everyone.

Lee had introduced me to his wife, April, via MSN, and once she contacted me while he was out on a mission.

'I'm worried about, him, Shane. Something doesn't feel right,' April tapped into her computer, half a world away.

'Nah,' I replied; 'Lee's a good man. He knows his stuff. He'll be fine, April.'

The team had stayed out for longer than originally planned and I guess April's imagination had got the better of her. Lee came back from that mission safe and sound, but now he had the bad feeling, right before we were due to leave. I felt a bit of a shiver down my spine as I loaded Benny on to the back of the GMV and climbed up behind my 240. I tried to shake off Lee's concerns. He loaded Spaulding and gave me a wave.

As we drove out of the base, I told myself there was nothing to worry about. It was a MEDCAP, so it wasn't as though we were going out to pick a fight with the Taliban. However, we were passing through an area where other vehicles had been hit by IEDs, which was why there were Afghan minesweepers and us two dog handlers along for the ride.

The convoy drove off road, as usual, but after we crossed the Sakhar River we had to go on to the road for a while, down the long Yakhdan wadi that had been christened, for good reason, IED alley.

We came to a halt, and the Afghans dismounted with their minesweepers and began sweeping the road ahead. The word came down the line that the Afghans had found something and also needed a dog handler to search and, as Lee had lost the toss, he and Spaulding got out and started to work. At the time, head office had told the civilian dog handlers working for American K9 that we were not to do roadside searches. As handlers and dogs had been injured by IEDs and pressure plates along roads, we'd been instructed to confine our searches to compounds, buildings, open fields, choke points and wadis. The greatest danger to the team, as far as I could see, was roadside IEDs, so I ignored the company rule and always searched a road when it needed to be done or, as was the case today, when it was my turn to do so. There was no point, I thought, trying hard to win a team's acceptance and then saying, 'No, I can't do that job to protect you because my company says it's too dangerous.'

I stood in the back of the GMV, stretching my legs, and grabbed a pair of binoculars. I focused and could see the ASG guys with their minesweepers, moving very slowly up the road.

'They're taking their time,' I said to the staff sergeant in the gun turret.

The two Afghans stopped in the middle of the road and appeared to be having a discussion. Behind them, I could see Lee and Spaulding. Spaulding was straining against his lead, and Lee had obviously kept him attached because of the close proximity of the Afghans, and to stop the dog from roaming ahead of the sweepers. Surprisingly, the team captain had also dismounted, and was walking along next to Lee and Spaulding. I could see one of the Afghans gesticulating with his hands to his comrade, as though they were arguing.

'What the fuck are you doing, Lee?' I whispered to myself.

Lee, Spaulding and the team captain were moving past the two arguing Afghans, apparently impatient with their lack of progress. This was a really unsafe practice, and there was no reason for the team captain to be out walking around while the road was being cleared.

I shook my head. 'Shit, man.'

Behind me, Benny was stirring and whimpering. I put the binoculars down and turned to my dog. 'What's wrong, boy? You're not spooked too, are you?'

Boom!

I scrambled back to the turret and snatched up the binoculars, which had vibrated off the ledge where I'd left them. Dirt was raining down on the wadi, and a cloud of black smoke was twisting and turning up into the clear blue sky.

'What the fuck was that?' the gunner in the turret said. The intercom radio was squawking with urgent conversation, but I couldn't focus on what people were saying. Benny was barking, as if asking me the same question the staff sergeant was.

'I think Lee's just been killed,' I said.

FIFTEEN

You know something can happen to you...

'Man, that scared the shit out of me,' Lee said, as we sat outside our hooch back at Cobra, sipping coffee. He was still shaken by what had gone down in IED alley.

'I thought I was going to find you and Spaulding dead,' I said.

Lee nodded. 'Me and the team captain got tired of waiting for those Afghans, and when we got about 20 or 25 metres past them, Spaulding started showing a change in his behaviour. We'd already cleared about a mile of road by then, and Spaulding was tired, so I thought that was what was up with him, so we pushed on a bit further.'

I drew hard on my cigarette. I had thought I'd lost my best friend, and if I was shaken by the experience, it was no wonder Lee was jittery.

'Then the explosion went off. All I could see was smoke and I could smell the fucking dirt... you know?'

I knew the smell. It was like the earth was wounded when a mine or an IED went off, or was blown, as though the ground were bleeding or having the life ripped out of it, and the smell was like that of a human or animal body being ripped open. Mixed in with the burning chemical odour of explosives was the raw flesh of Mother Earth, and there was nothing nice about it.

Miraculously, the two Afghan minesweepers had lived, but they'd had their eardrums blown; there was blood coming out of their noses, and they'd been injured by flying rocks and dirt and shrapnel from the IED. They were loaded into a vehicle and raced back to Cobra, while the rest of us set up a perimeter so that a search for more devices could be made.

Benny and I were called forward to help out with the search and I was pleased to see that Lee was OK, if a little shaken. We searched the roadsides, working in tandem with Lee and Spaulding.

Spaulding sniffed out a spider device, which was an electronic receiver with an aerial made of a coil of very thin wire. The insurgent who had set the IED would detonate it by sending a signal to the spider with a remote-controlled transmitter. There was a further delay while the explosive ordnance disposal men from the team set a charge to blow up whatever the spider was attached to.

We continued clearing for five hours as the rest of the convoy inched along behind us. By that time the team captain, who had also narrowly escaped being blown up, called off the mission. We'd been going out to treat sick and injured villagers and two of our Afghan guys had been wounded, so the mood towards the village on the convoy was 'fuck you'.

From the size of the crater and fragments around the explosion site, it appeared that the IED had been a buried 107–millimetre rocket that had been detonated by remote control in a bid by the Taliban to wipe out the trained minesweepers, as well as Lee, Spaulding and the captain. Lee set his coffee cup down and looked down at his hands. 'Scariest day of my life, man.'

*

I've been lucky in Afghanistan and, apart from the death of Scott, the ETT, in the Baluchi Valley, no coalition soldiers or civilian contractors were killed or seriously wounded on any of the missions I took part in. However, Lee's near miss with the IED reminded us both that dog handlers and dogs have been among the many casualties in Afghanistan.

There was a dog handler from American K9 who was walking along the side of a road when his dog stood on a pressure plate that set off an IED on the road's edge. The IED was pointing in towards the centre of the road, but the dog was killed instantly and the handler badly injured by the back blast of the explosion. He nearly died, and he's still carrying shrapnel from that day. A female handler at Kandahar was given the task of going through his gear, and found bits and pieces of the dog's hair and flesh in it. She had to pick them out before his gear could be sent home.

What made a lot of us feel sour about that incident was that there was a delay getting him flown back to the US military hospital at Ramstein Air Force Base in Germany for advanced medical treatment, because he didn't have his passport with him and it took a while to find it. As he was a civilian, the Americans wouldn't let him into Germany without the document. As it turned out, he'd been evacuated by chopper direct to the military hospital at Kandahar but his passport was back at the outlying FOB where he'd been based. This situation highlighted the fact that while the Americans were happy to have contractors fighting and, potentially, dying alongside their troops in the field, they would never bring them into the fold completely.

An American K9 handler was killed when an IED hit the SF truck he was travelling in, while another one of our colleagues had a miraculous escape while travelling in a turtle-back humvee. The dog handler was sitting next to an Afghan who had his hand up, holding on to the door frame through an open window. The Taliban opened fire on the vehicle as it was driving, and a bullet passed through the Afghani's hand, taking off a finger or two, and hit the handler in the head. Because the bullet's momentum had been slowed by it having hit the other guy first, it lodged in the handler's skull. If it had penetrated into his brain, the handler would probably have died. As it was, he made a full recovery.

My mate Guy had nearly taken a bullet on the TIC out of Cobra, when Apis was shot in the foot. Guy played it down, but something like that happening had to have disturbed him. A while later, he resigned from American K9 and took a job as a security contractor with Canadian firm Tundra. The fact was, in Afghanistan there was probably more chance of a dog handler than a security guy doing personal protection getting involved in TICs and coming under fire. Because we were working with SF, out in the remote mountains and deserts, we were often at the forefront of the war against the Taliban.

You know that something can happen to you, but you rarely think about it or worry about it. It's not like you can't afford to dwell on it, it's more that you just get used to the environment around you – and death is something that always happens to someone else. Still, every time a military or civilian handler or dog is killed or injured, I do have a reality check. It's the same when I hear about something happening to one of the SF guys I've served with. Like I said, I was lucky, or perhaps I have a guardian angel looking out for me. I do know that after Nat and I got together, I carried an angel with me. Nat bought me a tiny silver one, and had it blessed by the priest at the hospital where she was working in Perth. I've never been anywhere without it since.

When you're living in Afghanistan, it's actually hard to judge whether things are getting worse over there or not. There is always more fighting and dying going on as soon as summer – the fighting season – comes around, and then you're lulled into a false sense of security as the weather gets colder.

When an Australian soldier is killed or wounded in Afghanistan, it's front-page news back home, but the rest of the time the general public has no idea that there are guys going out on missions every day, sometimes killing Taliban and often getting shot at.

When I was about to leave Cobra, Deh Rawood and Spin Boldak, the team captains made certificates of appreciation for me, in recognition of the work my dog and I had done. There is no official acknowledgment of the services that contractors provide to the coalition, but those certificates probably mean more to me than any medal could.

Contractors in Afghanistan are paid well, yes, but few of us are there solely for the money. We're also there for job satisfaction, and we provide a service to the coalition that is, at least in the case of dog handlers, exactly the same as the work done by the US Army special search dog handlers. We live, fight and face the risk of death alongside our uniformed comrades. Our dogs and handlers are helping to keep coalition soldiers safe.

There are unlikely ever to be Australian military contractors marching on Anzac Day, but I've held on to the certificates I received from the Americans, and to other bits and pieces from my time in Afghanistan, mostly for my kids' sake. They're going to grow up knowing their father served in a war, but they'll never be able to march with my medals when I'm dead.

SIXTEEN

Afghans

'Shane, look!' Bari, the team's Afghan terp, walked into my room carrying a small brown Afghan puppy.

'Hey, man, when did you get it?' He handed me the puppy and I took a look at it.

'When I was on vacation.'

I showed the pup to Benny, who sniffed at it, but otherwise didn't seem too bothered by him.

Bari was a pretty good guy. He'd been at Cobra since before my first visit, which meant that by the time I ended up back at the FOB, he'd been there for nearly two years. He'd loyally served a number of teams during that time. The fact that he was living in the team compound, instead of in the terp hooch in the main Afghan compound, by the time I returned to Cobra was testament to his ability to fit in and to his professionalism. He had his own room, two doors down the hallway from me, and internet access, courtesy of the team.

He was in his mid twenties, and, like many of the other terps, he'd got a decent education and learned English while studying in Kabul or Pakistan. It was interesting, I thought, that the SF guys, including the Australian SAS, grew beards in acknowledgment that facial hair was usually a sign of maturity and of respect for old customs in the outlying villages of Afghanistan, yet many of the Afghan government soldiers and terps, like Bari, were clean-shaven in defiance of the Taliban's former harsh laws on such matters.

Bari rode along on all our missions, armed with an AK. When the shooting started, he would always join in, and a couple of times he was allowed to get behind a 240 and have a go at the Taliban. He'd get stuck into it and the fact that he would show a bit of aggression was another reason the Americans liked him.

Bari had parlayed his close relationship with the Americans into a business one; as well as being the terp, he was the middle man in some commercial deals. He had got himself into the business of vehicle rentals, and was part of an operation that leased four-by-fours to Cobra for use on and around the base. He also owned a jingle truck, which he used to haul stuff to and from the base, again on a contract basis. Bari was on the make, but no-one begrudged him making a few bucks. It did seem, however, that Bari's closeness to the foreign soldiers had caused some envy, or animosity, among the Afghans working for the government. As well as living in the US compound, he tended to avoid his countrymen when he wasn't out on missions.

'You can help me train my dog, yes?' Bari asked me.

'Sure.' I went through my spare gear and found him a collar, a dog lead, and a couple of tennis balls, and started giving Bari a few basic pointers on training his puppy.

Unlike most of the other terps and ANA, Bari never showed any fear around Ricky and Benny, and seemed interested in

215

them. Bari would happily jump in the back of a gun truck with my dog and me, but none of the other terps would want to and, if they had to, they'd sit in a corner as far from the dog as they could. It was no real surprise that Bari had found himself a puppy while on vacation.

Several times, Bari came out to the range where Mike, the combat controller, and I were training with Benny, so that he could pick up tips on how to work with his dog. I wanted Bari to bring the dog up properly and look after it, as most Afghan dogs lead a pretty hard life.

I saw some beautiful dogs when I was out on missions, and I saw some that were in a terrible state. Generally, the Afghans did not treat their dogs well, and dogfighting was still common in the villages. The owners would cut their dogs' ears and tails off, so as to deny its opponent in a fight something to get hold of. It was hard for me to believe that people could be capable of such cruelty, even in Afghanistan, where killing seemed to be a national pastime. I never went to a dog fight, and never would. I think it's barbaric to make an animal suffer as a form of sport. I love animals, and so I'm a softy when it comes to seeing a dog, or any other animal, in pain.

Occasionally, when I was searching a village or compound with Ricky or Benny, a local Afghan dog would start snarling or try to pick a fight with my dog. I couldn't afford to have my partner distracted during a search, so I'd find a rock and chuck it at the other dog, to send it on its way.

Before Apis was shot, I was on board a gun truck on a mission Guy and I had been sent on. He and I were taking it in turns to search, and he and Apis had dismounted. Over the intercom radio, I got word that a huge Afghan hound was hassling Guy and Apis. They tried tossing stones at it but it kept coming for them. Sadly, the SF had to shoot it, as it was becoming a threat to Guy, his dog and the mission. I heard the gunfire from further up the line – it had taken five 5.56-millimetre bullets from an M4, fired into the dog's head, to put it down. It wasn't a sad situation, but a stark reminder that we and our dogs were in Afghanistan to do a job, and that our mission, to search for explosives and IEDs was paramount.

There were a couple of Afghan hounds that lived around Cobra that were named Tali, after the Taliban, and Carl, after the Carl Gustaf anti-armour weapon. They were pups when I was first at Cobra with Ricky, but had grown to be fairly big dogs by the time I made it back to the FOB.

Tali and Carl had been adopted as unofficial mascots by the SF team, and roamed the compounds at night as extra security. They hated Afghans and when the gun trucks rolled out of base, Tali and Carl would follow us. Carl would usually give up after a while and walk back to base, but Tali would cover huge distances, up to five or six kilometres, trotting along behind the convoy. When we reached our night harbour position, Tali would hang around, keeping curious Afghan kids away from us.

During one mission that I wasn't on, Tali got too close to Lee and Spaulding and tried to bite Lee. Perhaps she was jealous of Spaulding, but the upshot was that one of the SF put Tali down because she was becoming potentially dangerous. This was a shame, as Tali had been a dog that was playful and protective at the same time, but it was a similar situation to that of someone getting a pet and then not caring for or training it properly. There was really no place for Tali or Carl on a FOB, particularly when there were other dogs there that had a job to do. As much as the SF guys loved dogs, nothing could ever get in the way of a mission.

At the same time Bari got his dog, one of the medics adopted a puppy but, like many dogs in disease-ridden Afghanistan, it soon contracted distemper and he had to put it down. It was just another example of the difference in care between strays and our working dogs. Dogs such as Ricky, Benny, Apis and Spaulding were in tip-top condition, and looked after by handlers who lived with them 24 hours a day. Soldiers love pets, but they can't always be there for them and, eventually, a dog's owner would have to rotate home.

It saddened me to see any dog being put down but that was life in this sometimes brutal, always unforgiving country.

Bari persisted with his dog's training, but it wasn't progressing well, as the puppy continually crapped in his room. I could sense he was losing interest in the animal. Sadly, the dog contracted distemper, not long after the team medic's pet did, and it also had to be put down.

Even though we didn't now have the connection through the dog, Bari and I still chatted occasionally. I was working on my computer one day when he knocked on my door frame. 'Hello, Shane, hello, Benny,' he said. Bari had his laptop clasped under his arm. 'Shane, I have pictures of my vacation, if you are interested?'

'Sure,' I said. Anything to break the monotony of life on the FOB in between missions, I thought.

'You have pictures of your vacation?' he asked me.

I clicked on a folder of pictures on my laptop that I'd taken during my last vacation. I showed Bari some shots of the beach at Port Kembla, the new, old, house I'd bought and was renovating, a picture of Nat, and a group shot of all my kids and me.

'You have many children; that is good, yes?'

'Yes, very. I miss 'em.'

He nodded. 'Australia looks so beautiful. I would love to go there one day and see it.'

I wasn't surprised that he thought Australia was beautiful. As much as I liked the wild beauty of Afghanistan's empty plains and jagged mountains, I couldn't imagine living there permanently.

Bari clearly wanted to get out of his own country and the US soldiers at Cobra were trying to help him achieve his dream. He'd put his life on the line for a succession of SF guys and, in recognition of his commitment, the current team had applied to get him US citizenship. If all went according to plan, Bari might very well visit Wollongong one day, as an American tourist.

It was Bari's turn to show me on his laptop pictures of his recent vacation to Pakistan. I wasn't anticipating I would be wowed but they were something different.

Fucking different.

'Have a look at this beautiful picture, Shane...'

I was expecting to see a scene of snow-capped mountains or something, but instead he started up a video that had been shot on a Handycam. It was of a young, attractive, coffee-coloured girl, smiling at the camera and doing a bit of a dance. She started undoing the buttons of her blouse and, with Bari encouraging her from behind the camera, she showed her bare breasts. What the fuck?

'This is a girl I met in Pakistan,' Bari grinned.

I took another look. Everything I'd learned about Muslim people and their culture told me that this Pakistani edition of *Girls Gone Wild* was totally wrong. I put it down to Bari wanting to fit in. When there was booze on the base, he would take a drink. He also swore, and ate pork – something he made a point of mentioning. Maybe he thought Americans liked to show each other pictures of their naked girlfriends. If that were the case, I hadn't seen any.

I didn't know what to say to him, other than 'Um…nice'.

I would sometimes eat with the ANA and Afghan Security Group guys. They were hospitable people, but also very nosey. Over a meal of lamb and rice, washed down with Pepsi or bottled water, they'd start asking me if I was married, how many kids I had, how old the kids were, what their names were, and anything else they could think of.

Like Bari, the Afghans were fascinated by life in Australia and if you struck up a conversation, via an interpreter, with one guy, the next thing you knew, there would be half a dozen of them there, all asking you questions. They also weren't afraid to talk politics and history.

'Ask him what he remembers about when the Russians were here,' I said to an interpreter one day. I wanted him to put the question to an Afghan soldier who looked old enough to have been a young man during the Soviet invasion.

'This man says that was a good time,' said the interpreter.

'Are you sure?' That was the last thing I had expected to hear an Afghan say.

The soldier nodded his head, saying, via the interpreter: 'It was a good time for our country, when the Russians were here. The Russians built roads and dams and housing, and our women were free to wear skirts and high heels and make-up, and to go to schools and university.'

The other soldiers grinned and nodded at the references to women not having to cover themselves. I'd seen some stunning Afghan women, with beautiful, piercing blue or green eyes, when I was on foot patrol or searching a village. While the women were generally very shy and hidden from view, if their husbands or fathers weren't around some of them would stick their heads out their front doors and peek at us, while others would gather in groups of three or four and stare at us. We were told not to make eye contact with the women, but it was obvious that some of them were just as curious about us as we were about them.

The soldier's comments about the Russians got me thinking. The more I thought about it, the more I realised that the coalition was trying to do what the Russians had tried, and failed, to do. We were supporting a moderate government and, while the Americans were encouraging the Afghans to embrace democracy rather than communism, their agenda was similar. We measured progress in the same way the Russians did – how many roads and schools we could build, and how many women could get away with wearing western clothes and getting an education. The Russians, depending on whose view of history you took, were either trying to expand their empire, or to bolster a friendly government and create a buffer between them and the rise of radical Islam. Weren't we doing exactly the same thing?

Most of our interpreters, or *tajiman*, as they called themselves, had learned English in Kabul or Pakistan, either in school or university, and their grasp of the language varied enormously.

'Mr Shane, can I ask you a question,' one of the terps who was on call outside the SF headquarters at Cobra asked me one day.

'Fire away.'

'What is nougat?'

'Nougat?' I had to think for a moment. 'Nougat? It's a lolly, I think.'

'A lolly? Please?'

'Um,' I scratched my head. 'A sweet.'

'Sweet? It is good, yes?'

I shrugged. 'Why do you want to know?'

'One of the Americans, he called me his "nougat".'

'He what?' This was weird, I thought, even for an SF dude, and they sometimes displayed an odd sense of humour – for example, shitting in kitty litter or wearing their beards as wigs, as George had. 'What did he say to you?'

'He said, "What is up, my nougat?".'

I racked my brains. Nougat. Noogar. Niggah? 'Ohh. Did he say, "Wassup, my nigger"?'

'Yes,' the interpreter beamed, 'yes, "What is up, my nigger?". That is good, this nigger, yes?'

I worked hard to hold in my laughter. 'Yes, very good, in context.' And, of course, in a very non-politically correct way, I'm sure it was.

There were some very good interpreters in Afghanistan and some very bad ones.

They tended to be young and often I wondered whether they were giving us the full story. I'd be listening to ANA or, sometimes, Taliban spotters talking to their commanders over the intercom radio, and the Afghans would talk for ages. I'd ask an interpreter to translate a five-minute conversation and he'd say something like 'This man says he has nothing to report.'

Some Afghans seemed genuinely to hate the Taliban, while you had to wonder about the motivation of other soldiers who were fighting for the government. There was an Afghan police commander at Deh Rawood; he was a middle-aged guy, who had a reputation for being a real hard arse. I asked around about him and the word was that his family had been killed by the Taliban, because he was working for the government. The policeman had rounded up a few of his mates, so the story went, and gone hunting for the Taliban who had shot his wife and children. Apparently, he found the rebels, and he and his men killed them all. The Americans greatly respected him for his motivation, his local knowledge and his no-nonsense manner.

By and large, though, I got the feeling from talking to the ETTs who worked with the ANA that the coalition advisers had their work cut out for them in getting the Afghans motivated to take the fight to the enemy. You couldn't blame them for being reluctant, I suppose. They were expected, rightly, to get stuck into the dirty business of clearing compounds and houses, and if there were going to be coalition casualties during a TIC, the odds were that they would be the Afghans and the ETTs. Also, the Afghans loyal to the government were probably concerned about retribution from the Taliban against them and their families if they were ever caught.

Commentators always like to compare what is happening in Afghanistan with the Vietnam War, but I don't know how valid that is. One thing about the conflicts that does seem to be the same is that the war in Afghanistan is not one that the Americans and their western allies can win by themselves. Victory, if that's even possible, will only come if the Afghan people can decide for themselves once and for all that they don't want to live under Taliban rule, and if they then develop their army, police and civil authorities enough that the Taliban can never again gain the support of the people.

For every business-minded, loyal Bari, or the police commander who wanted to kill as many Taliban as possible to avenge the shooting of his family, there was a traditional farmer out in a village somewhere who saw nothing wrong with the Taliban's fundamentalist approach, or a wild-eyed boy who wanted to emulate his dad's heroic deeds against the Russians by killing as many coalition -soldiers as possible before he went to Allah.

Lee and I needed some help from the Afghans at Cobra to keep our dogs' training interesting and relevant for them. We went down to the ANA compound and sought out the commander. In true Afghan style, he was very polite and hospitable, inviting us to sit down and drink some chai with him before we could get down to business.

The commander was a stocky guy with dark wavy hair and a neatly trimmed moustache. After the pleasantries were out of the way, I asked him if we could borrow some of his troops' ammunition and weapons, such as RPG rounds, grenades and any explosives they had. Our training aids, I explained, were getting contaminated. Lee and I were always using the same spare chunks of explosive to train our dogs, and they were getting too used to the smell of Lee and me on the stuff they were looking for. As the ANA used the same weapons as the Taliban did, and as the soldiers who used them would smell the same as Afghans fighting for the other side, Lee and I figured the dogs' training would be more useful for them if we used Soviet-made munitions.

The commander agreed, and also offered the use of his compound for training. We took RPG rounds and other types of ordnance, and buried them out the back of the FOB, in the open area we used as a rifle range and drop zone for the C-130 resupply missions, and later stashed some stuff in the rooms the Afghan security forces used. The dogs found the new locations and scents fascinating, and we completed some good, rigorous training with them.

A couple of days later, the Afghan commander had a meeting with the team in their compound there. As he strode across the compound, the commander saw my dog and me, and detoured to come and say hello. Knowing that Benny could be unpredictable, I pushed him to one side as the commander approached us. As the Afghan officer reached out his hand to shake mine, Benny leaped up and bit him. I apologised profusely and called the medic out to bandage the commander's hand, but he was seriously pissed off.

Benny was funny like that. Whereas Ricky liked to bite any Afghan he met, Benny was very selective. I could usually work him off-lead, even in villages and compounds, but every now and then he'd single out someone from the crowd who he didn't like. I wondered if he were picking up on something; some ill feeling towards me or the guys I was working with.

*

Not even Benny's sixth sense, however, picked up the traitor who was living among us.

It was about six-thirty in the morning when a noise in the corridor outside the door to my room woke me. I rubbed my hand over my face. Benny stirred at the foot of my bed and there was a knock at the door.

'Shane?'

'Yeah. Joe? What is it?' I swung my legs over the edge of the bed and reached for my trousers. Joe was one of the sergeants on the team. 'Come in, man.'

'Get your dog, Shane. We need you to do a search.'

I shook off my sleepiness. 'Sure. Where?'

'I'll show you.'

I pulled on a T-shirt, slid on my boots and first took Benny outside for a quick piss while Joe waited. There were more voices down the corridor when I got back inside and I was keen to find out what all the fuss was about. Nothing like this had ever happened on the FOB before.

'This way.'

I thought I was being roused from bed to go out on a mission or something, but Joe led me just two doors down the hall from where I slept. 'Search this room,' he said.

'What the fuck? That's Bari's room.'

'Yup.'

I took Benny in there and he started sniffing around the bed. There was no sign of Bari, but there was gear all over the place and it looked like someone had already been through the interpreter's room.

As Benny and I were searching, Lee appeared in the doorway.

'What's going on?' I asked him.

'Doesn't look good. I got woken about six and told to go search the terps' hooch in the other compound, then Bari's room.'

It looked like I'd been brought in to do a double check in case Lee and Spaulding had missed anything. 'You find something?'

Lee nodded. 'Weapon, ammo and detonation cord – plus a detailed map of the base.'

'Shit.' Detonation cord was explosive cord used to link a number of charges so that they all went off at the same time.

'Word is,' Lee said, 'that Bari was arranging for a suicide bomber to attack the next team to come through, either in the camp or in the village bazaar.' Bari would still have needed to get hold of some C4 or TNT, or some other explosive, to make a bomber's vest, but there was no reason why he should have had detonation cord in his room.

Benny and I searched Bari's room thoroughly as the incredible news started to sink in. Later in the day, as events unfolded, Lee and I discovered that the intelligence people had been monitoring Bari's mobile phone conversations for some time. The allegation was that the plan was that he—or someone else—would execute a suicide attack against the team using the vest that Bari had been assembling, piece by piece. He'd been PUCked—arrested as a person under consideration—and taken to the cells in another part of Cobra. When the next 'Brown Ring', the regular scheduled resupply and transport flight, came through, Bari was taken to the landing zone, handcuffed, had his eyes covered by darkened welder's goggles, and was put on a Chinook. I have no idea what happened to him after that.

As Lee and I sat and talked about the morning's amazing events, we started putting the pieces together.

'He showed me a video of this girl in Pakistan with her tits hanging out,' I said. 'It was like he was trying too hard to fit in—to be one of the boys.'

Lee nodded. 'I've seen him in some pretty good TICs—shooting back and all. He'd always turn up some pretty good intel, or so it seemed, but now that I think of it, nothing much ever came from it.'

Bari had been the consummate actor—lulling the Americans into a false sense of security and getting them to accept him almost as one of their own, even to the extent of conning them into applying for his American citizenship, while all the while he was hatching a plot to kill them. It blew me away, the way he'd appeared to leave his Muslim beliefs behind and become Americanised, and then sucked everyone in. I wondered if his not being accepted by the other terps was due more to their fear of him than to jealousy over his unusually close relationship with the Americans or his wheeling and dealing.

The word around camp in the days that followed was that Bari the likeable interpreter was actually a senior Taliban commander. With the access he had, this one man could conceivably have destroyed an entire Special Forces A-Team.

SEVENTEEN

Indiana Jones

I went out on a mission with Brad, the other American K9 civilian dog handler, who served at Cobra when Lee and I did. I was in the GMV behind the 240, with Benny at my feet, and Brad was riding inside the ETT Turtleback humvee with his dog, Rex. Brad liked Rex to travel in his portable kennel.

Rex was a creature of habit, who went out for a shit at precisely seven every morning, come rain, hail or shine. We left the base on the mission in what the Americans called hours of limited visibility – in this case, just before dawn. We weren't expecting that much would happen until we reached our objective a few hours later, but not long after leaving Cobra, we drove into a TIC.

The rounds started coming in like a swarm of angry, deadly bees and I let rip on the 240. The Taliban, so I learned later, had zeroed in on the Turtleback, and Brad was firing back from the turret. Brad could hear bullets pinging off the chicken plate armour that surrounded the gunner's position.

Never ones to shy away from the fight, the team continued pouring the fire back on the insurgents, chugging away with their Mark 19s and sending back a fierce storm of .50-calibre slugs. As the fight dragged on, so did the time, and before Brad knew it, seven o'clock had come and gone.

Rex was going crazy in his travel kennel. The din inside the Turtleback was unbearable for man and animal alike, and he started spinning around, trying to get away from the noise and the rain of empty brass cartridges falling around him.

Unable to hold on any longer, Rex crapped in his kennel. The problem was that as the poor animal did so, he continued to spin around madly, and chunks of dog turd started hitting the wide steel mesh of the door and spraying around the inside of the humvee. It was getting hot inside the enclosed vehicle and, although Brad didn't notice much from his position in the open turret, it was getting too much for the driver and the other guy inside.

'Holy shit, man,' the driver yelled. 'Do something about that ... do something about that fucking dog!' He was gagging while getting pelted by shredded dog turd and empty brass bullet cartridges. Humans have pants to crap in during a TIC – dogs don't.

While they were all part of the same army, each SF team was subtly different in its ways and idiosyncrasies. Much of that difference came from the people in command, some of whom were real characters.

Paul, the US SF team sergeant, wanted to be an Australian. He had served down-under on exchange with the Australian Army and loved it there. He told me he would have loved to live in Australia, and asked me, jokingly, if there were any way he could become an honorary Australian citizen.

Wanting to be an honorary Australian wasn't the only thing that set Paul apart from some of his comrades. To start with, he wasn't your typically pumped-up, weight-lifting hard-arse American SF solider. He was tall and lean, and a bit older than the rest of the guys. To look at him, you might think he was a slightly nerdy-middle-aged school teacher rather than a Green Beret. All the same, he commanded the respect of everyone in the team and took no bullshit from anyone.

Paul dressed differently, too. Some of the guys carried so much gear they looked like robo-soldiers, but he lugged the bare minimum of equipment. He didn't wear body armour or a helmet and, instead of a combat vest, he wore the old-style military webbing consisting of a belt, a harness, a couple of ammo pouches and two water bottles. It was the sort of gear that dated from the time I'd joined the army.

If his webbing was old, his rifle was a museum piece. He carried an M-14 that had been designed for the US Army and Marine Corps back in the late 1950s. It was an updated version of the old M1 Garand rifle that the Americans had used in World War II. It had been re-chambered to take the 7.62-millimetre NATO rimless cartridge and fitted with a 20-round box magazine, on account of the fact that, unlike the old Garand, it could fire on full automatic if required, and therefore needed more ammo. The M-14 had been super-seded early on in its life by the lighter, mostly plastic M-16, which became the standard infantry weapon in Vietnam and, in its various forms, right up to today. However, the M-14 had gained a reputation for being a very accurate weapon and, with a cartridge bigger and heavier than the M-16's 5.56-millimetre round, it saw service in Vietnam as a sniper rifle. I'd heard that the M-14 had come back into fashion in Iraq, where insurgents had started wearing body armour, which could withstand the 5.56--millimetre round but not the M-14's larger bullet. Engagements could be fought over much longer distances in the open fields and mountains of Afghanistan than in the streets of Baghdad – another reason for Paul's choice of this reliable old weapon.

Paul wore a non-regulation camouflage smock that hung down low, almost down to his knees, but even more distinctive than that was his trademark broad-brimmed hat. It looked exactly like the battered old hat Harrison Ford wore in the Indiana Jones movies, so Paul's nickname, naturally, reflected that.

Indiana Jones had his own way of operating on missions. While the majority of the team headed out on patrol in their gun trucks and turtlebacks, Paul and four or five other Americans, and a few Afghans, would set off cross-country on foot, sticking to the ridge lines. As we were mostly driving off road, to avoid mines and IEDs, our progress was slow, so the foot patrol could keep us in sight. Despite all the armour and guns on a GMV, it was somehow reassuring to know that this old-school warrior was walking the mountain paths and rocky ground above us, keeping overwatch.

The Taliban would usually have spotters hiding up in the hills, and Indiana Jones and his followers were playing them at their own game, sneaking up on them while the enemy were watching our vehicles trundling through the passes and valleys far below. He was using the same tactics as the bad guys, which showed he could think outside the box.

After prayers one afternoon, I went to Paul's bedroom and knocked on the door. 'On behalf of the people of Australia, Paul, we'd like to present you with a token of our esteem.' A couple of guys in the hallway were grinning because they already knew what was coming. The rangy team sergeant stepped up, and I produced the certificate that I'd asked Nat to bodgie up on her computer back home. 'It gives me great pleasure to officially proclaim you as an honorary Australian.'

'Thanks, Shane,' he said, surprised by the presentation. He read Nat's certificate, which bestowed honorary citizenship on him and gave him permission to visit any time he wanted. 'I'm very grateful and proud to be an Aussie.'

In many ways, Paul was just like an Australian SF soldier. He was quiet, mature and intelligent, and, while he could draw on some of the most modern and fierce technological weaponry in the world if his guys ran into trouble, he knew that it was just as important for soldiers to be able to go up into the mountains, armed with not much more than a trusty rifle, and seek out their enemy, man-on-man.

We went into a village in the mountains a couple of weeks later, and Indiana Jones, who arrived on foot, told the rest of the team that he and his men had seen from a distance some males of fighting-age bug out when they saw our approach. The men had run off to hide deeper in the mountains.

The village was empty by the time we got there and had a spooky feel. Benny and I were tasked to search the houses and a small bazaar. The shutters were down on the stores, so one of the guys got a pair of bolt cutters from the GMV and we busted in to the small stalls.

I didn't find anything in the buildings, but the team guys discovered an aqueduct that was channelling water into the village. It was quite an elaborate system of trenches, which led into a tunnel that had been excavated in the face of a slope. It looked like a place where insurgents could hide out, perhaps during an air strike, or move from one firing position to another without being spotted if the village were under attack. Given the suspicious behaviour of the men who had left earlier, and the eerie emptiness of the village now, we had no doubt that this was a Taliban hide-out.

'Blow the water supply,' Paul said.

One of the demolitions specialists, Billy, got to work rigging up an explosive charge and, as an ex-engineer with an interest in blowing things up, I offered to help. Once the charges were ready, Billy and I had to wade through and crawl up into the tunnel to place them where they would cause the maximum amount of damage to the water supply and the tunnel network.

Taking water away from your enemy was an almost medieval way of fighting. By the same token, one of the ways to win hearts and minds was to go out and sink a borehole or install water tanks in a village. It seemed that we were giving with one hand and taking with the other. By removing a source of fresh water, we'd deny the Taliban this hiding place, yet the village was also home to civilians. Where they were now, though, was anyone's guess.

In Afghanistan, the Americans had the same problem as had the previous generation of soldiers in Vietnam – it was often impossible to distinguish friend from foe unless they were shooting at you. The Taliban dressed the same way as ordinary Afghans did and many Afghan males carried weapons. Even if an Afghan decided not to wear a turban or have a beard, that was no guarantee he was pro-American. What had happened with Bari had taught us that lesson. We presumed the fighting-aged males who ran from us were Taliban. I suppose it was possible that they were just scared, but this didn't cross my mind at the time.

I concentrated on working with the explosives. The TNT was in place, with a number of charges linked by detonation cord–the same stuff with which Bari had been planning on blowing us up. We cut enough time fuse to give us three minutes to escape, then fitted an M60 igniter.

I got to turn the ring on the plastic tube of the M60, starting the timer, and Billy and I sloshed out of the cave and irrigation channel, back up to where the GMVs were parked. The charges went off with a satisfying boom that echoed through the mountains and, I hoped, sent a message to the Taliban that we were not to be fucked with.

In some parts of Afghanistan, there was a point to trying to win hearts and minds, through, for example, medical and humanitarian aid, but out here we were in Taliban country. It wasn't as though the Taliban had forced themselves on the people of this village, or were intimidating them. Here, the people *were* Taliban and all we could do was deny the fighters a place to hide or water to drink. We weren't going to win a single heart or mind of the villagers in that place.

Blowing the water supply in the village might sound harsh but we had nothing on the Taliban in that respect.

I was in a TIC some time after the mission on which we'd destroyed the water cave, and the team called in air support after making contact with some Taliban on the ground. A pair of Dutch Apache gunships circled above the head of the valley where we were operating, like birds of prey impatient for the kill.

The gun truck was facing forward and the .50 cal in the turret was hurling rounds down at a compound. I couldn't bring the 240 to bear, so I was watching the action and helping to spot for the gunner.

'Check your fire, check your fire, there's kids in the doorway, kids in the doorway,' the JTAC said over the intercom radio.

I picked up the binoculars and zeroed in on the entrance-way to one of the compounds we were targeting. The controller was right. I could see a young boy, maybe ten or eleven years old, crouching there, his hands over his ears. Even from 500 or 600 metres away, I could see the fear on his face. Tracer arced out at us from one of the windows.

'Fuckers are using the kids as human shields,' the gun truck driver said.

'They can see the Apaches,' I replied, recognising the heartless strategy for what it was. The Taliban had reasoned, correctly, that the Americans wouldn't play their trump card and call in an air strike if they could see children were present.

'There's some more!'

I looked to where the gunner was pointing, and clearly saw a little boy and a girl, aged no more than eight, running across an open field between two compounds, holding each other's hands.

I was furious at the gutless bastards who would pull this sort of stuff during a TIC. It was no secret that the Taliban mingled freely among the populations of some villages, using the presence of women and children to ensure we came in peace rather than starting as a fight, as the Americans would if they thought a village were empty of civilians. It was also true that coalition forces would throw lollies from their vehicles, like an aircraft dispensing chaff, to keep kids close to a convoy and lessen the chance of an IED being detonated or someone opening fire. What was happening now, however, was a new low – dragging kids into the firing line, or making them run from cover to cover, during a TIC.

How hard, how cold, could a man be? I couldn't imagine any cause in the world that would prompt me to do something like that – to put my kids, or someone else's at risk. I'd rather face an air strike and die like a man than use a child as a shield in a fight.

I watched the little boy and girl running, and could only imagine their confusion and fear. I doubt that an eight-year-old could comprehend why an adult would make them run among bullets. These people; life was so fucking cheap to them. It was bad enough that they would burn or blow up schools and kill teachers, but this was something else again.

EIGHTEEN

After-action reports

February 2008

I think that the things I was seeing and the constant grind of life on operations was desensitising me to the dangers of living in a war zone.

In the depth of winter we went back into the Yakhdan wadi – IED alley – where the Afghan minesweepers had been wounded and Lee had nearly been killed by the 107-millimetre rocket. As a Ford Ranger pickup carrying an ANA squad somewhere up the front of the convoy crested a hill, an IED detonated, sending a storm of rock and dirt into the back of the vehicle and a plume of smoke into the air. I reached for my helmet and soothed Benny.

The GMV pulled to a halt, along with every other vehicle in the convoy, and I got out and coaxed Benny down. 'Come on, boy, time for work.'

The blast had been command-detonated, and whoever had activated it misjudged his timing and barely missed destroying the ANA vehicle. Either Allah had smiled on the government troops in the back of the Ranger, or they'd been kissed on the arse by a fairy. I moved forward, but stayed behind the pair of ANA minesweepers who were walking slowly along the road. Benny and I started searching the ground on either side for more IEDs and booby traps.

Because of the way the IED had been detonated, I knew that the Taliban had their eyes on us. Someone had pushed a button, or something, to set that thing off—it wasn't as though it were a land mine. It was a freaky feeling knowing that the enemy was watching me, but this was the job I was being paid to do and so couldn't let it get to me.

The shaken but unharmed soldiers from the Afghan Security Group and ANA dismounted from the scratched-up Ranger and pushed out to the flanks, looking for command wires, Taliban spotters and, hopefully, the bastard who had set off this remote-controlled explosion. I concentrated on my job and on my dog, making sure that Benny kept his nose to the ground and kept on sniffing. As I'd done with Ricky, I'd trained Benny to work off-lead, even though it was against company standard operating procedures. Like his predecessor, Benny enjoyed working this way. He had more freedom to move and we worked faster, rather than having him straining at a lead. As harsh as it might sound, the other benefit of working your dog off-lead is that if, God forbid, he does trip something, you're a lot further away from him than you would be if you were hanging onto his leash.

Benny stayed about fifteen metres ahead, which was a good distance for me. With some dogs, if you teach them to work off lead after they've worked on-lead, they'll be reluctant to put too much distance between you and them. Benny wasn't like this and if he ever did start to crowd me, I knew it was his way of telling me that he was getting tired. I watched him closely for any change of behaviour that might indicate he'd found something.

'Sook, Benny.'

Benny knew exactly what I wanted him to do and it was all a game to him as he bustled along, quartering the road in a zigzag pattern, eagerly looking for something that would give him a chance to play with his ball. Even so, I made sure he overlapped the edges of the road each time he crossed, so that he didn't miss a thing. I kept his face turned into the wind, to help him scent whatever might be out there.

I also kept an eye on the minesweepers, keeping my pace and Benny's in line with them, so that I didn't get too close to them or drift ahead. As the sweepers, Benny and I moved slowly down the road, the convoy of trucks inched along behind us.

Boom!

A fountain of dirt and rock erupted maybe 80 metres ahead and to the right of me, and the smell of gutted earth rolled across the road.

Boom! Boom!

'Incoming! Mortars!' someone yelled from one of the gun trucks behind me.

Benny whimpered and I stood there on the side of the road, watching the explosions as more mortar bombs detonated. 'Sook, Benny,' I said to him, telling him to get back to work.

As far as I was concerned, we still had a job to do, but the Afghan minesweepers were running down the road towards me. As they passed me, running for their lives, I suddenly realised that if they were leaving their post, then maybe I should get back to my GMV as well.

Benny didn't need any encouragement to do this; when I re-attached his lead, he was straining at it to get back to the truck. He was whimpering and whining again, and when we climbed aboard, I took him in my arms and buried his head in my embrace. 'It's all right, boy; it's all right.'

Back at the FOB, days later, I typed up my after-action report of the incident, and the subsequent four days for American K9, keeping it simple and factual. No adjectives were required to describe the grind and the danger of days on patrol.

Mission after-action report – 28 Feb, 2008
Day 1
IED detonated near lead vehicle. I assisted with searching behind sweepers. Mortared while searching. Returned to vehicle. Artillery called on mortar site. Established remain overnight position overlooking village of keshay.

There was no room to mention the way I'd stood, staring at the mortars, wondering for a moment why all the Afghans were running away; my brain somehow suggesting that it was OK for me to be standing in the open in the middle of a mortar barrage. No mention, either, of the scream of the 105-millimetre shells called in by the US soldiers in retaliation. I can still hear that sound, of the projectiles tearing the sky apart, now.

I started typing again.

Day 2
Moved through westside of keshay village. Engaged sniper in Keshay. Enemy sniper neutralised. Enemy contact in vicinity of keshay bazaar. Special search dog handler located ak-47 and mags in compound. Received enemy fire from ridgelines. Returned fire. Close air support called.

This had been a busy mission. After we'd started taking fire from the hills, the team captain had summoned a B1 bomber from out of nowhere to drop a 2000-pound JDAM – a Joint Direct Attack Munition, the military name for a guided 'smart' bomb – on a -village that might have been there for a thousand years.

The after-action report didn't describe the pounding hearts, the adrenaline rush and the screams of elation. There was no room to describe Benny's barking and the smell of burning after the bomb went off.

Day 3
Continued to move south towards the village of saraw. Searched compounds with explosive detection dog Benny and Ana. Pkm and ammunition located. Large pharmacy used for enemy fighters was uncovered. A-Team vehicle damaged and unrepairable. Vehicle towed back to cobra.

I couldn't put it in the report, but I was actually annoyed that the Afghan soldiers had found the PKM Russian light machine gun and ammo. Benny and I entered the building about ten seconds after the ANA guys found the weapon. It would have been so valuable for Benny to make a real find, which would also validate his training – and mine.

We still had to search the mud-walled house, in any case, and Benny kept coming back to the PKM. He sat by it, indicating he knew it was an enemy weapon. This was pretty amazing, when you think about it. The ANA all carried the same weapons and ammo as the Taliban did, yet my dog knew that this particular machine gun had belonged to the bad guys. It might even have been firing at us the day before.

Even though the weapon had already been found, I rewarded Benny for doing a good job by letting him play for a while before we continued searching.

It was eerie, coming across hard evidence of this elusive–enemy's presence; to know that the Taliban were here, treating their wounded, and cleaning and oiling their PKM machine guns, just like we did between missions.

The vehicle damage referred to in the report was due to overloading, rather than to anything so dramatic as a roadside bomb or a mine. The humvee in question was carrying so much weight that its rear axle collapsed. We couldn't leave it there, so we were ordered to skull-drag the stricken vehicle all the way back to Cobra, its broken rear end slowly ploughing the dirt all the way home. It took forever, and we were tired and cold, by the time we got back to the FOB.

Day 4
Depart FOB Cobra with intent to return to keshay. Crossed sakhar river and entered village of yakhdan. While crossing Yakhdan wadi 2 x tm-62 Russian anti-tank mines located. I searched wadi for two hours. All mines destroyed in place. Takes another four hours to search and reach keshay.

After the brief respite of a few hours' sleep in our beds at Cobra, we saddled up and headed back out to IED alley and Keshay. Searching for two or four hours at a time is tiring work both for man and dog. You're not moving fast, but you're concentrating and communicating with each other all the time. To add to that pressure, we were heading back somewhere that we knew the enemy was, and where we had been attacked previously. Still, the SF guys got up, headed out and went looking for another fight without a murmur, because it was their job.

Once we got to the village and searched it, Benny and I had a bit of downtime, as we were both knackered. The team had parked its vehicles on some high ground over-looking the village, and I walked Benny down the hill to a small stream, about 100 metres from the compounds we'd just finished searching. The ground was rocky and barren, with just a few hardy shrubs managing to defy the odds. The stream was flowing, although it was only about a metre-and-a-half wide.

'In you go, boy.' I coaxed Benny into the shallow water and he stood there, tentatively at first, then lowered his head and lapped some up. 'Good boy.' I scooped up handfuls of water and drizzled them over him, then massaged them into his coat. He'd worked hard that day and deserved a break. Eventually, he sat down in the water and grinned at me as he cooled off. I sat on the rocks at the edge of the stream. It was great just spending some quiet time with Benny.

An Afghan soldier came down to the stream and drank from it, using his cupped hand, but Benny didn't pay him any attention. He was good like that – Ricky would probably have tried to kill the guy. The soldier then left us, which I was grate-ful for. In a place like Afghanistan the camaraderie of working with a great bunch of professionals is a beautiful thing, but sometimes you just want to be alone with your dog.

That night, Benny reminded me how he'd earned his origi-nal nickname, the Bouncer.

He was fiercely loyal to and very protective of me. As the sun started to settle behind the mountains, I took Benny for his evening piss and then up to the gun trucks, which were still positioned on the high ground overlooking the village. I fed him, then laid out my sleeping bag and tied Benny to the gun truck. He settled in for the night.

I walked around to the other side of the truck, where one of the SF guys was tucking into a Meal Ready to Eat. I selected a meal for myself, popped it into its heater bag, then carefully extracted the piping-hot foil package, tore it open and started to eat. While I was chatting in between mouthfuls, another one of the team sergeants started to walk around the far side of the truck, where I'd left Benny.

I didn't think anything of it until I heard a low growl, then a short, high-pitched yelp of pure fear. I dropped my food and ran around the other side of the gun truck. Benny was straining at his leash, barking, and the shocked sergeant was standing with his hands in front of his privates. Benny had taken a piece out of the crutch of the man's camouflage trousers and his undies were showing.

'I'm sorry, man,' I said to the sergeant and looked at Benny. 'Bad dog!'

'It's OK,' the sergeant said, his forgiving words barely hiding his realisation that he'd just come within millimetres of losing his crown jewels.

He was good about it, though, understanding that Benny was just protecting our little patch. I couldn't be too hard on the dog, but if he'd injured the guy, things might have been different. Psycho Nero, Jason's old dog, was eventually retired for being too aggressive. Benny the Bouncer could be as nice as pie, but it seemed that his original nickname could still be appropriate.

Day 5
Dismounted element including myself searched compounds and keshay bazaar for possible caches. Nothing was found. Returned to fob cobra. End of mission.

I smiled as I thought of the last day of that eventful mission. In the compounds at Keshay there were a number of farm animals, cows, goats and chickens, wandering around. There were also some Afghan dogs tied to trees. The dogs yapped at Benny but he paid them no mind, carrying on with his work.

At one point during the search, though, a baby goat walked up to Benny and then started following him around. Benny stopped and looked at me with a 'What the hell does this young punk want with me?' look on his face. I shook my head and laughed. It was like the goat was in love with him.

Benny tried to get on with his job, but the baby goat wouldn't leave him alone. The next time he stopped, the goat moved underneath him, trying to find a teat to suckle on. It was one of the funniest things I'd ever seen. Benny showed no aggression towards the little goat, but kept looking up at me for some sort of explanation. I just shrugged.

By the end of the mission, we were both exhausted, and it was an effort to stay alert as the GMV bounced along the dirt road. The dust coated my skin and invaded the weave of my clothes. My hair, and Benny's, was matted stiff with the stuff by the time we got back to base. There was no place in the report to mention the scary stuff or the funny stuff that had happened, or how good it felt to come back to a hot shower and a bed, and have your dog settle across your feet for the night.

The missions continued and when I think about them now, they tend to blur; to roll into one long, hazy memory punctuated by the odd mortar round falling, a mine being blown in place, or the sound of spent brass casings falling around a whimpering dog. The war showed no sign of ending, and the teams came and went. The job hadn't changed, but I had. I'd been going on missions for two years and something had to give.

I'd come back to Afghanistan with the intention of giving American K9 another four months of my life, and then as that time came to an end, my Canadian friend Darryl, who had been the camp sergeant at Spin Boldak, and who I'd holidayed with in Thailand, offered me a job with Tundra, the security firm where he was now working.

Tundra was Canadian-run and the people involved seemed to be a good mob; Guy had gone to work with them after Apis had been shot. The work, however was all security based and Tundra had no dog teams. I would change from being a dog handler to being an armed security guard—still working in Afghanistan, but based in Kabul and earning more money.

I flew back to Kandahar from Cobra with Benny at my feet in his travel kennel on the floor of the Chinook. I tried not to look at him.

When I got back to Kandahar, I found that things were in a mess at the American K9 kennels and offices. I'd left some personal gear in the supervisor's accommodation building at Kandahar airfield and now couldn't find my stuff. I was told it was in the company office.

When I got there, I found my gear lying in a pile, and it was obvious that someone had gone through it. I was missing a set of Peltors, which are expensive noise-cancelling headphones. I asked around and was told they had been taken for 'safe keeping'. It was a minor thing, but it pissed me off nonetheless and helped me justify my decision to move on.

As much as I would miss Benny, I thought it was time for a change in my life.

I got my dog out of the kennels and took him for a long walk. I hadn't worked with Benny for nearly as long as I had with Ricky, but Benny and I had formed a very tight bond in the four months I'd known him. I'd been able to socialise him to the extent that I could work him off lead around Afghans, unlike Ricky, who wanted to kill most locals and all motorcycles he met. Benny had suffered at the hands of his last handler and accordingly had some baggage, but I'd been able to calm him and turn him into an excellent working dog, through training, love and attention.

Benny and I went to the chai house across from the kennels, where US soldiers and Afghans would mingle and chat, and after a cup I took him up the road that paralleled the airfield. I wanted to spend as much time with him as I could, because I knew that after I returned him to the kennel, I'd be getting on the C-130 to Kabul and would probably never see him again. I let him off lead and he trotted contentedly along, just ahead of me, looking back every now and then to make sure I was still there.

His tongue lolled out and he grinned at me. I tried to tell myself that he would be fine, and that my wish would come true that he'd get a good handler, who would look after him and let him sleep on the end of his bed, as I'd done. In my heart, though, I had the sad feeling that Benny was a one-man dog, and that I'd had the fortune to be that man.

With every step Benny took, his feet sent up little puffs of dust. He stopped and looked back at me, like he wanted me to do or say something, like it was just another job or another day of training. He ambled off and started sniffing some empty wooden ammo boxes, and trotted over to near the hescos to see if I'd hidden some explosives there for him to find.

Benny looked back at me again, and my heart hurt. As far as he knew, after we'd finished whatever we were doing here, we'd stroll back down the long road that ran alongside the airfield and he'd go to sleep, and he'd wake up tomorrow and I'd be there to take him out for his morning walk.

'Come on, mate,' Benny seemed to be saying to me. 'What are we doing here? You gonna play, or what?'

Whether it was play – training – or the real thing, he'd stuck by me all the way, and never shirked from doing his job or run away from danger. They're not all like that – even explosive detection dogs get shell shock and go AWOL sometimes.

But Benny was a good dog. And now I was leaving him.

'Come on, Benny.' He stopped sniffing around a stack of sandbags, turned and trotted back to me, his tongue lolling out of his mouth, grinning up at me.

I dropped to one knee. 'Good boy. Good dog, Benny,' I said as I ruffled him under the chin and hugged his face close to mine. 'It's time to go, boy.'

NINETEEN

Kabul

July 2008

When CAI had folded and been taken over by American K9, Uncle Buck had left and set up his own company, Vigilant Canine Services International, or VCSI. He called me while I was still in Afghanistan and offered me a job as the trainer at the new Kabul power plant, where he had a contract to provide explosive detection dogs and handlers.

It was a good job, but I'd already agreed in principle to work for Darryl at Tundra. When I'd said goodbye to Benny, I'd gone to Kabul and then to Zubal, where Tundra had a base, and had begun doing some on-the-job training as a security contractor while I waited for the Canadian company to come through with a firm offer.

Tundra was offering good money, but it's never just been about the money. Pretty much any military contractor would be lying if he or she said the money wasn't important at all, but it's not the end game. Afghanistan helped me get my finances, and my life, back together, and while there were countless times I wished I could be back home with my kids and Nat, there was no way I was going to go home to a job that paid badly and start going backwards. My last days with American K9 had left me with a sour feeling and I needed another break back home, away from Afghanistan and the war, before I started my new job.

I headed back to Australia without a firm job offer from Tundra, but hoping that they would keep to their end of the verbal deal. As much as I was enjoying my break from the war, being home with Nat and seeing more of the kids, my financial situation started to look grim again. I was renovating a house and if you've ever done that, you know where the term 'money pit' came from.

Although I'd given my word to Darryl, things were getting desperate, so I emailed Buck to see if he'd filled the position he'd offered me. He replied straightaway, telling me the job was still mine if I wanted it. I took it; while Tundra did eventually come back with an offer, it was too late.

Fate, and dogs, had taken me away from Australia again, but now I found myself in a very different part of Afghanistan, in the capital city, Kabul.

It was a dirty, crowded, chaotic mix of the modern and the medieval. The traffic was crazy and drivers relied on the magic horn to get them out of every near-miss situation. If you took the horn fuse out of every car in Kabul, I swear, the whole city would grind to a halt. The streets were jammed with rusted second-hand reject cars from Pakistan, new Toyota pick-ups and ancient Russian Kamaz trucks. As well as the richly decorated jingle trucks, there was the odd sleek new European sedan, weaving in among three-wheeled motorbikes that each have a tray on their back that is loaded with farm animals or people.

The air was choked with blue exhaust fumes from the cars and clouds of dust, especially in summer. I heard estimates that up to 20 per cent of the particles in airborne dust in Kabul were human faecal matter. That would account for the smell that pervades the city.

In the poorer parts of town, they had a neighbourly system of sewage disposal. You and your family crapped in a bucket, then took it outside the family compound and emptied it up the road near your neighbour's place. There were wide, deep drainage ditches full of effluent on either side of the roads. Any vacant block of land in a neighbourhood would be filled with shit.

The capital was far more secular than other parts of the country, and I saw men in western-style suits and women in dresses, though the women would usually have a headscarf covering their hair. Women went to work, school and university, and shopped in the brand-new shopping centres that are being built amid the bullet-pocked compounds and old concrete Russian apartment blocks. There were shops selling state-of-the-art computers and mobile phones, and others that had a sheep's carcass hung up outside them, dripping blood on to the pavement.

My first managerial job in Kabul was in quality assurance for VCSI. Affable Buck had used his people skills and experience to build the company up while other canine companies fell by the wayside. He had networked with the various military establishments and other contracting companies in Afghanistan to win contracts and so gradually expand the company.

Buck resisted pressure to pay bribes to win contracts – corruption was rife in Afghanistan – and he did well by sticking to what he knew, and proving his worth and his honesty to his clients. Buck was supported all the way by another good guy, a Mexican–American ex-police dog handler, Luis Montalvo, who also served in Iraq and came to Kabul at the same time as Buck.

Part of my role as QA manager was to train people to be operational dog handlers and, much as Mark did for me, I paired up handlers with dogs, to make sure they complemented each other. The dog handlers I was teaching in Afghanistan tended to be Nepalese, Filipino and Afghans. If I got a handler who was a bit introverted, I would look for a dog that was calm and easygoing. There was no point in giving a slower person a dog that moved at a million miles an hour, although, as happened with me and Ziggy, I would sometimes mix it up and give someone a dog that was quite different from them, to help hone their skills.

A South African woman, Tracey, was our dog trainer, and I concentrated on the people. Once we had teamed up a dog and a handler, I travelled around to wherever they were based to make sure they were doing the job well. The other part of the QA role was assessing the teams in the field to make sure their operational standards were up to scratch.

Training people from all around the world had its challenges, particularly in terms of communication. The students spoke English, but when I first started training contract dog handlers, I found they were having a hard time understanding me, because of the Australian slang I was using and the speed at which I was talking. Also, I got sick of repeating myself every time I spoke to an American, so I slowed down the pace at which I talked.

A lot of people from countries such as the Philippines couldn't wait to get to Afghanistan and work as contractors, as, for them, the money was out of this world. Inevitably, people would sometimes exaggerate the experience they had in order to get a job with us. I taught a dog handlers course for 20 Filipino ex-Marines and while there were some very experienced soldiers in the group – some of them at sergeant-major level, and with combat experience – it was clear that most of them had little or no experience as dog handlers. In fact, when I assessed them, some were hopeless.

One of the things I did to try to gauge the level of experience new recruits had with working dogs was to give them an introductory lesson in caring for a dog.

I got a dog up on the bench in front of one group of new recruits, and showed them how to check for parasites and lumps, running my fingers through the animal's fur while i addressed them.

The students all nodded, as though this was pretty obvious stuff they had all been through before.

'Now, you usually won't have direct access to a vet, unless you're working somewhere like Kabul or Kandahar,' I said to the group. 'If you're out at a FOB you'll have to know how to recognise symptoms if there's something wrong with your dog. OK?'

There were nods all round from the eager students.

'You won't be issued with a thermometer, but I'm sure you all know how to tell if a dog has a high temperature?'

At this point, the nods became slighter, with some of the students glancing at each other to see if anyone did actually know the answer. I was searching them as well.

I gave the dog a pat, then gently lifted his tail. 'What you do is stick your finger in your mouth,' which I then did, giving it a good lick, 'and stick it in the dog's ass. If you feel your finger getting very warm, then you know your dog has a problem.'

I fought to stop from breaking into a grin as I surveyed the looks of horror on some of their faces. I didn't perform the action myself, but looked for who seemed to be the biggest bullshitter in the group and called him forward. 'OK, you first.'

Over the times I did this simple test I was amazed by the number of so-called experienced dog handlers who stepped up and started licking their finger, before I stopped them.

I didn't go on missions anymore but I still carried a pistol and, when I went out, a 5.45-millimetre Russian AK-74 for personal protection. I thought my days of getting shot at would be pretty much over when I took the job in Kabul, but not long after starting, I was nearly killed – by some coalition troops.

In Kandahar, while on a quality assurance check, I met up with an old mate of mine, Brian, whom I'd met while working for American K9. Although the military part of Kandahar airfield was dry, we knew there was alcohol for sale in a contractor's compound, just outside the main gate on the highway. We headed out in a pick-up and when we got to the company bar, proceeded to down a few beers. As it was getting late, we tried to buy a carton of beer to take back with us. The barman wouldn't sell us takeaways, so we left disappointed.

It was night time by this stage and as we approached the main gate at Kandahar airfield, someone in the guard post flashed a bright light at us. I'd never seen anyone flashing a light like that before. We stopped and the light winked again.

'What the fuck's all that about?' Brian asked.

I shrugged.

Brian, who was driving the pick-up, started to move forward slowly and we heard the *crack-thump* of a rifle shot.

'Holy shit!' I said. Brian hit the brakes and we heard another bullet whiz over the top of us.

'What the fuck is this?' Brian yelled as he rammed the car into reverse and, as we started to back up, the guard in the bunker fired a third shot at us. We didn't know what this fucker wanted – to come to him, to stop or to reverse.

Brian was scrunched down below the dashboard as he drove.

'Is that shit I can smell?' I laughed, for some reason, as it all seemed pretty funny at the time, with Brian ducking down and glancing out the rear window as he weaved the truck in reverse.

Brian stopped again and we wound down the windows. 'What the fuck are you doing?' I yelled back towards the gate. 'We're contractors, you dumb arses! Stop fucking firing!'

Brian was yelling as well, and finally someone stepped out into the light and waved for us to come forward. We drove forward slowly and when we got to the gate, exchanged words with the guards, who spoke in a thick Eastern European accent. It turned out they were recently arrived Slovakian soldiers, on their first night's duty manning the gate.

'We flash light at you to tell you to stop, but you move,' one of them said.

'That's bullshit,' I said. 'No-one's ever used that signal before.'

As we were talking, another vehicle approached the gate. The guy behind the spotlight flashed it, and the vehicle kept coming. No-one opened up on this car. 'See?' I said. These pricks didn't have a clue what they were doing.

A German military policeman was summoned and, after talking to everyone, he escorted us to the Military Police post at the airport's pax terminal, where Brian and I made full statements. We were later exonerated completely, and I hope that the Slovakians got a major kick up the arse.

Although I was no longer in combat in Kabul, I felt like I could never relax. I knew that any hour of the day or night I could get a call to tell me one of my handlers, or one of their dogs, had been caught in the blast of a command detonated IED and been killed or wounded. I would get stressed wondering if the handlers were doing a good job and if they were being accepted by the teams they'd been placed with. Sometimes I wished I could just go out there and take their place and do the job myself.

VCSI had a contract to supply dog teams to the headquarters of ISAF, the International Security Assistance Force in Kabul. I regularly went there to check on our handlers and dogs, drop off dog food, and to make sure the client was happy.

ISAF was about ten kilometres from my location; 20 minutes' drive in good traffic. On one of these trips I was giving a lift to Mark Wilczynski and a handler named Clint. Mark, who was my instructor on my army dog handler's course and the person who recruited me to Afghanistan, now worked with Buck and me at VCSI. I drove the company Hilux along Jalalabad Road, turned right at Freedom Circle and continued towards Kabul city until I reached Masood Circle, where I turned left.

The neighbourhood around ISAF was also home to the US embassy and to some other consulates. The streets were flanked with trees and high walls, and there was plenty of security given the number of foreign diplomats who lived and worked in the area. I stopped at an Afghan police checkpoint, showed my ID badge, and was allowed through. The second checkpoint I had to pass through was closer to the US embassy, and manned by expat security contractors from a company called ArmorGroup. A grey armoured car with a turret-mounted machine gun on top backed them up. Finally, after passing through the contractor's checkpoint, I had to go through another boom gate, to get to the actual entrance gate to headquarters.

Once inside the complex, the security was handled by Macedonian soldiers – part of the international force – rather than by Afghans. I could see a group of military people in British camouflage uniforms, who looked like they were getting a tour of the headquarters, wandering around. I went to yet another gate, the 'badge gate', where I was given a vehicle pass, and from there to a final stop, a vehicle checkpoint where soldiers checked under my car with mirrors.

Finally through all the security hurdles, I drove through the complex, past offices, and a small café where, incongruously, some uniformed people were sitting, sipping espressos. I headed for the back gate, where our kennels were located.

Just as Mark, Clint and I got out of the Hilux, there was an almighty explosion that rocked the ground like an earthquake. Three British soldiers near us dropped to the ground and at first I thought it was a mortar attack. The three of us started walking back towards the accommodation blocks we'd just passed, to the gate. A pall of black smoke and dust began to rise from the area we'd just driven through, and Mark got out his digital camera and started taking some video footage.

'IED, front gate,' I heard an American soldier saying.

When we got closer to the gate, it was chaos. The windows of buildings around the gate had been blown in and I could see a car, maybe two, burning on the other side of the boom. 'Over here!'

We were ready to help, and a couple of Americans and I lifted a female Macedonian soldier and carried her to the medical centre. She was a tall and solidly built girl in her late twenties, with dark hair, and eyes that were open but empty of expression. She didn't appear to have been injured physically, but was covered in dust and in deep shock. It was as though she were conscious, but unable to walk, talk or move at all under own steam. Once we dropped her off, I went back towards the gate.

'Stay inside the base,' an American major was yelling at people as he tried to coordinate the first aid effort, 'stay away from the gate!'

There were wounded people everywhere, lying, staggering around, moaning. I found an Afghan soldier wandering around with his hand to his head. He'd been hit in the scalp, probably by flying glass, and his face and upper half of his shirt were soaked in blood. 'Come on, mate, let me give you a hand.' I put his arm around my shoulder and half led, half carried him back to the aid post.

A loudspeaker message was warning everyone that the base would be in lock-down for the next two hours, in case there were more IEDs out there. As I came out of the medical centre, I saw Adam, one of our dog handlers, and his labrador, Betty. Adam hadn't been on duty, but was already kitted out and had come to the gate to see if he could help search for more bombs. Adam was an Australian Army dog handler, and I was impressed with his motivation and his attitude. He hadn't needed to be called to go there, not shirking despite a mother of a bomb having just gone off.

Six minutes.

That's how long after Mark, Clint and I passed through the boom that the IED went off. It turned out that it had been a suicide bomber driving a Toyota 4Runner packed with between 150 and 200 kilograms of explosive. How the hell he'd passed through the previous security checkpoints was anyone's guess. Perhaps someone at the boom had finally noticed something was up.

Three people died that morning. The bomb had gone off at about eight-thirty and had vaporised another two cars. The people killed were Afghan civilians, apparently, and a further 85 civilian and military personnel were injured, mostly by flying glass and other debris.

I didn't dwell on how close I'd come to being killed. If I gave it too much thought, I would never have gone back to my job in Afghanistan.

Not long after the suicide bombing at the International Security Assistance Force headquarters, I got a call and a follow-up email from my eldest son, who had turned fifteen. He told me that, as far as he was concerned, we didn't have a relationship as father and son anymore.

At first, it felt like a kick in the guts to hear him say that, and then to read it in his email, but on reflection, I realised he was just saying what I already knew. He told me that I hadn't been there for him as he was growing up, and that I was missing out on the younger kids' best years. He was right.

My kids had never asked me much about what I did for a living, or what I had seen or done, in Afghanistan. When I was away, the kids and I talked on the phone, and on Skype, but I was always sure they would rather have been talking to their friends, so the conversations were usually short.

There was a 10-year age gap between the youngest and eldest, so they all had different priorities. I liked to think of my only daughter, Demi, as Daddy's little girl, but I had missed so many important moments in her life. She and Kyron both went to dancing lessons, but even when I was home and had the chance to drop Demi off at her class, I was not allowed in, as the teachers didn't like parents hanging around. The only time I would have been able to see Demi dance was at the two recitals she did each year, but I was never in Australia for those, so I never got to see my daughter dance on a stage.

As well as not being there for my children when they were having problems, like when Lauchlan wrote to me, I missed seeing them play sport and being there to read their school reports. I'm sure the kids would have talked to me more if I had been home more often but, as it was, I could feel the relationships between us becoming more strained by my absences.

Perhaps, as my son said, the gap between my kids and me had widened too much, but I hoped I could make it up to them. Some of my vacations home coincided with the school holidays in Australia and it was great to have the kids around me all day and night, even if it was crazy, but during my last couple of trips back home from my QA job with VCSI they were at school, which made it hard for me to spend quality time with them.

There wasn't a day that went by when I didn't think about my kids or look at their pictures, and feel guilt about not being there for them. I was lucky, though, as were they, that they had good mothers and they were all very well looked after. There was, I would tell myself, no point in having a father who was always around but had no money to support them. That wouldn't have been fair on my kids or their mothers.

While I was stuck in Kabul, my canine friends, Ricky and Benny, were still soldiering on in Afghanistan. After Nero the dog was retired for bad behaviour, my mate Jason Bergeron, who had accompanied me to Cobra on my first trip, was looking for a new dog. Fortunately, Benny was between handlers and available, and was teamed with Jason in March 2008.

Jason and Benny were deployed to Cobra, where it had all begun for me, and while working there, Benny was credited with finding an IED made up of two 105-millimetre artillery shells rigged to a pressure plate. If a vehicle had driven over that device, it would have been obliterated.

In October 2008, Jason and Benny were redeployed to a new forward operating base, Tombstone, in Helmand Province. While there, they took part in the largest Special Forces operation of the war to that time, around Marjeh. Benny and Jason uncovered numerous caches of explosives.

Ricky was lucky enough to end up with another friend of mine, a South African named Werner. An ex-police dog handler, Werner had also gained extensive experience in Afghanistan and Iraq. In my opinion, Ricky couldn't have gone to a better handler.

Werner and Ricky were attached to the Canadian military. One day, they were searching a choke point when Ricky exhibited a change in behaviour, stopping and looking.

When Werner called some engineers forward, they realised that Ricky had found – and very nearly stood on – a pressure plate connected to a buried bomb. For their good work that day, the Canadians gave Ricky and Werner a commendation, and Ricky was made an honorary lance corporal in the Canadian Army.

Life continued on as what passed for normal for me three months on in Afghanistan, followed by three weeks at home, until the day I almost died, and things started to unravel.

TWENTY

Near Death

October, 2009

"What, are you going to fucking shoot me as well?"

Face bloodied, and bruised all over, I took a ragged breath and looked down the barrel of an AK-47. The Afghan in uniform had his finger curled through the trigger guard, ready to shoot. His eyes were as wild as mine must have been.

How the fuck had this happened?

I'd spent the morning in Kandahar airport doing a quality assurance check on one of VCSI's handlers and his drug and explosive detection dogs who worked in a search bay at the entry to Kandahar Airport. Our company was contracted to provide canine services to Global, the firm that had the airport security contract.

The handler was due to leave the country, but didn't have his passport. Our HR people had it in Kabul and I had brought it with me to Kandahar to give to him. However, I had left it in my bag at the main Kandahar military base. After the assessment was done I told the handler that I would fetch his passport for him.

At about three in the afternoon I returned. At the ECP, the security entry control point, there were two border policemen in camouflage fatigues sitting in folding chairs near the boom gate, along with a couple of men in civilian clothing.

As I approached them I held up the handler's passport. 'Hello,' I said, 'passport – for dog handler.'

I'd been working in the area all morning, so I hoped the officers might have recognised me. I was out of luck. One of them said something loud and aggressive at me, in Pashto.

I pointed to myself. 'Global,' I said, indicating that our company was part of the group who handled security.

'Za!' the guy yelled, which I knew meant 'go'.

'I just want to deliver a passport.' I started reaching into the left hand pocket of my cargo pants, to get out my identification wallet and show him my Global airport security pass and my ISAF ID.

Without warning or provocation, from him, the second policeman got up and shoved me in the chest. That took me aback, but the guy then drew back his arm and smashed his fist into my nose.

Blood poured from my nose and I lost it. I grabbed the policeman with my left hand and started belting him, punching him in the face in retaliation.

More Border cops appeared from inside the airport and I was dragged through the checkpoint and behind a blast wall, where no passers-by could see me, and a crowd of between eight and 12 of them started laying into me.

"Global... ISAF..." I tried yelling, but it seemed everyone of these guys wanted a piece of me. Some were using AK-47s as clubs, sticking the barrels into me, or punching and kicking me. Another officer smashed the butt of his rifle into my back. I heard the mechanical snicker of rifles being cocked at least three time. Shit, I thought, one of these guys is going to accidentally shoot me.

In the scuffle I dropped the handler's passport and one of the Afghans must have picked it up. I wasn't about to give in. I kept swinging at them, but the more I fought back, the more they gave it to me.

At some point I went into survival mode and stopped fighting back. I realised I just had to suck it up and take what they wanted to give me if this was ever going to end.

In amongst all the punching and kicking I was able to get myself to my feet again, wincing with pain, blood flowing from where I'd been hit in the nose and head. One of the policemen raised his AK-47, cocked it and pointed it at me, although a few of his mates were still lashing out at me, so he couldn't get a clear line of sight.

It dawned on me that I was no longer at risk of being accidentally shot, this man was going to execute me.

"What, are you going to do, fucking shoot me as well?" I said to him.

It was entirely possible that he was going to do just that. The border police were not appointed because of their intelligence or sensitivity – an expat had been shot dead at the airport just three months' prior. This guy could have just decided that he was going to kill me to impress his mates. He was about 10 metres from me, lining me up.

All I could think of was that I hoped they didn't take the handler's passport, and that they would let him leave. I wasn't scared of dying; like I say, I had, to a certain extent, lost all feeling. I was numb.

I'm pretty sure the policeman would have shot me if an Afghan National Army soldier hadn't shown up and got between us. The soldier was well turned-out, his uniform smart and ironed. He spoke to the mob and calmed things down, but I was then put in a vehicle and driven further into the airport to the office of the general commanding the border police.

At one point we passed a Global vehicle with the handler – the one whose passport I had fetched – inside it. Despite my protests the people in my vehicle wouldn't stop or give him the passport.

I was half marched, half dragged into the general's office. The crowd of abusers had grown to nearly 20 now, civilians and police, and they all seemed to be yelling their version of events to the general, even though most of them hadn't been anywhere near where the fight kicked off.

I couldn't understand what was being said, except when man said: 'fuck off and punched him in the head'.

'I did not tell anyone to 'fuck off',' I told the general. I tried to explain that I had done nothing wrong and had not thrown the first punch, but it was useless.

I was dragged outside again, not knowing what would happen to me, and bundled into a vehicle. A chubby guy in traditional Afghan civilian dress got in the back of the pick-up next to me.

Kandahar was Taliban country. You could never tell just where any of the locals' allegiances still lay. This guy could also have been taking me somewhere to put a bullet in the back of my head.

The chubby man stared me in the eye and delivered his verdict.

'You are never to return here,' he said to me, in perfect English. 'If you do, the police commander will kill you, himself.'

I was taken back outside the airport perimeter and dumped, battered and bleeding, on the main road. All I could think was: *thank fuck I'm not going to prison*. I did not fancy my chances of surviving in a jail in Kandahar.

I hauled myself to my feet again and started stumbling down the road, towards Kandahar military base on foot, which was crazy enough in itself. This was Indian country.

People in the street stared at me in my dishevelled state, and after a while – I was too dazed to remember how long – an Afghan ambulance pulled over and the driver ushered me inside and asked me where I wanted to go. He dropped me, dazed, at the front gate of the base and I called Darryl, who worked for Tundra and was stationed there, and he and some others came out and collected me and took me to the base hospital.

Even now, years later, I see the eyes of that police officer and the tip of the barrel of his AK-47 pointing at me. I see it often.

I broke up with Nat in 2010.

My fly-in, fly-out lifestyle was tough on everyone – my kids, myself, and my relationship. Nat had left her family and friends in Western Australia and when I was home in Australia I was surrounded by my kids. We grew apart and ended up more as friends than people who were ready to commit to each other.

The war in Afghanistan just kept getting busier, and bloodier. VCSI picked up more contracts, running dog teams to provide security for the Danish, Canadian, British, and Australian embassies, and the European Police and US military bases in Kabul.

We had ramped up to a force about of 56 handlers and 84 dogs and as their manager I was acutely aware that any of those people or animals could suffer injury or death at any minute of the day. On top of that, like a salesman, I had to make sure our customers were happy, and to keep in their good books.

Along with the extra work came more responsibility – and added pressures – for me, now as country manager. It was a war of a different kind, trying to make sure clients paid their bills on time and that handlers received their wages. Like any business that grows quickly there were challenges and I was burning out.

I needed to go home for good, but what would I do for money?

I resigned from VCSI and returned to Australia in 2012, worn out and tired, but determined to find a 'real' job and to spend more time with my children. I found, however, it wasn't as easy and I thought to leave the war behind.

Just as I had when I had been going home to Nat I found myself suffering from depression alternating with hyper-vigilance. I had spent so much time in a combat zone that I found I was continually on edge, waiting for something to happen.

If you think of a 'level' for awareness or anxiety, a normal person might operate, say, on a level of three or four out of ten, and then when they come under pressure or get anxious about something their level might creep up to a high of about six or seven. My resting rate, when I was in Afghanistan or home in Australia, was a six or seven all the time and I found that I could redline, to ten very quickly. That's what hyper-vigilance was.

Being on edge all the time was incredibly exhausting, so I tried to manage it, as best as I could. When I was younger, and even when I had first started working in Afghanistan, I was a shit stirrer, a larrikin, the loudmouth life of the party. I found that as time went on I withdrew into a shell I had created for myself. If I did not engage with people, if I did not get drawn into discussions that might turn into arguments, or express my frustration at the seemingly minor things that people worried about I would be able to stop myself from red-lining.

I remember being in a car full of friends on a long drive and the people on board were laughing and talking all the way. It was just small talk and jokes, but the noise was driving me crazy. It was all I could do not to pull over, get out, throw away the keys and walk away. No one on board knew that, though, they just saw quiet Shane, who was another person to the younger me.

I found a job close to home, working as a wharfie at Port Kembla. Plenty of people would have been happy to land it, but loading coils of steel wire into ships and driving car after car on and off transporter ships was not for me.

I was doing 12-hour shifts and it was fucking monotonous. I had wanted this, to come home to something predictable and safe, but I had been living on adrenalin for years and I found myself missing it.

Of course, one of the main attractions of being home in Australia was that I would be closer to my kids and able to spend more time with them, but that didn't work either. When I'd been in Afghanistan I would be given all of my children at once, to spend my leave periods with them, but now I had to fit in around their schedules and it seemed to me that without the periods of enforced isolation with me there was always something more important that they would rather be doing, or some other activity they had to attend.

I remember turning up to see some of the kids at Christmas time, but they were playing at a neighbour's house and I had to stand there, on the street, and hand their presents to them from the boot of my car. It was gut-wrenching.

As troubled as I had been in Afghanistan, I had at least had a sense of purpose, and now that was gone. The only thing in life I was good at, I realised, had been working as a dog handler, or training dogs and managing other teams. Back home in Australia I felt like I was contributing nothing to society, not even to my children. I met another woman, but couldn't even hold down a relationship.

I was lost.

Before I'd gone to work for Buck at VCSI on my last stint in Afghanistan I'd had an offer from the Canadian security company, Tundra Group, but they hadn't been able to get anything concrete to me before I'd accepted the job with Buck. When I was in Australia Tundra contacted me and offered me a new position in Canada, training dogs for operational deployments.

It sounded like a dream gig, complete with a cottage in a ski resort and I said yes. The company organised a work visa for me, but I hadn't read the fine print. I had assumed that I would get paid leave, to return to Australia for a few weeks every three months, as I had in Afghanistan. I figured that at least that way I could go back to having some quality time with my kids on a regular basis. It turned out that wasn't part of the deal and if I wanted to return to Australia on my leave periods it would be at my own expense. I turned the job down.

However, slowly, but surely, I was being drawn back to the place that had been such a big part of my adult working life, and where I had truly felt, if not at home, at least valued. I was contacted by a British private military company, Hart International, and they said that they wanted to develop their own K9 division. Up until then Hart had been outsourcing the use of dog teams for their security contracts in Afghanistan and Iraq. Hart's management agreed it was time for them to expand and I was employed as their operations director.

Hart's quartermaster, an ex British military guy named John Sheppard, was a huge help to me in setting up this new capability for the company. John came across as a real tough bugger, but was a salt-of-the earth guy who would do anything for you. We became good friends and I even travelled to the UK for his 60th birthday.

John started work on designing and building new kennels at Kabul even before I got there. Once more I had a mission and a purpose in life, and felt like I was making a difference again.

We got off to a flying start. The company picked up some good contracts and I got to reunite with some of the handlers that I had trained years before. As well as managing handlers and dogs again, part of my job was to go out and win new business for Hart International. Fortunately I had a good manager to assist me, a Zimbabwean named George Chiutsi. George was one of the best dog handlers I had met and he was around to run things when I was away from Kabul.

Travel was a big part of my new role. I flew to Egypt to meet with a canine company by the name of Anubis K9, in Cairo. to see if we could set up a joint venture. The owner Khaled El Hiatmy and I became friends and while we didn't end up going into business it was a good networking opportunity and we have continued to stay in touch and assist each other.

I also accompanied Hart executives to Pakistan to talk to potential new military and police clients, and went to Iraq, for the first time, to assist with the training of new dogs and handlers.

Hart was operating at Basra, in southern Iraq, where most of the UK military commitment was focused. John and I were setting up the K9 unit there, continuing the training and accreditation of our newly recruited handlers, many of whom came from Nepal and the Philippines. While the kennels were being built the dogs slept in our rooms, air conditioned portable cabins.

Iraq was the hottest place I'd ever been to – daytime temperatures could top 50 degrees. I was working with some dogs and handlers in the open and the heat was sucking the moisture from my eyeballs. It was so hot the sweat would dry on your body before it soaked into your clothes. After one session I went back to my cabin and took off my shirt, enjoying the aircon. I felt a stinging on my stomach and when I checked I found my skin was burned from where the sun had heated my metal belt buckle.

Outside of the base it was checkpoint after checkpoint, making travel anywhere slow and frustrating. It was an urban environment, too much concrete, and buildings that looked either half finished or half destroyed. *Give me Afghanistan any day*, I thought to myself as we sweated through yet another VCP. At least in Afghanistan the scenery was better, with the snow-capped mountains and wide open desert landscapes.

Afghanistan might have been easier on the eye than the bits of Iraq that I saw and we still had good freedom of movement on the streets of Kabul, but it was still dangerous. I was at home, back in the familiar rhythm of three-months on and three-weeks off when I got the news there had been an attack on Camp Hart, our main base in Kabul.

A vehicle-borne IED (VBIED), a truck packed with explosives, had been driven into the rear wall and detonated in order to breech Hart's fortified compound. The point where the explosion occurred – and by all accounts it was a mother of a blast – destroyed our gym. Luckily for our guys the attackers had chosen a time when the gym, often packed, was empty.

The attackers were also slow off the mark or disoriented by their own explosion. Their two-phase plan called for terrorists in suicide vests to run through the gap in the wall caused by the VBIED and then detonate their own devices to cause even more death and destruction. However, our guys had time to grab their weapons and rally. The bombers on foot were gunned down and killed as they entered the compound.

Although I was in Australia, Afghanistan was never far from my mind. Usually, I was out of the conflict zone and home within three days, with no time to decompress or chill. I was worried for the guys there, and I flew to Kabul straight after the attack happened. As a result of the increased threat level we had to change our SOPs and put in extra security. An Afghan security guard was killed in the initial blast and one of our Eastern European operators, who was in a room closest to the breeching explosion, was thrown so violently by the shockwave that his neck was broken, leaving him paralysed. I later heard my European colleague took his own life.

The threat of death and injury had become part of my everyday life over many years. One Hart operator I served with was killed by a car bomb in Kabul and another British guy I knew was gunned down in a restaurant while he was working as a close protection operative.

There were some guys, those who were close to the ones who were killed, who were massively affected by the deaths. My way of coping was to keep myself numb – and quiet – so I didn't have to dwell on what was happening.

*

On one of my leave periods I was invited to my friend Dan Richardson's 40th birthday. Dan and I had been police dog handlers together during the Sydney 2000 Olympic Games and had become good mates. He stayed in the police and ended up rising through the ranks – I admire how well he has done in his career.

At the party I was introduced to a woman, Bernadette, Dan's wife Sharon's best friend, and it turned out she had heard about me. In fact, I got the feeling this might have been a set up. Bernadette was also separated and had one son, by the name Kalani. She worked as a national account manager for a company called Bugaboo, which sells high quality prams.

I had been on a massive fitness kick for the previous three months, but in Dan's honour I decided to break my booze fast and take a bottle of vodka to the party. Bernadette was chatty and friendly and we got on well; however, I was pretty pissed by the end of the night.

I had withdrawn into myself and I did not think I was in a place where I was ready for another relationship. Bernadette, however, kept in touch with me, as I went to and from Afghanistan. We communicated by text and messenger and over the following six months I got to know her.

She had been out of her relationship for 12 months, but also wanted to take things slow and steady. I learned that she was a kind-hearted soul, with never a bad word to say about anyone. She was the sort of person who could see past a person's flaws and offer them support whatever they were going through – just a gorgeous human being.

We got together, but it wasn't long before Bernadette learned what things were like for me. She was very understanding, as I tried to explain to her why I found little things, like going into a crowded supermarket, or being around too many people in a social setting unnerving.

My anxiety levels would ramp up and I'd become anxious and nervous. I kept myself to myself, knowing that if I didn't I might easily blow my top.

As my kids grew older the full impact of me being absent for such long periods became more and more clear to me. I had missed out on so much of their lives.

If I had still been in the Australian Army it might have been different. If I had been the brave soldier going overseas to defend his country they might have been proud of me, might been forgiving, with a mum who said "daddy's a hero, over there doing his job, keeping us all safe, and doing his best to keep a roof over our heads," but real life wasn't like that.

All my kids saw was a father who was absent, and it was no wonder that they probably sometimes thought I didn't care about them.

As well as being distant from my kids, the other thing I learned was that civilian military contractors are shut out of the Anzac tradition and shared experience that puts a value on what our servicemen and women do. Very few people in society know what we do, what we've been through, and apart from our pay cheques there's no recognition for the work done by tens of thousands of civilians in war zones. At the peak of the war in Afghanistan private contractors, employed in both frontline and support roles, outnumbered the number of US troops there by a ratio of about three to one. It was a similar in Iraq.

A few years ago I travelled to Niangala, a small village near Walcha, on the edge of the New South Wales Northern Tablelands, for the opening of the Sergeant Andrew Russell

Bridge. Andrew was the first Australian serviceman to die in Afghanistan, killed in 2002 after his SAS Long Range Patrol Vehicle Land Rover detonated a landmine. Despite a valiant effort to save him, in which a US military surgical team parachuted into the remote area where he had been injured, Andrew succumbed to his wounds.

Before joining the elite SAS Andrew had been an engineer and I had served with him in 2 Troop, 1 Field Squadron. One of our fellow soldiers, Corporal Paddy Ireland, was from Niangala and as part of our ongoing training Paddy asked the Army if our unit could do something for the local community by rebuilding a derelict bridge. Approval was given and we all hooked in and built the bridge.

In 2015 Paddy and some of the other guys approached Walcha Council with a request to rename the bridge in Andrew's honour. The council agreed and I was home on leave from Afghanistan in 2016 when the renaming ceremony was to take place. I flew up to the nearest airport, hired a car, but the flight was late and I ended up arriving just after the ceremony.

Quite a few of the guys had been to Afghanistan or Iraq by then and some were still in the army. They were all gonged-up, wearing their medals. We had all shared a bond of friend-ship with Andrew and many of us had seen combat, but I felt somehow left out of it, having nothing visible to show for my service despite the fact that I had been serving in Afghanistan for most of the previous 10 years. To put it in perspective, the amount of time I spent in-country would have equated to an Australian soldier doing almost 20 tours of duty, which would be unthinkable in the military.

The US military has a Defense (sic) of Freedom Medal that they award to civilian contractors who are wounded in action, or who perform an act of gallantry, and the UK awards a service medal to contractors employed by their Ministry of Defence or government bodies, but for people like me there's nothing.

Sure, the money is a big reason contractors seek employment in war zones, but we also feel like we're making a difference, supporting our military and the coalition in the fight against terror. However, when I die there will be nothing for me to leave my children of my wartime service, no medals for them or their kids to wear on Anzac Day.

Hart wanted me to try and help them win business in Australia. We knocked on the doors of the big sporting stadiums and event venues, trying to convince them of the need to have canine teams as part of their security, to check for weapons and bombs and to act as a deterrent.

At every meeting we met with pretty much the same response: "If we need sniffer dogs we'll call in the police."

That was the mindset in Australia – someone else would take care of it. The terrible terrorist bombing of the Ariana Grande concert at Manchester Arena hadn't happened at that time, but even so I felt that Australia needed a wake up call when it came to security. I was sure that if we did ever suffer a major terrorist attack there would be a knee-jerk reaction, with everyone calling for more security, including more dogs than the police or military could muster, but no one wanted to listen, or make a decision.

The business development role added to my stress and anxiety. My way of coping with post traumatic stress disorder – because I had come to realise that what I was suffering from was PTSD – was to withdraw, yet here I was in a job that forced me to go out and meet new people and win them over.

I had never had the gift of the gab and was useless at making small talk and being a salesman.

I told Hart I was having problems and their human resources people organised some Skype sessions for me with a psychologist. It wasn't enough, but it did confirm what I'd long suspected, that I had PTSD.

It was time for me to reassess my life. I knew that If did not make a massive change I was not going to get past this injury – and PTSD is now recognised as an injury. How long, I wondered, could I keep going back to combat zones before it killed me, literally? I also felt like I was butting my head up against a brick wall trying to win new business.

I had also, once again, decided to try and make things right with my kids. Even if they didn't particularly want to spend time with me, I wanted to at least be in Australia for them.

If I thought going into combat or knocking on the doors of executives to present a sales pitch was stressful, I was about to step into the biggest and most nightmarish ambush of my life – the hospitality industry.

I figured that running a business would be a good way for me spend my time in Australia, and help me get ahead. I looked at franchises and picked a burger joint. The idea, which I was sold on, was that there would a system in place that took care of pretty much everything and that I would invest my money and be successful in my new found business.

How hard could running a restaurant be? I thought it would be a walk in the park. I was wrong. I had picked a job that did not suit me in the slightest. Instead of sitting in a room counting my money I ended up having to be the chef, waiter and barman at various times. I had stress dealing with staff, trying to pay expensive rents and cover the costs of supplies and I ended up working long hours, seven days a week.

I put everything I had into the place, financially and emotionally, and tried two different locations, at Wollongong and Dapto, but I failed. In the end, when I parted company with the franchise owners, I had lost every cent I had earned in the 10 years I had spent in Afghanistan.

My mental health was also taking a nosedive.

Even before the drama with the restaurant, I had decided to address my PTSD. With Bernadette's support, I reached out for help. Through my private health insurer I was able to get into a PTSD treatment program run by the health provider, St John of God. I signed up for three months' worth of meetings, once a week.

The meetings were mostly group-based. I was the only ex military person; most of the others were police or paramedics, and other people who had experienced trauma in their lives. We all told our stories at different times. It wasn't easy, but I did find it helped.

I wasn't alone at the meetings. As well as the other group members I took along a new mate, a kelpie named Rex. I got Rex as a rescue dog when he was two and he became my little shadow. I understand what people see in the concept of companion dogs, for people who have suffered in their lives, or are lonely. Rex turned out to be a real favourite with the other members.

I was asked if there was one incident, or one image, that I kept coming back to, that might have been directly related to my PTSD. I had seen some bad things in Afghanistan, and I had known quite a few people who had been killed or injured. Time and again, however, I found that when I closed my eyes it was the image of the Afghan border police officer pointing his AK-47 at me during the scuffle I'd had while trying to get the dog handler's passport to him at Kandahar Airport.

That incident still runs through my mind. It could have gone south very easily, with either me being locked up in prison – with God knows what happening to me there – or being shot by the border policeman.

These things happen in war – the trauma of being apart from family and friends, and the disruption it causes to lives on both sides of the world. The unusual thing about military contracting, as opposed to military service, is that it would have theoretically been feasible for me to go on as I was for as long as the war lasted. I could have kept on going back until, one day, my luck ran out.

A friend, Stu Sulter, threw me a lifeline after we sold the restaurant, and saved me from having to go back to Afghanistan by helping me find a job in a coalmine, not far from where I live. This was a really tough time in our lives for Bernadette and me, and I was extremely grateful for Stu's support and the opportunity he gave me. I fitted in well at the mine and have met some awesome people there, including Kane Formosa who helped me make the transformation from military contractor back to civilian again, which has been a massive, but important change in my life. As a result Kane and I have become really good mates.

My children are growing into adulthood now. We have dinner nights together, when we can, and I'll text them to ask them if they feel like a coffee.

I love them all, and I now feel like we have made huge leaps and bounds, in terms of reconnecting. I understand I still need to rebuild and that it's an ongoing process that I am committed to. I have recently become a grandfather and the feeling is unreal. I have so much love to give my kids and my grandkids and I look forward to sharing that with them.

Bernadette and I have been together for eight years now. We have a house and I count my blessings that I have somewhere to live and that she is the shining light of my life. I wonder, though, what life has in store for me next?

There is no magic cure for PTSD, but I have learned what works and what doesn't. I have been on several types of medication, but they all seem to turn me into a zombie. I have found that keeping fit, working out in the gym, and being in the outdoors is what works for me, what helps me keep my demons at bay. Exercise is not therapy, but it is better than sitting indoors, thinking, over and over, about the things that happened.

To anyone who has served and is having trouble adjusting to 'normal' life, I would offer these few words from my own experience: this injury that we suffer is not immediately visible to anyone but yourself, but the pain is deep and real and is the result of war. You can only mask it for so long before the cracks reveal themselves to others. You continue pretending to yourself that everything is OK, but your loved ones knew you before you were injured they will know. Please remember you are not alone, and that your deployment has come to an end. There is no need to continue to relive the past; it's the here and now where the healing begins. You owe it to your friends, your family and, more importantly, yourself, to be open, honest and real, as this is where you will find the peace in your life. Reach out, ask for help, now is the time to heal.

I was asked to talk at a local football club, to the players, about my experiences in Afghanistan, and with coming to terms with my mental health problems. I would have liked to, but the thought of addressing even a small audience made me nervous. I found myself torn between wanting to do something to help, and overcoming my own anxiety. I've enrolled in a Toastmasters course and want to learn how to become more at ease with addressing crowds, so that I can tell my story to more people.

My story is shared by many. A 2013 report by the US-based think tank, the Rand Corporation, surveyed 600 private military contractors and found that 25 per cent of them showed signs of suffering from PTSD. Many were still employed, in Iraq or Afghanistan, and while they knew they were showing symptoms a majority had not sought help from their employers, because they feared it would harm their employment prospects. At the time, the baseline rate for PTSD in the general community was six per cent, and among US military people it varied from eight to 20 per cent. In the years that followed the report's release many tens of thousands more men and women from around the world would serve as military contractors. Who knows just how many more people there are like me out there?

In one respect, the numbers are not surprising. A little publicised fact, revealed in a 2019 report by Brown University in the US, revealed that 7,950 military contractors had been killed during America's various wars in the Middle East since September 11, 2001. That figure was more than 900 higher than the number of US military people killed in action. With little public recognition, fear for their jobs, virtually no support, and ongoing exposure to action, it's little wonder contractors are more likely to suffer PTSD than their uniformed brothers and sisters.

Here in Australia, at the time of writing, the issue of military veterans' mental health is coming to the public's attention. Between 2001 and 2017 419 serving and ex-serving

Australian Defence Force members took their lives – nearly 10 times the number of men killed in Action in Afghanistan. The suicide rate among Australian male veterans is 18 per cent higher than that of the general population. Among female veterans the rate is even higher, a phenomenal 115 per cent.

Defence Force veterans in Australia, as in the US and UK, have access to veterans' affairs medical and mental health care for service related injuries, after they leave the military. Private military contractors are entitled to nothing.

I am not complaining. I am an ordinary bloke who went to war. I knew the risks when I signed up and I took a job as a dog handler in Afghanistan all those years ago not for medals or glory, but to challenge myself, contribute to saving lives, and to pay my bills. I knew what I was getting into, and I do feel that I did my bit stop the spread of hatred and extremism and, with the help of the dogs who served faithfully alongside me that we did our job, to keep those who depended on us safe.

I am thankful that my private health insurance gave me access to counselling services when I needed them and I'm also grateful to the NSW Police for giving me half a dozen sessions based on my prior service. However, I worry for those forgotten civilian soldiers of the wars in the Middle East. There are plenty like me who came home not to welcome home parades or medal ceremonies, but to their day-to-day lives and families who may not have understood why they spent so much time away. I wonder how many of these men and women, finding themselves unable to cope, took their lives.

My job, as a dog handler, was not to kill, but to protect and I was probably at my most content, most fulfilled, when I was doing that work. I don't know what happened to Ricky, but Benny retired from active duty fit and well. Jason Bergeron took him home to his family, in Texas, where Benny saw out his days until he passed away at the age of 14, a very good innings for a dog.

I feel like maybe my new purpose in life, through this book, is to record the fact that not every man and woman who served in the post 9-11 wars did so in the uniform of their country. Good people, many of them ex-military, have served and suffered and some have paid the ultimate price.

If I can work on keeping my PTSD at bay and learn to speak out in public, not just through the pages of a book, perhaps I can do something to help the many more people who were in my situation and are now paying the price.

I would like more people, including my children, to know that men and women and dogs did their duty in places such as Iraq and Afghanistan, and did it well. Despite the dangers, it was easier for the dogs than the humans. For Ricky and Benny work was a game, something to do in order to receive the reward of play and joy.

The dogs asked for nothing other than my friendship and loyalty and in return they gave their all, not for a cause, but for love. Their purpose, although they never knew it, was to save human lives. It's the same with my dog, Rex. He gives me unconditional love, has a calming effect on me, and expects nothing in return.

Rex gets plenty of exercise, but if I was a dog I would want to be a working dog, like Benny and Ricky, helping people and spending my time in the outdoors, with a friend by my side, exercising and doing the job I was trained for, with a feeling of purpose and the love of a partner by my side.

Want more? We want to hear from you.

Shane Bryant and Tony Park, the authors of 'War Dogs' are on Facebook at facebook.com/pg/War-Dogs-Book or just go to Facebook and search 'War Dogs Book'. You'll find pictures and videos to accompany the story, and feel free to leave us a comment. Shane is also on Instagram at war_dogs_international.

Shane and Tony are also interested in hearing from serving or former private military contractors who may have experienced difficulty in adjusting to civilian life.

You can find more information about Tony Park's novels and other non-fiction books at www.tonypark.net

ACKNOWLEDGEMENTS

Shane would like to thank:

Many people have stood by me and helped me during my time in Afghanistan and beforehand. I would like to thank my family: Mum and Dad, and my siblings Aaron, Nicole, Kristin, Reece and Naomi for always being there for me during the happy and tough times. I couldn't ask for a more loving family.

I'd also like to thank my children's mothers and their partners; they have brought up beautiful, respectful children in my absence.

A special thanks to Gavin Lawrence; Gav has always been there during times of needs and is a reflection of the true meaning of mateship. Dave and Chris Piper always had a bed for me whenever I needed one, and were more like family than friends. Without Mark Wilczynski, who first trained me as a dog handler, I wouldn't have had the opportunity to work in Afghanistan, so I thank him for that and for the guidance he always gave me when I needed it. Thanks, too, to another great mate Daryl Crane for his help whenever I stayed at Kandahar and to Chris Arp for his recollections of our time together in the army.

Tony Park is not just a great author, but a genuine Aussie bloke with a lot of patience and I like to think I have made a mate for life.

Tony would like to thank:

Thanks to Shane, for telling his story so honestly, and John 'Robbo' Roberts, who introduced Shane to me. It's not the first time John has helped me with one of my books. Your lunch is in the mail, mate.

And thanks to Nicola, who stayed strong for me when I was in Afghanistan.